Beyond the Blogosphere

Beyond the Blogosphere

Information and Its Children

Aaron Barlow and Robert Leston

 PRAEGER

AN IMPRINT OF ABC-CLIO, LLC
Santa Barbara, California • Denver, Colorado • Oxford, England

Library of Congress Cataloging-in-Publication Data

Barlow, Aaron, 1951–
  Beyond the blogosphere : information and its children / Aaron Barlow
and Robert Leston.
    p. cm.
  Includes bibliographical references and index.
  ISBN 978-0-313-39287-0 (hardback : acid-free paper) —
ISBN 978-0-313-39288-7 (ebook)
1. Information technology—Social aspects.   2. Internet—Social
aspects.   3. Digital media—Social aspects.   4. Social media.
5. Swarm intelligence.   6. Information behavior.   7. Intellectual
property—Social aspects.   I. Leston, Robert.   II. Title.
  HM851.B367   2012
  303.48'33—dc23   2011032444

ISBN: 978-0-313-39287-0
EISBN: 978-0-313-39288-7

16   15   14   13   12   1   2   3   4   5

This book is also available on the World Wide Web as an eBook.
Visit www.abc-clio.com for details.

Praeger
An Imprint of ABC-CLIO, LLC

ABC-CLIO, LLC
130 Cremona Drive, P.O. Box 1911
Santa Barbara, California 93116-1911

This book is printed on acid-free paper ∞

Manufactured in the United States of America

Instead of learning about our technology, we opt for a world in which our technology learns about us.

—*Douglas Rushkoff,* Program or Be Programmed

Mass production is an admirable thing when applied to material objects, but when applied to matters of the spirit, it is not so good.

—*Aldous Huxley, "The Outlook for American Culture"*

Contents

Preface   ix

Acknowledgments   xv

1. For the Love of *Zoe*   1

2. Knowledge and Beauty, Perceptions and Contexts   31

3. Intellectual Property in a Digital Age   65

4. Smart Mobs or Mobs Rule?   109

5. Getting Savvy, or Draining the Information Swamps   135

6. The Fault of Epimetheus   169

7. Education Amid the Digital Revolution   195

8. The Excess of the Internet
   and the Waste of Information   229

Notes   237

Bibliography   251

Index   259

Preface

People began to take notice of Web 2.0 in 2004, the year of the blog. As a result, American Individualism began to take a major hit. The pressure of the crowd started to be felt even in our most private places.

There have always been periods of collective strength resulting in movements for social change in American history, so we should not have been surprised to see the power of grassroots organization rise up once again. But this time something was different.

The opening lines of the U.S. Constitution continue to be a rallying cry for Americans, guaranteeing certain "inalienable rights" for each individual. Today, we understand these to apply to every person regardless of race, sex, or creed. What carries the "spirit" in this document is that each human, because of his or her humanity, is equal at a level of nature. Consistent with Rousseauian "rights of man," each individual American has the right to better his or her own life; the rules and laws are made not to favor any one group or individual over another. Throughout the course of U.S. history, movements for social change, such as abolishment of slavery, equal rights for women, and civil rights were all movements where the collective organized so that each member of the group could share in the American *ideal*. Collective organization had always occurred in order to empower the individual.

How much easier would it have been for past freedom fighters to organize if they had the communication tools that we have today? How many more people would have gotten involved? At the same time, how much stronger would the status quo have been with the same communication tools?

The fact of the matter is that, in the past, groups organized *for the sake of the individual.* That's no longer the case. With the rise of the blogosphere, social media, mobile networks, and the generalized convergence of media into the digital sphere, a different phenomenon has begun to appear. All of this communication and exchange of text, visuals, and sounds is now being produced to give power to the collective—not so the individual could have more rights but just so the collective, the group, could express itself *as a group.* Yet this extraordinary change is not yet generally recognized. Certainly, it is not yet reflected in our ideas of ownership still favoring the individual, not the crowd or commons.

Under traditional broadcast media, the power always lay in giving voice to the few in order to influence the minds of the many. Now, we can all broadcast. Every individual has the opportunity to extend his or her voice through electronic media. Whether any one particular voice will be heard is another matter altogether and, we are finding, maybe not even relevant.

In the old model, if you were lucky enough to get a place from which to speak, the many would hear you. Imagine going to the town square where you live, your own soap box and bull horn in tow, complete with permits (of course) in hand. But things have changed. Now imagine a soap box and speaker every five yards, everyone speaking at the same time, each listener also broadcasting a message.

Voices only count as voices if they can be distinguished from the noise. The crowd has a voice, but the voice is not unified. It is noise.

Of course, some voices raise above the din, people begin to listen and filter out particular voices because, in the end, while everyone can now have a voice, not every voice can be received.

The rise of the blog and Web 2.0 resulted in an explosion of books in the mid-2000s, books drawing attention to the idea that we now have an unprecedented ability to communicate on a massive scale. Modern technologies, these writers argued, are finally bringing people together in a way and with an ease that had never been accomplished in the past. Writers implored us to recognize the good that lies within these developments and to see that the benefits outweigh the costs. Our societal and cultural fabric has changed, they said, for the better. It is finally time to recognize that there is an intelligence to our collective wisdom, a voice of the crowd: one that we have failed to recognize while we have been absorbed in our concerns with the individual.

In response, one of the things we explore here is the distinction between crowd intelligence (conceived of in complex networks) and how humans exhibit crowd intelligence. Rules governing crowd behavior are largely different from the rules governing individual conduct. Some are now taking the argument a step further, arguing forcefully that network technologies are creating the conditions for a collective intelligence to take place on the internet, claiming that the internet itself has begun to express an emergent behavior, one with its own kind of independent agency and desire. It's more than just that the people on the internet are exhibiting a particular kind of intelligence. The noise is not only the cacophony of crowds. If we can differentiate the signal from the din, there is something else that the machines seem to be saying.

In *The Information: A History, a Theory, a Flood,* James Gleick notes an ominous progression:

> After "information theory" came to be, so did "information overload," "information glut," information anxiety," and "information fatigue," the last recognized by the *OED* in 2009 as a timely syndrome: "Apathy, indifference, or metal exhaustion arising from exposure to too much information, esp. (in later use) stress induced by the attempt to assimilate excessive amounts of information from the media, the Internet, or at work." Sometimes information anxiety can coexist with boredom, a particularly confusing combination. David Foster Wallace had a more ominous name for this modern condition: Total Noise.[1]

But, of course, everything is just noise unless and until we work to understand its patterns and possibilities. This is especially true when we are faced with something new, something completely beyond our experience, as is happening now, as the crowd finally asserts itself; it takes time for the unknown and apparently chaotic to arrange itself into order. But time, in face of a flood, is in short supply. For good or ill, the crowd is moving. And growing.

According to a 2010 report by the International Data Corporation (IDC), "Between now and 2020, the amount of digital information created and replicated in the world will grow to an almost inconceivable 35 trillion gigabytes as all major forms of media—voice, TV, radio, print—complete the journey from analog to digital."[2] The report goes on: "So, if you have ever suffered from information overload or been bombarded with emails, texts, instant messages, documents, pictures, videos, and social network invitations, get ready, this is just the beginning."

And so it is.

But get ready how? What should we get ready *for*? And what does it all mean, anyway? When information extends beyond any individual human ability to conceive of it, let alone make use of it, what has it become? Has information become the crowd? Part of the crowd? Should we be worried about what is happening? Or should we be looking forward with enthusiasm? Or should we be looking back within, to see who we are among the crowd?

There is no time and no way any single book can adequately answer these or any of the other major questions we try to address here, all of which are part of an urgent conversation going on over the internet (and elsewhere) about the internet (and elsewhere). Fortunately, this discussion already reaches beyond any of us, each bit or byte, book or blog, merely a small contribution to a whole now forming around all of us—and a whole that, if we are prepared for it, we will be able to step back from one day, to view it, make sense of it, and use it—a whole that, in a real way, is taking on a life of its own and continuing to change at the same time as we strive to understand it.

No matter how solid our scholarship, how perceptive our observations, how deep our thought, there is no way this book (or any) could accurately predict just what the new world that we and our technologies are creating will look like. So, we don't try to do that. All we can do is help each other and our readers get ready by increasing our understanding of ourselves, of our relations to the tools we have created, and even of the evolution of our tools into something that may not prove simply to be tools at all.

In his 1954 science fiction story, "Fondly Fahrenheit," Alfred Bester tells the story of a man, Vandaleur, and his android, telling it through the third person, the first person of two singulars, and through first-person plural. The android turns killer from heat, it seems, killing a little girl at the start of the story. But the situation is a great deal more complicated. At the end, the android "dies," destroyed in a fire too hot even for it. But. . .

> Vandaleur didn't die. I got away. They missed him while they watched the android caper and die. But I don't know which of us he is these days. Projection . . . . If you live with a crazy man or a crazy machine long enough, I become crazy too. Reet!
>
> But we know one truth. We know they were wrong. The new robot and Vandaleur know that because the new robot's started twitching too. Reet! Here on cold Pollux, the robot is twitching and singing. No heat, but my fingers writhe. No heat, but it's taken the little Talley girl off for a solitary walk.[3]

This may not be our future, but our relations to our technological creations are already proving a great deal more complex than once we imagined they could be. Perhaps they are moving to another realm completely, something more like what Bester imagined than anything our more prosaic images of human/machine relations can muster.

Whatever. We just don't know. Again, however, not knowing the future does not mean we cannot prepare for it by learning a little more about ourselves and the present, about what has made us and our creations. And a little more about how we react as part of a crowd and about how machines do. This book, instead of trying to provide a look ahead, tries to give us a heads up through a look at us—as we are as we head into a future that is going to be different from what we have known, as different as 1950 was from 1900.

Only more so.

Acknowledgments

The completion of this project was made possible first of all through the collaborative process. When Aaron asked me to come onboard and work on this project with him after he already had completed the first two installments to this trilogy (*The Rise of the Blogosphere* and *Blogging America*), I was delighted. What followed was 18 months of productive and enjoyable collaboration. We spent hours discussing matters of the impact that telematics were having on our lives and the lives of our students. We debated, we disagreed, and we informed each other in ways that allowed us to both grow. Cheers! I would also like to extend my thanks to my wonderful colleagues in the English Department of the New York City College of Technology as well as my many supportive friends and colleagues around the country who have helped shape my intellectual development over the years, especially Sarah Arroyo and Geof Carter. Special thanks must also go to our patient editor, Michael Millman, and the publishers at ABC-CLIO. Thanks to my family for your enduring support, and tons of gratitude to the patience of my partner and collaborator in crime, Toni Leston, and special thanks to my whip-smart daughter, Alexandra, who was always willing to lend an ear, allow me to take ideas for walks around the block, and never failed to provide critical and insightful feedback that undoubtedly helped to make my thinking about the issues within sharper and more focused.

Robert Leston, Brooklyn, June 15, 2011

If it hadn't been for Robert Leston and Michael Millman, our editor at Praeger, this project would never have seen the light of day. After two books on New Media, I was getting tired of the subject, and tired of the cyber-utopians whose work threatened to bury me—and tired of their opposite (but smaller) number, the doubters of the value of the new digital possibilities. Something was missing on both sides, and I just couldn't see what it was. Robert showed it to me, and Michael made it possible for us to explore it.

As always, I couldn't have completed this book without the support of my wife, Jan Stern. I would also like to thank Laura Kodet, whose patience and help in the City Tech office where I do much of my work kept me from falling into complete disorganization. Also thanks to the two scholars who share my nook, Caroline Hellman and Johannah Rodgers, both of whom were willing to stop their own work to listen to my complaints and explorative rantings.

Aaron Barlow, Brooklyn, June 15, 2011

ONE

For the Love of *Zoe*

We open our book with two anecdotes that come from very different times. Both of them are recounted by Kevin Kelly: technology writer, speculative thinker, and founder of *Wired* magazine. And both help place the discussion of group intelligence as a real, and not simply speculative, concern.

The first story begins in Las Vegas at the dawn of the internet. In his book *Out of Control,* Kelly describes attending a 1991 conference for computer graphics experts. Attendees walked into the large conference room and were each given a cardboard wand—red on one side and green on the other. Hanging at the front of the auditorium was a display screen that all 5,000 attendees could view. Video cameras, linked up to a host of computers, scanned the audience and registered each wand into the display. Show the red side of the wand, and it shows up on the screen. Flip it, and the green side shows up. Kelly goes on to describe Loren Carpenter, the graphics wizard running this presentation, initiating an illustration of how groups of people can act like swarms under the right conditions.

First, Carpenter loads what Kelly describes as the "ancient game" of Pong, one of the first popular computer games, so that it can be displayed on the screen. After a few instructions, each member of the audience chooses which team to be on and becomes either a red or green paddle. "The audience roars in delight," and "without a moment's hesitation, 5,000 people" divide into two groups and begin the fierce battle of knocking the digital ball past the opposing team.[1] They learn to play so well that Carpenter speeds up the game, and the groups adjust. "The participants squeal in delight," and when the game is sped up again, "the mob learns instantly."

Carpenter challenges the group to another activity; this time he draws a huge circle around the screen and asks the audience if they can make a green number five in the center of the screen. Slowly, the number begins to take shape. Each wand holder decides whether she should be part of the background or the centerpiece. Wands flip back and forth from green to red, and the numeric shape becomes discernible. Those on the edges decide whether they are part of the numeral or not, and the number sharpens into view. Carpenter then asks them to become a four, then a three—the audience catches on, and the countdown takes on a life of its own; they become a two, then a one, then a zero.

The next maneuver is slightly more challenging. This time Carpenter loads a flight simulator and tells half the crowd to control the pitch and the other half to control roll; and in an instant the plane is airborne. The horizontal axis is controlled by 2,500 audience members, the vertical by the other 2,500. In the distance, a runway appears, and so all 5,000 participants attempt to land the plane. They make their approach, but they are about to land on the wing. They can't straighten the plane out and still land in time; groups on one side of the room begin to yell commands to the other side and vice versa, but landing the plane appears to be a maneuver too complex for the mob. They are about to crash, and so they instantaneously pull up, circle, and attempt another approach. Kelly notes that while audience members barked commands at each other to straighten the approach for the landing, nobody spoke when they collectively pulled up and began to circle. Who decided? Why this way and not that way? They begin the second approach.

This time, the alignment is better. Unfortunately, 5,000 people working in concert still express too much error in a maneuver that has very little gray area between safety and devastation. Again, they pull up and begin to circle. This time they tilt as they circle, and the tilt becomes exaggerated. Something comes over them, and "at some magical moment, the same strong thought simultaneously infects five thousand minds: 'I wonder if we can do a 360?' "[2] The group continues their roll and, without directions, it takes on an autonomy and control of its own; it exaggerates the roll, flips the plane on its head, and rights itself again. Five thousand amateur pilots have just completed the first collective horizontal roll. To celebrate, the crowd erupts into a standing wave of self-applause.

The Vegas computer graphics conference Kelly attended in 1991 and wrote about in 1994 foretold the possibilities that graphics engineers would come to witness on the Hollywood screen only a year later. In 1987, a computer graphics researcher by the name of Craig Reynolds had invented a flocking program he called Boids. Boid refers to a bird-like object. Through this computer simulation, Reynolds was able to show that the behavioral rules of flocking and schooling were easy to duplicate. Although it seems magical the way dozens of birds or thousands of fish can behave as though they are governed by a single mind, high-speed film has shown that there is actually a delay of about one-seventeenth of a second between a member and its neighbors.

The phenomenon of flocking and schooling relies on allelo-mimesis, of mimicking your neighbors. Reynolds had discovered three simple rules that could be applied to groups—whether actual or simulated—to show flocking at work:

1. Separation: don't get too close to your neighbors,
2. Alignment: go the same direction as your neighbors, and
3. Cohesion: keep equidistant from your neighbors.[3]

Following these simple rules, Reynolds designed the first computer simulation that showed how flocking behavior could be duplicated by computers. The program can still be viewed from the site that Reynolds continues to maintain (red3d.com/cwr/boids/).

Observing Reynolds's algorithms illustrated by the Boid program, director Tim Burton employed Reynolds and his program to design the flocking behavior of penguins and bats in the 1992 film *Batman Returns.* Not only does flocking behavior work with a group of intelligent graphics engineers, but it also works with the graphics themselves. Most importantly, it can be controlled.

It was around this time in the early '90s that significant advancements were beginning to be noticed with the study of self-organization and complexity. Stuart Kauffman's *The Origin of Order* had been published the year before Kelly's book was released, and Kauffman's more accessible *At Home in the Universe* would be published a year later. Kauffman explains, in *At Home in the Universe,* that the rules governing the process of ontogeny (how life begins) and cosmogony (origins of the universe) are the same principles: ones that are at work for all self-organizing systems. It would appear, then, that certain principles governing life now could be understood. And if they could be understood, they could be simulated.

Given the connections between hive mind and network culture that Kelly was pioneering, it should come as no surprise that Kelly's *Out of Control* was one of the three books the Wachowski brothers required actors to read in order to prepare for *The Matrix,* the famed dystopic film where the world is overtaken by machines and humans are turned into bat-teries.* Arguing that the internet acts like a superorganism, Kelly wrote:

> Nets have their own logic, one that is out-of-kilter to our expectations. And this logic will quickly mold the culture of humans living in a networked world. What we get from heavy-duty communication networks, and the net-works of parallel computing and the networks of distributed appliances and distributed being is Network Culture.[4]

He then added:

> Alan Kay, a visionary who had much to do with inventing personal com-puters, says that the personally owned book was one of the chief shapers of the Renaissance notion of the individual, and that pervasively networked computers will be the main shaper of humans in the future. It's not just individual books we are leaving behind, either. Global opinion polling in real time 24 hours a day, seven days a week, ubiquitous telephones, asyn-chronous e-mail, 500 TV channels, video on demand: all these add up to the matrix for a glorious network culture, a remarkable hivelike being.[5]

The example of the 5,000 attendees helps to illustrate how this connection between technology and nature takes place while illustrating the role that humans might play in serving as a link between the two. Recall Kelly's depiction: "the participants squealed in delight"; one could get a sense of a bright new world of interlinked networks and technologies just waiting to be tapped.

To tap it successfully, however, we need to know a lot more about our-selves and our machines, the networks we create with other humans, and those we build through machines. We need to attempt to understand the

---

* Outside of offering an interpretive reading of the film—something that lies outside the purview of this book—one can only speculate why the Wachowski brothers chose to anthropomorphize machine intelligence into a human visage resembling a Buddha baby surrounded by a Christian halo (*Matrix Revolutions*). If there's one thing that needs to be learned from the power of technology, it is that all things are not reflections of Man. Perhaps these choices contributed to the failure of the final two installments of the *Matrix* trilogy. The essential point, however, is that under the influence of Kelly and similar think-ers, the Wachowski brothers tried their best to show how swarm logic has the potential to reach the point of organization.

role the connected actor plays in the formation and maintenance of the group, and we also need to recognize the group as a composite, and not simply an undifferentiated whole.

Seventeen years after *Out of Control,* Kelly still believes in "glorious network culture," but with the 2011 publication of *What Technology Wants,* he also makes clear that he recognizes that this "hivelike being" may have another side to it, a recognition that brings us to the second of our Kelly anecdotes. In this story, Kelly describes making a visit to Willow Garage, a start-up company near Stanford University, which had designed the PR2: an open-source, personal robot. The PR2 is quite a sophisticated accomplishment, even in the world of robotics. One can see the intricate tasks the robot has been trained to perform on YouTube (willowgarage.com), from receiving internet commands to fetching beers for programmers, to playing billiards, to discerning dirty bottles and cups and clearing them from the office space, to folding towels, and to a host of other domestic activities.

One of its more impressive pieces of programming gets the PR2 to plug itself in when its batteries run low. Kelly writes:

Before the software was perfected, a few unexpected "wants" emerged. One robot craved plugging in even when its batteries were full, and once a PR2 took off without properly unplugging, dragging its chord behind it like a forgetful motorist pulling out of a gas station with the pump hose still in the tank. As its behavior becomes more complex, so will its desires. If you stand in front of a PR2 while it is hungry, it won't hurt you. It will back track and go around the building any way it can to find a plug. It's not conscious, but standing between it and its power outlet, you can clearly feel its want.[6]

A machine that exhibits a desire? This desire is unlike a human desire, but it is a desire nonetheless—and is a significant development in human attempts to understand our machines and ourselves. On a first look, we might think that, like the Wachowski brothers, Kelly is attributing to technology an anthropomorphism that it does not possess, as though unfeeling technologies could experience the feelings of desire that humans experience. Such a move would elevate the status of technology considerably, bringing the world of technological tools onto the human playing field, even if the levels of this field remain unbalanced.

In order to show *how* technologies are able to have wants, Kelly makes a helpful and strong distinction between individual technologies and the ecology to which those technologies belong,[†] something contingent to the autopoiesis, or self-making, that Humberto Maturana and Francisco Varela explore in terms of biological systems. Kelly suggests an analogy to the difference between a bee and its hive. The bee exhibits one set of traits and the hive another. No matter how hard or how long you study the bee, you will not determine the behavior of the hive.[7] Carry the analogy to individual technologies and their associated worlds: Just like you cannot determine the ecology to which the bee belongs by dissecting the bee, you cannot determine the ecology to which the technology belongs by dissecting the gadget. The ecology that both creates and is created by the world of all interconnected technologies is what Kelly chooses to call the "technium." But the analogy only goes so far, since bees are only one species, and Kelly is speaking about the comprehensive network of *all* human-created technologies. The entire animal kingdom would be closer to the scale Kelly is trying to get at. The technium is a massive technological leviathan constituted by complex adaptive systems, superorganisms, and informational chaos. It is not conscious of itself (not yet, anyway) but is both the mother and granddaddy that interlinked complex systems create from the bottom up. In keeping with complex adaptive systems, the children (individual technologies) give birth to the parents (the technium).

What are we to make of this so-called technium that, even today, seems to have its own desires independent from our own? Should we be frightened? Shall we be turning to something like "war in the age of intelligent machines" any day now?[‡]

What does it *mean* to say that a robot has a desire? It's silly to say my blender desires something, right? But what about my bicycle? Or the guitar that sits, waiting patiently on its stand? Does the book that you are reading have a desire different from your own? If we do not dismiss out of hand the idea that technologies and their ecologies exhibit a desire, then these questions must also open a whole host of other questions about what it does and will mean to be a part of technologized society.

Kelly's definition of *want* is outside ordinary usage of the term, where *want* is commonly thought of as a desire to meet a perceived lack, as in

---

† One might be surprised to use the singular form of *ecology*. It would be commonsensical to presume that if you are talking about technologies in the plural, then you would also be talking about the ecologies to which they belonged: ones that are distinct from each other. Kelly is more interested in increasing the scale to observe (or imagine) how all the ecologies form a grand system, what he calls "the technium," discussed below.

‡ We borrow this turn of phrase from Manual De Landa's book by the same name.

I *want* a new pair of shoes or a cool jacket. So, to get a handle on what Kelly means, it's necessary to dispense with the typical notion of desire as a tendency exhibited only by the self-aware—by humans. Though he never cites them, Kelly's understanding of desire shares important affinities with the notion of desire presented by the philosopher-psychoanalyst duo Gilles Deleuze and Felix Guattari. Their ideas provide a broader context for Kelly's notion of desire and allow us to draw very necessary distinctions.

Deleuze's concept of desire is in part forged through his study of 17th-century Dutch philosopher Baruch Spinoza, along with a variety of other thinkers, including Spinoza's younger German contemporary, Gottfried Leibniz. Spinoza is an interesting figure because, unlike other philosophers and theologians writing in the middle of the 17th century (the so-called age of enlightenment), Spinoza did not believe that God transcended or existed beyond the natural world, a stalwart belief that provided the basis for the formation of his philosophical system. In contrast to beliefs of *transcendence* that continue to be the most widely held, even to this day, *immanence* is a term used to describe metaphysical systems in which God is understood as internal to or "immanent within" all things. Of course, many religions do include notions of immanence in order to say that God is in all things, but they generally subordinate that idea to transcendence so that God can also be an external cause of nature, acting on it from outside instead of acting on it from within. Spinoza was not concerned with attempting to rectify the separation between the world and God but rather in explaining how God and the world are "univocal," from the same voice. For Spinoza, the cause or genesis of the world is not and cannot be external to nature. Rather, as Reidar Due explains, the expressive cause is an "internal or a 'genetic' principle."[8] In addition, by borrowing the concept of "expression" from Leibniz, Deleuze argues that for Spinoza the principle of immanence means that "divine nature expresses itself in all things."[9] Thus, God and nature exist in one, and God is expressed in each thing.

Deleuze's reading of Spinoza explains that to be is to belong to nature. Nature is a self-generating infinite substance that has its cause within itself and produces both itself and other things in nature. Since the cause of nature is produced within itself and it produces those things that are finite, there is no rupture between those things that are finite and those that are infinite. This is what Deleuze refers to as the "univocity" of Spinoza's modalities—that all things are connected because the cause is within the source that brings them all into being and that source is self-generating.

God cannot exist apart from this structure, and it is for this reason that Spinoza deems self-generating nature as divine infinite substance—because nothing, especially not God, can exist apart from this structure. From a Spinozist point of view, we are (part) God, and we are living among Gods, and we are born directly and continually from God. As cultural critic Michael Hardt says, immanence over eminence. Pantheism over transcendence.[10] Nature and God are univocal, of the same voice, of the same source.

It is easy to see that if your metaphysics establishes that God is not transcendent and is internal and coequal with nature, it is possible that some might interpret this position as a form of atheism or pantheism. Spinoza suffered such accusations and, before composing his treatise, was excommunicated by the Sephardic community of Amsterdam.[11] This expression of internal genetic cause is echoed in later thinkers who also influenced Deleuze and Guattari, particularly two influential theorists of the early 20th century: philosopher Henri Bergson and psychoanalyst Carl Jung. Bergson called this causal agent, this gush of the raw energy that produces life, *elan vital,* a force that accounts not only for the process of evolution but also for the creative impulses found in nature and in humans.

Bergson's account of *elan vital* also had strong resonances with Jung's work. After having broken his relationship with Freud, Jung found an intellectual cousin in Bergson, particularly in the echo to Jung's theories concerning libido.[§] Libido is typically understood to mean sexual desire, but Jung's version of libido differs from the accepted Freudian definition. (As the story goes, it was partly their disagreement concerning the libido that led to the dissolution of the relationship between Freud and Jung.) In contrast to Freud, Jung laid out a view that libido was much more comprehensive than sexual desire; sexual desire, to him, is only one of the expressions of a more generalized desire, which should be considered a genetic, pre-evolutionary cause.

Helping make the connection to Deleuze, Christian Kerslake explains:

> The rechristening of libido as "desire" (without specifying it be *sexual*) is one of Jung's first moves against Freud. Jung points out that, in classical

---

§ Commenting on the affinity of their two, independently produced ideas, Jung writes: "When I first read Bergson a year and a half ago I discovered to my great pleasure everything which I had worked out practically, but expressed by him in consummate language and in wonderfully clear philosophic style." In Henri Bergson and Arthur Mitchell (trans.), *Creative Evolution*, xv.

times, the latin word *libido* had the more general sense of "passionate desire" or simply "desire.". . . Deleuze's understanding of desire in *Difference and Repetition* is explicitly indebted to Jung's conception.[12]

It would be overambitious to attribute a direct and causal connection between Jung's theories of libido and Deleuze's theories of desire, especially since Deleuze was influenced by a dizzying number of philosophical, psychoanalytical, scientific, mathematical, and artistic movements and thinkers (and has influenced perhaps just as many). The point is that there is a strong history of thought that links desire to a productive self-generating energy of life. Sometimes Deleuze calls this energy "desire," but many also call it becoming, immanence, intensity, multiplicity, the virtual, and so on.

When speaking of a human context, Deleuze frequently uses the term *desire*. But while desire may be a term used to discuss how it (immanence, *elan vital,* etc.) runs through humans, it does not originate from one's conscious choices, emotions, or experiences—all of which find their sources in human life. We are able, of course, to consciously influence our desires, but in this scheme, consciousness itself is inhabited by other desires influencing and being influenced by the desires running through us on emotional, neurological, psychic, neuronal, and other bodily levels. Different desires pass through us simultaneously: some in competition with another, some supporting one another, some redirecting others, some channeling others, some combining with others; we are conscious of a few of them, most of them we are not. In any of these cases, the individual is not their source, certainly not simply and not completely.

Following in this Deleuzian vein, cultural theorist Rosi Braidotti also distinguishes this force in this way so that it does not get confused with the life force that belongs singularly to human life, something with which much modern and even postmodern thought has been overly, narcissistically concerned. To distinguish this force from *biological* concerns, Braidotti calls this particular energy "*zoe.*"[13] Speaking in the context of the impact that advanced technologies are having on contemporary life, Braidotti writes, "What returns now is the 'other' of the living body in its humanistic definition: the other face of *bios,* that is to say *zoe,* the generative vitality of non- or pre-human or animal life."[14] Call it what you will, the raw energy of immanence (Spinoza) or *elan vital* (Bergson) or libido (Jung) or will to power (Nietzsche) or lamella (Lacan) runs through each of us and through all things. Desire comes from elsewhere, not specifically from consciousness; in this sense, it is *nonorganic* life.

But there is another interesting thing in what Braidotti says, something that turns us back toward Kelly—that the force of *zoe* is making a return. Why? Why now?

For the sake of being exact, it is not really a matter of *zoe* making a return, but that larger numbers of people have begun to notice that what was before generally an invisible force is now taking a more invasive and insidious role in daily life and having increasing influence on the direction of society. The increased power of computing over the past 30 years has led to myriad technologies and inventions that are having an impact on our world. For the worse or for the better? It is still difficult to say, and, as with many issues where there is no clear-cut course of action, sides are being taken, arguments being made, lines in the sand being drawn.

If we look to Kelly and his followers in order to measure Braidotti's suggestion that the technological ecology expresses desire, we will soon discover that we must be assured that we are exploring in the right direction. Of course, technological inventions of the past have expressed desires before, and people have also gotten alarmed at the way the progress of technics seemed to change the shape of culture. But desire, we see today, clearly is not limited to the conscious individual and, in this sense, is beyond our control. Is this bad? One of the favorite arguments of social media apologists is the proposition that people have decried new technologies in the past, saying that they would ruin culture and change everything for the worse. Yet, the apologists quickly point out, so-called technological progress has actually often made things *better* even as some things are lost. "The sky didn't fall," they say. "Culture is alive and well, thank you very much." Are they right?

We would never suggest that our current technologies are creating a doomsday situation, but we would say that the change that is occurring now is, for better or worse, like nothing that has occurred in modern history. It is on a scale of change that has only been seen two or three times before in all of human history: the first time some 50,000 years ago when homo sapiens acquired language. The second came about roughly 4,000 years ago with the invention of the alphabet. This most recent historical shift, the revolution we are currently experiencing, is certainly just as significant as the shift that Walter Ong outlines: from a world primarily comprised of oral culture to a world primary comprised of literate cultures, the third great change. To see a clear example of how significant and revolutionary this last shift is, one needs only to look at the contrast between the way people live and behave in Western culture (founded on literacy) against tribal culture (founded on oral tradition). In 2012, it is becoming more and more difficult to find examples of tribal, nonliterate peoples who continue to live in an oral culture—a fact that itself shows that, though the shift is slow and gradual, it is also pervasive, almost universal.** The shift that is now happening is one that has been underway at least since the invention of electricity. Some people call this a shift toward *digital literacy,* but that term captures neither the sense of scope nor the quite real glacial nature of the shift (and glaciers, remember, move slowly seen in the aggregate but sometimes quite quickly, in the particular).

As Marshall McLuhan pointed out, modern Western civilization is grounded on being literate. Everything about the order, linearity, hierarchy, and efficiency of modern thought—from the divisions of the sciences, to the economy, to the structures of cities—would not have been possible without the abstraction and linearity that comes from the printed word. This most recent evolutionary stage, however, may even prove to be an undoing of literacy and, in that case, it might also be an undoing of the foundations of Western civilization. If you feel like our culture no longer seems to have any ground to be sure of, you can at least be confident that it's not just you who feels that way. It is literacy itself—the ground beneath our feet—that is shifting. Fortunately, much of the movement, though often seeming fast, is slow and gradual, so we have the opportunity to learn to reinvent the old ways of doing things for the new milieu. The difficulty is that the speed of technological change *does* follow a pattern of acceleration. As with glaciers, the changes, even when slow, happen faster than we might think.

The time will come when this book will be like a scroll from the past. Books in the future will go through periods of what Jay Bolter and Richard Grusin have called "remediation" before the past vestiges fall away like an old skin and the new form blossoms, continues to evolve, and then hits a plateau of little to no change.†† But the change of the form of the book to whatever the book will come to be in 100 years is only one side

---

** However, while there are few tribal cultures left, 20 percent of the world's population is illiterate, a situation revealing that while the machine of civilization is good at upsetting tribal ecosystems, it also wastes human potential at alarming rates (discussed in the final chapter).

†† Remediation: generally defined when a new medium or technological form borrows vestiges of an older, established form to make it palatable to an audience, oftentimes without recognizing that it is acting as a remediator. An example is cars from the 1960s that used faux wood paneling or the notion of the "Web page" that for a long time resembled a newspaper page. Today, web pages have fallen to uninteresting and too easily producible templates that remediate convenience and little more.

of the story. The way we think, no longer influenced quite so strongly by alphabetic writing and linear thinking, is the other side of this change. In fact, it may be the way that thought occurs under periods of sustained writing that will really prove to be at the heart of the future of the book, not simply the physical manifestation (which will probably be myriad, anyhow).

Every technological innovation carries a loss with it. Take, for instance, one of the stories behind Eugene Burdick and William Lederer's novel *The Ugly American*. McLuhan recounts it, telling of a series of Indian villages that was "fortunate" enough to receive the "wisdom" and "generosity" of modernization efforts put forth by the United Nations Education, Scientific and Cultural Organization (UNESCO). In efforts to provide the villages with running water, a series of tubes and pipes were installed in the villages. After a short period of time, the elders approached those who had installed the plumbing and asked that it be removed. When asked why, the village leaders explained that they did not realize that the installation of the pipes was going to mean that it would remove the need to go to the central watering hole where they communed daily with their neighbors.[15] Westerners, put bluntly, do not think about pipes for the most part, not unless they are plumbers or if one of the pipes is leaking. If pressed, Westerners think about plumbing as a necessity; we are way beyond seeing plumbing as a convenience and, while we can sympathize with the villagers' objections and desire to preserve the ties of their community, we hold no such allegiances of community over such an important personal convenience.

The villagers recognized that they would lose an essential tie to communal life by accepting such an advancement. "We do not think of it [running water] as culture or as a product of literacy, any more than we think of literacy as changing our habits, emotions, or our perceptions. To nonliterate people, it is perfectly obvious that the most commonplace conveniences represent total changes in culture," wrote McLuhan.[16]

The question about the future of the book that must be asked is in what way will the thought process that accompanies the literate mind change along with the technology. Will the future book even stabilize into a constant, reliable form? Right now, books come in multiple forms: from e-books you can read on your computer; to ones that can be read on the Kindle, Nook, Sony Reader, or other similar device; to books that are being published in multimedia formats designed for the iPad. To be *computer literate* or *digitally literate* means being able to adapt to a variety of different applications and platforms both on and off "the cloud." Less and less does being literate simply carry the connotation of being able to abstract strong comprehension from that which is being read. Can you open a Kindle, find the correct page, and highlight a particular passage? This, today, is part of what literacy is becoming. Will there be a proliferation of forms and devices so that the word *literacy* in the traditional sense loses any meaning at all? The book is a good technological example for discussion of the slow/fast shift that we all are experiencing. As we have said, this shift amounts in the end to a shift in how future humans will think. Western civilization is founded on alphabetic literacy; the future will be based elsewhere.

When the *want* of technology was felt by humans in the past, the reasons were generally quite different from the reasons why humans feel the want of technology today. Still, then as now, one needed to be careful what one wished for. Take, for instance, the *want* of hand cranks for starting cars before the invention of the starter motor. It was a step up from pushing the whole vehicle, but it had its drawbacks. A person wishing to start the vehicle would have to apply a considerable amount of force while holding the handle in a quite unnatural way. If the owners were cautious enough to prevent being run over by their own vehicle, they would have already placed the gear in neutral, after chocking the wheels so the vehicle would not roll away. Owners were advised to hold the crank with the thumb next to the forefinger, gripping the crank handle with an overhand grip rather than a more natural style of grabbing the crank with fingers on one side and thumb on the other. This was because, on attempting to start the car, the cylinders in the engine might kick back due to improper positioning. A cylinder would rotate in the opposite direction and cause the engine to momentarily rotate the wrong way. A person holding the crank with a wraparound grip could easily break a thumb. Or consider the number of people it took in order for the early telephone to work. As recently as the '60s, a soldier making a long distance phone call from a remote location to a girlfriend in the United States would have to go through a number of human operators to complete the call. Prior to the telephone, the telegraph required operators who could signal and interpret Morse code. Traditionally, when new technologies are introduced into a culture, they quickly become apparent (unless they don't catch on) because they change the way we behave in ways that are evident, but also because they often do not work the way they should ideally work.

The presence of technology, clearly, has always made itself apparent. Tim Wu, who has written an account that speaks to the repeating historical patterns of the adoption of different technologies, echoes social media supporters when he writes that "the Internet wasn't the first information technology supposed to have changed everything forever."[17] Wu's point is an interesting one, and it is worth quoting further:

> Again and again in the past hundred years the radical change promised by new ways to receive information has seemed, if anything, more dramatic than it does today. Thanks to radio, predicted Nikola Tesla, one of the founders of commercial electricity, in 1904, "the entire earth will be converted into a huge brain, as it were, capable of response in every one of its parts." The invention of film, wrote D. W. Griffith in the 1920s, meant that "children in the public schools will be taught practically everything by moving pictures. Certainly they will never be obliged to read history again." In 1970, a Sloan foundation report compared the advent of cable television to that of movable type: "the revolution now in sight may be nothing less. . . . It may be conceivable more. As a character in Tom Stoppard's *The Invention of Love*, set in 1876, remarks, "Every age thinks it's the modern age, but this one really is."[18]

Wu takes a long view on the introduction of various technologies, finding that each new technology follows a consistent, cyclical pattern:

1. A new technology appears every few decades. A lot of hype occurs around the technology. People dream of a better future, but they also worry about the loss and destruction the new technology will cause.
2. The innovation brings on a period of economic chaos where multiple stakeholders bring different versions of the product to market. This chaos leads to instability and an overabundance of choice. (Early cars, for instance, were of numerous kinds, including not just different brands but those powered by wind, steam, water, coal, and petrol.)
3. Either through competition or through governmental regulation, the market stabilizes because, to borrow Wu's terminology, *the mogul* promises a more stable environment for the customers and also promises a steady stream of income for those who would benefit from market stabilization. (The gas-powered car wins out over the others.)
4. After time, this centralization ossifies to the point where innovation becomes stagnant, and people dream up other ways to accomplish tasks. A new wave of technological innovation, often coupled with governmental deregulation and decentralization occurs, and the cycle begins once more.

For Wu, the internet falls neatly into this cycle. He suggests that it won't be too long before Google takes over the world through a business model that gives software and applications away for free so that it can expand the territory that is conducive and friendly to Google. Google wants to be everywhere and involved in everything, and giving its developments away for free is one way of continuing its dominance.[19]

By drawing our attention away from the particular moment and asking us to take a longer view of modern information technologies, Wu helps us to put technological progress into perspective. This is not the first time people have said that a new technology would change the world. There is a significant difference, however, in the media corporations that Wu concentrates on from pre-internet days onward and the internet as a technology itself. Since Wu is primarily concerned with tracking the rise and fall of traditional media and telecommunications, it is important to recognize that computer engineers are well into the process of overcoming limitations in bandwidth both from the perspective of laying down more efficient cable and finding more efficient methods of delivery. Soon, we will have a situation where the internet is a medium where all forms of traditional media can be delivered: image, text, sound, and moving pictures, in addition to their combination, and ever more than can now be effortlessly and immediately shared. Wu understands this difference, and openly wonders whether the innovation of the internet, that it is able to deliver all kinds of information, is powerful enough to change the cyclical pattern that he has identified. In the end, Wu is confident that we are now in a position of individual openness and sharing like nothing that we have ever been in before. Perhaps it is even inevitable that history will shift in the opposite direction, a welcome day for those who feel lost and out of sorts in the information bomb.

But while these cycles do occur, and while it is true that each new technology brings with it both harbingers of doom and glory, it is worth remembering that although Nicolai Tesla, D. W. Griffith, and the Sloan Foundation all predicted that their technologies would lead to massive changes that would spell the end of individuality, literacy, and book publishing in favor of technologies that lead to collective wisdom, something else happened. We would do well to remember that, even a tenth of the way through the 21st century, the entrenched forces of literacy and the hold that they have on our institutions are not proving easily replaced.

Wu's suggestion that the cycle repeats itself throughout the course of history misses a critical component, the slow/fast shift we spoke about earlier. It's important that we read our Ong and our McLuhan, but you won't find mention of either in Wu's book, interesting and insightful as it is. The blind spot to the next horizon, what Paul Virilio calls the *third horizon* (after orality and literacy) is outside of Wu's scope.

Unlike the technologies of the past, internet technologies have the power and potential of authentic ubiquity. To think that one can use his phone to program his DVR to record the game while having dinner at the restaurant! The internet does not fit neatly into the cyclical patterns that Wu discusses, for it is not a technology that performs a function that could not be performed before. Rather than performing a function, it creates a space so that functions can be performed more easily, efficiently, and quickly, and so that new technologies can continue to be invented. It is platform, fabric, space, and network. It is one that carries previous media of film, photography, radio, television, news, magazines, and intellectual and academic work of all kinds as well as giving birth to new creations. The network also connects mobiles, ground transportation of all kinds, airplanes, maritime vessels, satellites, household appliances, and apparel. While it does not have the negative connotations suggested in the films by the Wachowski brothers, it is truly a global matrix. Consider that, as of 2008, the internet housed:

- 100 billion clicks per day
- 55 trillion links
- 1 quintillion transistors
- 1 billion PC chips
- 2 million emails per second
- 1 million IM messages per second
- 8 terabytes of traffic per second
- 65 billion phone calls per year
- 255 exabytes of magnetic storage
- 1 million voice queries per hour
- 2 billion location nodes activated[20]

What would cable television and the phone system have looked like if people on the network were able to add to programs onto the system? What if, from their own living rooms, people were able to create their own channels, their own shows, and instantly add them to the network that everyone else was receiving? If this potential had been built into the system from the start, what would have cable television evolved into?

Even in such a thought experiment, the medium of the cable TV would have limited the potential for the technology to do other things external to the cable media platform. You can't send analog video signals through a radio channel, but on the internet all of these media converge and strange things that no longer seem strange all—such as Twitter—become possible.

To return to the question of *zoe,* people are noticing a new force that does not belong to human knowledge or desire but belongs to technology. It is not because the internet is new (in one sense it is still an infant, and in another sense young people and children have grown up with it and have witnessed its changes), and it is not because it is expressing its own particularities and malfunctions—though it does make itself known for these reasons as well. People are starting to notice the desire of technology because it is already and always there. It is always on, and we are always connected, addicted. And here's the rub: the addiction is not individual as a person who is addicted to heroin. The addiction is worldwide. Soon, we will no longer call it an addiction; we won't even notice it. Soon it will be an integral part of who we are. Even today, try asking an iPhone user to go a week without it. Facebook and Google are becoming, and in many ways have already become, an infrastructure to global civilization.

As of June 2011, 311 million people were living in the United States.[21] Facebook alone has almost twice that number of people as active members on the site, with 1 in 13 people on the globe having an active account.[22] We feel the want of technology because more and more it is becoming the governing force in daily life, and we begin to feel lost without it.

We can predict with some degree of certainty three things:

1. The internet will continue to grow at breakneck speed.
2. Communication tools will tend toward being unseen and unnoticed, becoming part of the background.
3. Technologies will get better at satisfying human needs not only as they arise, but they will also attempt to anticipate what those needs will be in advance. This will mean that intelligent machines will talk to other machines about human desires even more frequently than machines will create customized ads and web pages for individual users.

French theorist of technology Paul Virilio has been drawing readers' attention to the crisis conditions brought on by what he calls "dromospheric pollution." *Dromos* comes from the Greek root meaning foot race. Virilio is keen on what we might best call the logic of acceleration and recognize that the current technological milieu has led to a general sedentary condition. For Virilio, the ways in which people of the modern world think and behave changed as a result of modern technologies, causing a reciprocal sense of loss and gain. These changes have occurred largely as a result of the light speed of real-time technology. In other words, as transmissions of all kinds become more and more dominant over modern life, the distances of traditional notions of time and space are erased. As we spend more time taking pictures, watching television, viewing film, and surfing the internet, light speed—the absolute now—dominates chronological time while instantaneous presence, the fusing of the here with the there, dominates territorial space.

The modern conveniences associated with the closing of time and space throw the modern world reeling into a crisis. Because more time is spent becoming familiar with those who are telepresent, those who are present become strangers. We gain a society that is present both here and there at the same time, but we lose the tale (and our interpretations) of the traveler who tells us about worlds afar. We gain instantaneous information but lose memory. Instead of volume, we now have just surface. Rather than the measure of the life-size object, we substitute the measure of the televisual image. Most importantly, these remote-control technologies, because they cut holes through time and space and unite the near with the far, sever any reason for us to move beyond our homes and offices. From an outside perspective, perhaps this is hyperbolic; but from the perspective of the viewer or computer user, Virilio's statement rings true: "This is the end of the outside world."[23]

One of the knacks technology often has is for attempting to fix the problems that it creates, as long as those problems can be fixed; but the problem here is more than the fact that computers tie us to desks. With the evolution of the ubiquitous smartphone in many cases replacing the laptop, which, in many cases is replacing the need for a desktop, it would appear that computers have gone mobile. And they have, at least in the sense that you can carry them from one place to the next, but nobody wants to if doing so isn't necessary.

In 2011, laptops could not be outside on a sunny day, as liquid crystal displays (LCDs) cannot accommodate bright light. In 2012, this is already changing with the advancement of active-matrix organic light emitting diode (AMOLED) displays. These displays use organic properties, and the screen itself generates its own light once it receives very low dosages of electrical current. Furthermore, the screens can be made so thin that they can be transparent and flexible. While the iPad, Kindle, iPhone, and smartphones do not have the computing power, size, or application functionality of computers, they still carry a powerful punch of computing power. Rather than people locked up in their homes and offices surfing the internet, we now experience the phenomenon of people looking at their phones while being with others, sometimes for extended period of times. It's common to see a gaggle of teenagers gathered around a table having lunch, each one of them deeply into their world inside their phones, no doubt on some occasions texting the same people they happen to be sitting next to. Now, we take our virtual worlds with us, and even as we experience the world we do not experience it.

Virilio's argument that modern telecommunications causes us to lose mobility because we can communicate more efficiently through computers screens should be updated with the information that those screens have themselves become mobile so that we can communicate with our 503 Facebook friends while on the move, or with our heads into a small screen while at the basketball game or at dinner with friends. The problem Virilio identifies remains, particularly in this separation between the virtual and physical worlds. So, what does one do? If you do define this as a problem, and you are either a computer engineer or a company looking to innovate, you develop an application that allows the possibility of bridging the physical and virtual worlds.

And so we enter the next stage of ubiquitous computing. Some of it is already here: BUMP is an application that can be downloaded to iPhone and Android applications that allows two phones to share information by physically tapping the phones together. Another application called Layars allows virtual information of all kinds to be superimposed on the physical world. To use it, one looks through a phone's camera screen and chooses a "layer." If one chooses the Starbucks layer, one can look through the screen and see the landscape. Superimposed on that landscape will appear location points for the coffee shops. If you choose the Wikipedia layer, anything within the vicinity that has a corresponding Wikipedia entry will appear as a link in the screen. When one of us tried Layars in a populated area of Brooklyn, NY, the Wikipedia entries for the local hospital, park, and other attractions appeared. The application contains layers for oodles of information, from real estate hunting, to finding blog posts written by friends or neighbors, to connecting with love interests, to finding dog parks, and more. If one chooses all the layers at once and is in a developed place, one's screen will offer hundreds of links providing information about what is seen.

Virilio's lament that the material world is lost for the virtual world is beginning to collapse: the two spaces are moving toward convergence. First, media converged so that it all could be delivered through the computer. Soon the physical world will also be delivered by the virtual one.

The onset of technologies that bridge the virtual and the physical seems like a natural step. Why shouldn't we use our phones to provide more information and interaction with the world that lies before us? We walk up to a university campus and, looking through the Layars program on our

Droid, we access the Wikipedia entry on the university. Hungry, we are able to check out the Yelp reviews of the cafeteria food.

Imagine a bird's eye view of 100 people simultaneously using the Layars application on a busy New York City block. It's not necessarily a pretty picture. A hundred people looking through 2.5 inch screens to navigate the busiest city in America. Accidents would happen. People would get run over by cars and buses. Mayhem. All these technologies working to close the gap between the tradeoff between those things gained and those things lost are really moving the user to spend more time looking through the screen.

Is it possible, as the applications suggest, to really bridge the gap between the physical and virtual worlds? At the moment, we look through the screens on mobiles to see the virtual world and all the information the internet has to offer about our particular location. Yet, who knows when or if we may tire of carrying gadgets. A phone screen certainly cannot replace a natural field of vision. The mobile screen should serve as a spatial calculation as to how large of window should be opened in material space to the virtual. At the moment, these screens are small. They only allow limited information. Bigger screens would allow more information to pass through, but they would be impractical to carry. Smaller screens, the size of contact lenses, would give a complete field of view and allow invisible integration of the physical and the virtual. The technology is underway. Professor Babak Parviz at the University of Washington has already invented such lenses and has tested them on rabbits.[24]

While mobile windows to the virtual are small today, the windows we look through at home and work are considerably larger. These are the places where we still work or where we still have a form of working. For while the internet causes media to converge, it also causes play and work to converge as well. As goes the media so goes humanity.

Today, the computer is where we do everything. No longer are there separate places for working, playing, relaxing, watching, listening, socializing, volunteering, or participating in civic or other forms of social life. Everything happens through the computer. Facebook may not be work, but it has the same *feeling*, the same bodily orientation to the computer as work. "Facebook is amazing because it feels like you're doing something and you're not doing anything," said a struggling high school student in a recent *New York Times* article. "It's the absence of doing something, but you feel gratified anyway."[25]

Information and its exchange are embodied in screens; machines; and what Donald Norman calls *information appliances,* a clunky term meant to designate a gadget that provides a transparent window between the user and the content. While the term may be ugly, the aesthetics of some of these so-called appliances are sometimes truly beautiful. While it is common now, remember the sense of awe the first time you saw the iPhone or iPod touch rotate its screen. We are bedazzled and bewitched by each new bauble. Seduced. What does technology want? It wants to be in your pocket. It wants a home. Like any parasite, it wants a host.

Apple has a commercial for the iPad2. While providing a close-up shot of the slim, sleek, pleasing profile—technology's version of a swimsuit model—a soothing, gentle, even sultry man's voice begins:

> This is what we believe. Technology alone is not enough. Faster, thinner, lighter . . . those are good things. But when technology gets out of the way, everything becomes more delightful . . . even magical. That's when you leap forward. That's when you end up with something like this.

The premise behind this commercial, that the technology should not be an obstacle between the user and the content, has a number of different layers. This commercial is a brave stroke from our vantage point. One should sense immediately that something is wrong, that they are being hypnotized. Seduced. On the other hand, there are plenty of people who believe that technology should get out of the way.

One of the foundational treatises about computer design, targeted specifically to companies who made computers and their offspring, is Donald Norman's *The Invisible Computer*. One of his central arguments is that technological products have a life cycle spanning birth, adolescence, and maturity. When a new technological product comes to market, the niche of the product is not typically immediately apparent. So-called early adopters purchase the product even though there is no clear, marketable need. In the early days of mp3 players, for instance, mp3s only allowed music enthusiasts to buy individualized songs rather than the whole CD, itself not a new idea. This allowed people to create playlists that jumped from artist to artist, just as a record stacker did in the days of the 45 rpm single, or a jukebox did. In this case, the consequence of cutting up albums into individualized songs for sale once more meant that artists generated less revenue through the sale of albums. Rather, the sale of albums now helps to fuel the markets that revolve around concert touring, product endorsement deals, and supplemental products such as t-shirts and the like.[26] When mp3s started appearing, it turned out there were enough people who would rather not be required to purchase an entire album and invest energy into developing a relationship with an artist, people who would rather develop their own musical interests independently. Top 40 radio already filtered the hits from the rest (went the mindset), and it's better to purchase a single song rather than have to pay for a whole album.

Of course, early mp3 players were high in price, low in storage capacity, finicky to use, and difficult to set up. It was a technology in its infancy, as Norman would say. Early adopters, however, are willing to pay high prices for glitchy products in order to stay on the cutting edge of technological change. As time goes by, technologies enter into an adolescent stage. Norman suggests that technologies at this stage seem to act as though they have been injected with testosterone and try to pack as many features as possible into a gadget, whether they make sense or not. Anyone who has ever purchased a computer has noticed all the "bloatware" that comes bundled with the operating system: software that eats up memory, slows the system considerably, and adds an extra, unnecessary layer of mediation between the user and the content.

The final level is maturity. When products enter a mature phase, the kinks have been worked out and glitches have become rare. The makers have gotten over the sense that they have something to prove by offering useless and redundant features that do little more than reinforce the brand. In the mature phase, the product's aim is to do its best to enable the user to do what she or he needs to do as quickly and as efficiently as possible.‡‡

In 1998, when Norman wrote this book, he argued that computers were still in the juvenile phase. He was dissatisfied with the difficulty associated with using computers, and he pitched his book as part of an overall consulting package meant to help computer companies develop better designs so they would be simple to use, the complexity disappearing into the background. He wrote:

> Today's technology imposes itself on us, making demands on our time and diminishing our control over our lives of all the technologies perhaps the most disruptive for individuals is the personal computer. The computer is really an infrastructure, even though today we treat it as the end object. Infrastructures should be invisible. And that is exactly what this book recommends: a user-centered, human centered humane technology where today's personal computer has disappeared into invisibility.[27]

---

‡‡ For all intents and purposes, computers are likely still in their infancy, though they have gotten sleaker and performed better over the years.

Right around the time Norman was writing this book, he left his position at University of California, San Diego and joined the team at Apple as a design consultant. Perhaps it should come as no surprise that his ideas are reflected in the philosophy Apple touts in the iPad2 commercial. Information appliances should get out of the way and become a transparent window that will allow a movie buff to enjoy her movies or a cousin to check Facebook, or the four-year old to be quiet while playing a video game.

But while we appreciate the use and elegance of Apple products as much as the next person, this idea of invisibility should also give us some pause.

It is actually quite fortunate the *zoe* is rearing its head now, at this critical stage, especially because technology is expressing its desire at the same time that its ubiquity is being felt by the cultural imagination. It will not be long before many of the technologies and gadgets we use today will become outdated and will surely and slowly disappear from use. It will be at that stage where there appears an invisible infrastructure where the internet, or what it will become, will have invaded every cavern—a massive growing nervous system, billions of cameras, terabytes, petabytes, exabytes, and zettabytes.[§§] Once computer technologies disappear from our concerns and anxieties, and once they disappear from reflection, then it will be very difficult to make significant changes. In effect, the iPad, the personal computer, and the Droid will have created a world we will be powerless to change. The scary part is that it will become a network inventing itself; we will no longer have any say in what it will look like or what kinds of people and minds it will birth.

Any interesting book about technology and media is in one way or another an expansion of the '60s McLuhanesque concept that the medium is the message. A medium is the technological apparatus through which the content is delivered, and according to McLuhan's laws, the content of a medium is always another medium. The content of writing is speech. The content of radio is phonography. The content of film is a novel or a play. We pay attention to the story being told through the film and, as we do, we miss the effects the film is having on our brains, bodies, community, economy, and so on.

---

§§ By 2015, annual global IP traffic will reach 1 zetabyte. According to Cisco's Visual Networking Index IP Traffic Chart, 400 terabytes is the equivalent of a digitized library of all books written by humans in all languages. Sixty-six zetabytes is the equivalent of all the visual information processed by the human brain—by the entire human race—in a year.

It may be said that the message of the medium is to be wary and attentive to the shaping force of the medium. Millions of women and men get manicures each year. What if the medium of nail polish were different? What if applying polish did not involve someone brushing the paint onto your nails with a tiny brush but rather offered you a bucket to dip your fingers into and then provided the service of cleaning off the polish from the surrounding skin? Why are the keys of the keyboard arranged as QWERTY in the upper left-hand corner of the keyboard, making it difficult for people to learn keyboarding? Why are the designs and applications of video games becoming more important as time moves on? Such speculations are infinite in their variety, but all of them question the effect that media have on configuring the world that we live in.

The greatness of McLuhan's apothegm is that it drew attention away from the content being delivered and caused people to become cognizant of the medium itself. The weakness of the statement, however, is that the influence of the medium is understated. A medium conveys something much more than a message. Messages are pieces of information that can be accepted or dispensed. Individual mediums are embodied and have physical presence. The news report can be ignored, but the television takes up physical space and serves as an organizing principle of interior design in millions of living rooms.

We can turn off the television and read a library's worth of books, but a hardcore gamer will notice our lack of fluency in the gaming medium. When the book that was to carry the title the *Medium is the Message* came back from the printer with a typo and was mistakenly titled *The Medium is the Massage,* McLuhan was delighted. By working us over, the medium did indeed give us a *massage* by allowing one to feel better momentarily, but the media also contributed to a false sense of security by simultaneously and paradoxically fostering a culture of anxiety. For McLuhan, *message* and *massage* opened to other forms of play that revealed other truisms such as the medium is also the "mass age" as well as the age that is also a "mess."

Friedrich Kittler, another influential cultural critic of technics, though agreeing with McLuhan's ideas on several points, pushes them in new, interesting, and rather insightful ways. He drives McLuhan's claim that the medium is the message to its logical limit, saying that the "media determines our situation."[28] In *Digital Matters: Theory and Culture of the Matrix,* Jan Harris and Paul Taylor illustrate how McLuhan explains the conceptual differences in thinking that result from two different ages, an explanation that applies perfectly to Kittler as well.

For both McLuhan and Kittler:

Media determine the ratios of man's senses and the structure of human societies; thus, [McLuhan] argued that the emergence of the phonetic alphabet
effects a cultural revolution: in substituting "an eye for an ear" it frees man
from the "tribal trance of resonating word magic and the web of kinship."
Likewise, the invention of movable type ushered in an entire "galaxy," one
of whose components was a certain expression of man, understood as a
rational linear thinker, while, as the "first uniformly repeatable 'commodity,'" printed matter provided a new paradigm for production. Similarly, the
global village was a direct result of the emergence of new non-textual media
that replicated the modalities of those senses that had been exiled by the
triumph of print, offering an omnipresent immersion rather than a discrete
sequence. Thus, for McLuhan [and Kittler], the attention deficit often im-
puted to the young was simply a clash between different media-determined
sensory regimes: the linear processing of an older generation born in a primarily textual age and the immersive sensibility of youth inculcated in a
multimedia matrix. Thus, media are matrices that determine the nature of
their epoch "by altering the environment, [media] evoke in us unique ratios
of sense perception . . . when these ratios change, men change."[29]

Kittler stresses the idea that since we are born in different ages, we will
have abilities and capacities suitable to the particular age. Ages are defined
by media—by information delivery and process—more than by anything
else. In the age of books and linear logic, the medium that determined the
age was the printed word. The word had given birth to an abstract linear
logic that followed a set of rules and methods. As a consequence, the logic
that culminated in the industrial age and the planning and foresight of
19th-century America was influenced and inspired by the letters, literature, logic, and philosophy of the day. The electronic age and the digital
age no longer follow these patterns so rigorously, though vestiges remain.

While McLuhan and Kittler are in agreement concerning the possibilities for human action in a particular techno-historical age, they disagree
over the relationship between the human and the technological. McLuhan
famously wrote that technologies extend the human body and as a consequence, the central nervous system. The axe extends what the hand can do
(allowing it to fell a tree). The automobile extends the speed and distance
humans can travel. Writing extends the voice by allowing its words to be
recorded, and it also extends memory and the brain by allowing thought
to be retrieved.

Modern media writer Nicholas Carr has recently argued that McLuhan's
point is considerably more than a metaphor—at least from the perspective

of recent neurological breakthroughs. Carr explains that the technologies we employ have the ability to physically change the composition and organization of the brain, writing of an area of neurological research called neuroplasticity. Supporting the phenomena that the brain is "plastic" (in the sense of adaptable and flexible—like a muscle), this research grew partly from studying the phantom limb experiences of amputees. Norman Doidge in *The Brain that Changes Itself,* for instance, tells the story of a man who suffered a stroke at the age of 54, one that damaged an area on the right half of his brain that regulated the left side of his body. While he regained some control of his body after physical therapy, his left hand remained severely crippled, and he continued to walk with a cane. After enrolling in an experimental study at the University of Alabama that concentrated on the relationship between physical movement and the neurological organization of the brain, the man was able to regain normal motor skills by performing mundane tasks over and over again: tasks such as washing a windshield or tracing the letters of the alphabet.

This therapy is based on research that has shown that the visual cortex does not simply stop responding in people who go blind, but that it is "taken over by circuits used for audio processing."[30] Nancy Kanwisher of MIT's McGovern Institute for Brain Research helps explain: "Neurons seem to 'want' to receive input. . . . when their visual input disappears, they start responding to the next best thing."[31] "Thanks to the ready adaptability for neurons, the senses of hearing and touch can grow sharper to mitigate the effects of the loss of sight."[32] The experience of the man tapping into other neurological regions to compensate for a damaged area to the brain is not something that has occurred in isolation or that brain scientists do not understand. Carr does a fine job of mapping out the history and changes in the established dogma that originally believed the brain was genetically hard wired where the scientific community believed that physical changes to an adult brain were impossible, to the earliest experiments on the brain's plasticity and ability to reorganize itself. The brain is a complex adaptive system; many of its secrets still remaining hidden from view. From a neurological standpoint, Carr argues that the shift that is happening from an age of literacy to an age of the network is quite literally changing the physicality of our brains.

Carr's points about the neurological changes that occur gain their full significance when we recognize that the brain also reorganizes itself according to the cultural milieu to which it belongs and inhabits. The plasticity that Carr discusses shows how the information that is part of an era becomes a major force in how cognition develops. So, it turns out that 'the medium is the message' is more than a simple catchphrase. While technologies may be extensions of humans in some cases, they have a way of reaching back into our neurological systems and physically changing the way brains are formed.

From the starting blocks, Kittler is one who has believed in the autonomy of technology and, while being a supporter of McLuhan, has also found that McLuhan's views toward technology, particularly in the rule or law that they are extensions of man, are lacking or at least are incomplete. As Kittler correctly points out, McLuhan is a humanist at heart, a condition that tends to make McLuhan's theories anthropocentric at their core.

Kittler does not believe that technologies and the media are only extensions of humans. For Kittler, contemporary media technologies "no longer reflect the performance of the peripheral sensory organs, [but] rather imitate the command centers themselves" such that "independent thought is cerebral software."[33] A distinctive anti-humanist stance emerges from this position: Kittler doesn't place the human in the center of the mediaverse and doesn't see any reason why humans might be in control of the media. For Kittler, "media are not pseudopods for extending the human body. They follow the logic of escalation that leaves us and written history behind it."[34] It may not be a position as comforting as McLuhan's, but it's a position that, as we see, more accurately reflects information's role.

For the love of *zoe,* what *does* technology want?

By bringing to the forefront the interconnected worlds of nature, humans, technology, and desire, the two stories that this chapter began with reveal something important about our relationship with technology and the way that relationship is changing. Kelly's early suggestion in *Out of Control* was that the evolution of technological systems is beginning to mimic the self-organizational patterns of natural systems. We would find in technology that the rules of complex adaptive systems—swarm logic—pertained to technological systems, particularly computers; and that from these principles an elevated level of self-organized complexity was beginning to take hold. Where the first example of human crowd behavior illustrates how to better understand nature and its connection to technology in order to understand how to harness that power to get what *we* may want from it, the second example of the robot wanting power is a bit more ominous. The first example looks to the unknown and sees the future loaded with potential; the second example hints at a progression in the development of technology for which we may not be prepared.

Kelly wants to paint a picture of what technology *is* and what technology can do. And in the process, it reveals to us that while technology may have a power and direction that is largely out of our own control, we should not fret. In the end, Kelly argues, technology wants the same 13 things that humans want: increasing efficiency, opportunity, emergence, complexity, diversity, specialization, ubiquity, freedom, mutualism, beauty, sentience, structure, and evolvability. To put us at ease, we should see that both nature and technology exhibit the same tendencies, following what Kelly describes as "directional evolution" that follows a "cosmic imperative."[35] This is all made possible because a larger, unseen organizing principle is at work. Kelly, however, comes short of calling it, well, intelligent design.

It's helpful to imagine Kelly's two anecdotes as two different poles on a spectrum of increasing complexity: the image of the human hive marking the beginning of a recognition for the potential of collective intelligence; and the image of the robot's desire marking another beginning of the potential of collective intelligence but on an increased scale of complexity— and one that does not necessarily include human desire.

Presumably a robot plugs itself in so as to free the human of needing to but, in so doing, the robot gains a degree of autonomy, and the human loses a degree of control. At first, such a trade may seem like small potatoes. The history of technology shows that humans are always bargaining with technics, a bargaining that is, indeed, one of the West's founding mythologies (back to Daedalus and Icarus). This bargaining is like a deal with the devil. Give me a shovel, and I lose the connection of my hands in the earth. Give me an ox-drawn plow, and I lose the sensitivity and directness of the shovel. Give me a gas powered tractor, and I trade the contact of the earth and my relationships with the animals for the efficiency of gas. Give me a company with hired labor. I sit at the desk and write in my ledgers.

At each level we gain the time and leisure that comes from employing a technology, and we also increase the distance that we have to our own place in the experience of being a human *animal* connected to the earth. Each technological innovation requires a trade-off. The trade of allowing your personal, open-source robot to plug itself in may seem minor compared to the very fact that someone may have a robot picking up his dishes and folding the laundry. Yes, the deal with the devil seems rigged, *in our favor*. This very *rigging,* however—this notion that technologies come along and seem to make life better and easier—helps us to forget that each technological innovation distances and alienates us from a more natural and less-technologized state. Under the promise of efficiency and simplicity, increased technologies do not necessarily make life any easier although they may make *tasks* easier. Just think about how much time most professionals now devote to email.

Revealing his awareness that technology often creates more problems than it solves, Kelly writes:

Most [of] the new problems in the world are problems created by previous technology. These technogenic problems are nearly invisible to us. Every year 1.2 million people die in automobile accidents. The dominant technological transportation system kills more people than cancer. Global warming, environmental toxins, obesity, nuclear terrorism, propaganda, species loss, and substance abuse are only a few of the many other serious technogenic problems troubling the technium. As technocritic Theodore Roszak says, "How much of what we readily identify as 'progress' in the urban-industrial society is really the undoing of evils inherited from the last round of technological innovation?"[36]

This question is important to consider, especially since the pieces of the puzzle are beginning to fit together. We know that complex adaptive systems exist in nature and that they can be simulated through mathematical algorithms, so they can and do exist artificially as well.

No matter how tempting it may be to dismiss it, the next step will be to determine whether the machines will spontaneously organize to form a self-conscious mind. Certainly, the logic of acceleration, the speed both of technological developments and the speed of informational flows, should tell those of us thinking about these issues that it would be irresponsible to dismiss the notion of self-organizing technology out-of-hand. As Virilio has shown, we are suffocating from the pollution of speed and can no longer clearly see where we are heading.

Anyone alive in the '60s and '70s can easily remember television programs such as *Star Trek* that portrayed face-to-face communications using live video feed (though it wasn't called that then), thinking that such a possibility was beyond technology's grasp. Then, signals through the television traveled in a single direction, and the apparatus required to broadcast them was massive, expensive, and prohibitive. In the analog era, the internet was not part of the cultural imagination, so it could not be part of any imagined solution. Now, not only is it possible to communicate face-to-face through live video feed, but doing so costs no more than having the right computer with an internet connection. Hovercars may not be on the short list of the next available achievements, but autonomous cars that drive and park for humans have already begun to appear on the market. The logic of acceleration indicates that it would be prudent to at least hold open the possibility that while some technological advances never come to fruition, many of the computational advances that seem beyond our grasp may be closer than we think. The rapid speed of technological change should give any reflective person some pause to think about the possibility that a jump in machine intelligence might occur beyond human control. Let's hope that Kelly is correct: that "technology wants what life wants."[37]

TWO

Knowledge and Beauty, Perceptions and Contexts

Speaking on the FoxNews show *The O'Reilly Factor* in 2004, former CBS executive Jonathan Klein said, "you couldn't have a starker contrast between the multiple layers of checks and balances [of the CBS news division], and a guy sitting in his living room in his pajamas writing what he thinks."[1] Soon, bloggers Roger Simon and Charles Johnson had established "Pajamas Media," tongues firmly in cheek, to turn blogging, which was fast becoming an important part of the practice of journalism, into a business. Klein's comment had come in the wake of the scandal that had led to Dan Rather's resignation from CBS, a scandal made known primarily by bloggers. Four years later, just after the 2008 election, Sarah Palin, apparently unaware of the derision that had been aimed at Klein, said (also on FoxNews), "kids in pajamas sitting in the basement of their parents' homes"[2] were responsible for negative comments about her. As a result she, too, was quickly the butt of new jokes.

Both Klein and Palin were behind the curve, trying to excuse situations through reliance on an image that had lost its power: the image of the isolate in underwear in the basement of his or her parents' house, a voyeur and parasite with no responsibility to anyone—but with a new megaphone. The asocial individual gone haywire. They were tapping into an image of what, 50 years ago, the visionary writer Philip K. Dick called "crap artists": "it was actually crap," Jack Isidore says in one of Dick's non-science fiction novels, "but I didn't realize it."[3] By doing so, they may have missed what was actually happening.

It is important to understand the crap artist in any attempt to come to grips with the digital world, for the crap artist is still here and certainly is amplified by digital technologies. He or she remains an important force, be it a lonely kid or Glenn Beck with his audience of millions. In a letter composed years after that long-unpublished novel, *Confessions of a Crap Artist,* was written, Dick commented on Isidore: "When I wrote *Confessions* I had the idea of creating the most idiotic protagonist, ignorant and without common sense, a walking symposium of nitwit beliefs and opinions."[4] Isidore is "an outcast from our society, a totally marginal man who sees everything from the outside only."[5] The type that Isidore represents has, in the decades since, become a commonplace (though Dick's character himself remains relatively unknown) and not simply because of the web. By the new century, it had indeed become the image of the web surfer or browser brought forward when someone like Klein or Palin wanted to be dismissive of the internet. Isidore and his kind are the antithesis of the truly educated and, in the minds of many, they are the people who the internet has unleashed, empowering them in their idiocy as never before.

The novel starts with a section that Isidore narrates:

> I am made out of water. You wouldn't know it, because I have it bound in. My friends are made out of water, too. All of them. The problem for us is that not only do we have to walk around without being absorbed by the ground but we also have to earn our livings.
>
> Actually, there's even a greater problem. We don't feel at home anywhere we go. Why is that?
>
> The answer is World War Two.[6]

Today, this is just the sort of non sequitur that one expects from the nuts who have learned to turn to the internet to support even the wildest of their beliefs. At the end of the book, unlike his brethren on the web (who just seem to get stronger and stronger, evoking the title of Cyril Kornbluth's old science fiction story "The Marching Morons"), Isidore comes to a realization that few of today's crap artists manage:

> I realized, sitting there, that I was a nut.
>
> What a thing to realize. All those years wasted. I saw it as clearly as hell; all that business about the Sargasso Sea, and Lost Atlantis, and flying saucers and people coming out of the inner part of the earth—it was just a lot of crap.[7]

It took death and destruction and disappointment for Isidore to come to his realization. So far, nothing comparable has happened to the vast majority of those using the web to amplify their crap. Not as a group, at least.

The image of the powerful internet fool persists. In 2010, BBC journalist Andrew Marr spoke at the Cheltenham Literature Festival, saying:

> A lot of bloggers seem to be socially inadequate, pimpled, single, slightly seedy, bald, cauliflower-nosed, young men sitting in their mother's basements and ranting. They are very angry people.
>
> OK—the country is full of very angry people. Many of us are angry people at times. Some of us are angry and drunk. But the so-called citizen journalism is the spewings and rantings of very drunk people late at night.[8]

But the internet has changed, and the crap artists have no more taken control of it than they took control of public discourse before its inception. They were around long before the digital age and have always been both a nuisance and something of a corrective, a necessary part of the crowd. They just seem louder now—though they are not as quite a dominant voice on the web as they might sometimes seem or as Marr's anger might lead one to believe. Something else is happening, and it can have positive results.

The vision of the crap artist as the dominant force in blogging, if not the web, had once been promoted particularly by professional journalists like Klein, many of whom saw bloggers taking the information that journalists had prepared and turning it into opinion (and foundationless opinion, at that)—while wanting credit for original contributions on par with what the journalists were getting. They didn't see that even these bloggers were, in some respects, re-creating the journalism of the Jacksonian era (when political opinion, often ill informed, was the engine driving almost every American newspaper and when reporting, as we know it today, was just being born). Nor did they grasp that observing—as distinct from collecting—can be an important part of the art of journalism, though they do participate in that themselves. For all their vaunted objectivity, journalists have always provided context generated far from the specifics of an incident along with (at least implied) opinion—which is exactly what many of the bloggers were (and are) doing, though with the opinion generally explicit, its value aside.

As blogging increased in popularity over the first five years of the new century, bloggers' postings were more and more frequently denigrated (sometimes fairly, often not) by traditional journalists—and with an increasing level of panic. Among other criticisms, blogs were depicted as resulting from nothing more than surfing the internet, an activity seen as lacking both the responsibility and the background necessary for any real contribution to intellectual and political discussion. Whatever their value, the bloggers didn't just use browsers, they *were* browsers quite literally, looking in at Windows and websites, observing whatever they could from the other side of their computer screens. And, yes, much of the time they were coming away with nothing more than jumbled images, a potpourri of unrelated information. In those early days, the idea that their surfing could also be a process of learning and discriminating was often ignored—by the bloggers themselves and by those who observed them in the media. Real work and knowledge, in the assumptions behind such attitudes, are brought *to* the web. What is taken *from* it was seen as ersatz, as replication, at best. For all its "connectivity," the internet was seen as a barrier between people and between people and knowledge. But surfing, common opinion notwithstanding, was beginning to generate something interesting.

In 2005, journalism professor Jay Rosen stated that "Bloggers vs. journalists is over."[9] Journalists had begun to be bloggers, and bloggers sometimes served the purposes of real journalism, especially for breaking stories. The distinction began to be something else, not a fight between different types of news providers but between a reliance on the world of the web and the world outside, between (if you will) Saussure's signifier and signified, though the signifier seems, to many, to have become a thing-in-itself, self-referential.

The world of the web, in some eyes, has come to be seen as an overlay, but a false one. Adam Gropnik writes that not even this is a new concept:

> The odd thing is that this complaint, though deeply felt. . . , is identical to Baudelaire's perception about modern Paris in 1855, or Walter Benjamin's about Berlin in 1930, or Marshall McLuhan's in the face of three-channel television. . . in 1965. When department stores had Christmas windows with clockwork puppets, the world was going to pieces; when the city streets were filled with horse-drawn carriages running by bright-colored posters, you could no longer tell the real from the simulated, . . . all of life had become indistinguishable from your fantasies of it.[10]

The people fascinated by the internet were fascinated by something other than the real, by a fake world of imaginings and bright colors—or so it did seem, until people began to see the internet as something more integral than simple shop windows and posters. Today, of course, the web has moved beyond the shop windows—it is the shop. The web is more than posters—it is also their subject and their designer. The browser becomes its nexus, its crowd, and possibly even its wisdom.

Though the earlier attitudes have disappeared, for the most part, they weren't completely spurious. Aside from the jealousies of the blogger/journalist divide, they were based, to some extent, on a misunderstanding of the function and form of surfing the web and of blogging, but that doesn't mean these attitudes should or can be ignored—especially as we are beginning to understand the relationships and knowledge gathered from the internet can never be sufficient in and of themselves—and that nobody, really, ever seriously claimed they were. The web and the world only become more intertwined; soon, we won't be speaking of them as separate entities at all. Signifier does not become signified but can no longer be so easily spoken of as distinct.

Those early disparaging attitudes toward bloggers arose not just from the crap artist or from the apparent separateness of online and physical worlds but from assumptions of passivity on the part of web browsers, an assumption carried over from the apparent passivity of those watching movie and television screens. It could be argued that the assumption goes back even further, to the bookworm whose life is supposedly centered on what he or she reads without actual experience of the world. Taken more negatively, it can be seen in the idea of the peeping Tom, looking in where he (or she, now) would not be expected or wanted.

Though elements of this image of the voyeur do remain today, the triumph of the blogs, the withering of a part of traditional journalism, and a suspicion that something more than surfing takes place online has changed most of our views. We have seen that the internet can be a conduit for real information from a wider variety of sources than ever before contemplated, and not just through the gatekeepers of expanded aspects of the news media; we have seen the web become a phenomenon much more powerful than anything imagined even way back at the turn of the century. We have come to understand that surfing the web can sometimes be a much more significant and different activity than anyone (except for a few, generally seen as crackpots or crap artists themselves) had envisioned. Today, through the browser, we are in the process of reorganizing and restructuring the ways in which we deal with information. This process is even at the heart of social networking, which has itself grown to facilitate browsing, making it into something a great deal more powerful than it was a decade ago.

The browser, we also are coming to understand, is much older than the internet—and not just as a viewer of film and a reader of books. Another seed of our changing conception of "browser" was identified by Charles Baudelaire a century-and-a-half ago, and he certainly wasn't the first to notice it. In his 1863 essay "The Painter of Modern Life," he describes the *flâneur,* the idler strolling and looking, not involved, though (as Baudelaire eventually shows) not always simply a spectator and not only merely living as a parasite:

> The crowd is his element, as the air is that of birds and water of fishes. His passion and his profession are to become one flesh with the crowd. For the perfect flaneur, for the passionate spectator, it is an immense joy to set up house in the heart of the multitude, amid the ebb and flow of movement, in the midst of the fugitive and the infinite. . . . The spectator is a prince who everywhere rejoices in his incognito. . . . Thus the lover of universal life enters into the crowd as though it were an immense reservoir of electrical energy. Or we might liken him to a mirror as vast as the crowd itself; or to a kaleidoscope gifted with consciousness, responding to each one of its movements and reproducing the multiplicity of life and the flickering grace of all the elements of life.[11]

Substitute "internet" and "web" for "crowd" and "multitude," and you have, here, an apt description of web surfer. Just as Baudelaire saw his flâneur as containing possibilities for becoming something more than simply the voyeur, even the laziest of browsers of the web can develop into an active, even contributory being. It's not a great stretch to bring the flâneur into our discussions of the present-age web surfer.

Making the connection even easier is the discussion a generation ago on the growth of the "leisure society," a discussion reflected in the essays of Eric Larrabee and Rolf Meyersohn's 1958 collection *Mass Leisure.* In their Introduction, Larrabee and Meyersohn write, "Our subject is the leisure which has become available, on an increasing scale, to the populations of the modern, industrial West. Since these are societies mainly oriented to work, leisure is seen in contrast to it; and, since they are prosperous and productive, leisure is not only time free by time paid for."[12] As a result of this work-oriented mindset, leisure activity, or activity with no clear purpose, is not only looked at askance from the point of view of European (particularly Protestant) morality, but from that of productivity and value: "Someone worked hard to pay for your leisure; it is incumbent upon you, therefore, to work hard." Thus, another source of the distaste toward the web surfer.

The internet certainly is today's siren call for the voyeur—witness the importance of pornography to its early financial success—much as the city once was, with Paris the exemplar to the 19th century. Though a rejection of aspects of the old goal-oriented work ethic is present, the reservoir of energy one can tap into through the web is proving active and transformative, just as the city was and did (and still is and does) for generations of ambitious youths. "In a similar style to the Flâneur, a web surfer hopes to gain novel experiences by following links that arouse his curiosity. Thus freed from the demands of targeted search, his navigation and reading of the material is not directed or tainted by expectations. Rather than judging information by preconceived criteria, he finds joy in assessing the material for its own merit."[13] When it works positively, that joy exceeds its own merit, creating new types of goals and pathways, new organizations of information.

Robert Luke describes one contemporary permutation of the flâneur, "the phoneur, the cell phone sporting, incessantly talking, e-urbanite whose identity is articulated within the mediated space of the mobile phone and the ensuing enculturation processes of the wireless web."[14] Such people have brought the web down from the ether and into life, another clear transforming action far beyond simply watching. The smartphone is becoming so popular that it may replace the computer as the primary access point to the internet quite soon, further integrating the online and the offline into one seamless whole. As Andy Clark writes, "the iPhones, Blackberries, laptops and organizers . . . transform and extend the reach of bare biological processing in so many ways. These blobs of less-celebrated activity may sometimes be best seen, myself and others have argued, as bio-external elements in an extended cognitive process: one that now criss-crosses the conventional boundaries of skin and skull."[15]

Extraordinary as these changes are, moving far beyond the simple pajama'd surfer, they don't abandon him or her (leaving behind only the crap artist, who does remain, but as a grim parody of the real flâneur). Something more, another level of perception and knowledge, has simply been added—or, more accurately, recognized, amplified, and integrated into our lives and understanding.

At the beginning of "The Painter of Modern Life," Baudelaire describes the visitor to a museum, the browser who stops only at the most known works, then believes she or he knows the museum. Baudelaire uses this as a lead-in, as:

> an excellent opportunity to establish a rational and historical theory of beauty; . . . Beauty is made up of an eternal, invariable element, whose quantity it is excessively difficult to determine, and of a relative, circumstantial

element, which will be, if you like, whether severally or all at once, the age, its fashions, its morals, its emotions.[16]

This last element requires knowledge and active engagement on the part of the viewer. The simple flâneur cannot operate in this way, ingesting both aspects of beauty. A person who only sees one or the other of the two can never appreciate the full extent of beauty—or, today, of knowledge or of the web and its possibilities. He or she remains the crap artist or that simple version of the flâneur, the dilettante museumgoer or one who is "rather like the whippet. . . who believed that if you ran fast enough round a corner, you were sure to put up something you could chase. But then the whippet was content that life should be a succession of patternless episodes."[17] This satisfaction with simply unexamined, random action can lead one to assume "that where you have so much circumstance and movement, you must surely have progress too."[18] But one doesn't, not necessarily, not unless understanding and recognition become part of the chase.

Beyond the crap artist, there are two flâneurs: the whippet or dilettante who simply observes what others have pointed out, and another who can comprehend and combine. The former might in fact be found in pajamas in the middle of today, but the latter "is not wandering aimlessly, but rather assembles 'raw materials' for the production of culture and identity. So, if early users of the initial incarnations of the web were more 'alienated' and passive, the active users of the Web 2.0 might reflect a desire to take control of the 'alienating space' by 'aestheticising' and 'colonising' it."[19] This is a far cry from idiot belief, passive observation, or simple utilization. It may even be the reward of our age for its expansion of leisure—and might be the real possibility for our future, for it takes leisure and turns it to use. Bertrand Russell has written:

> The wise use of leisure, it must be conceded, is a product of civilization and education. A man who has worked long hours all his life will be bored if he becomes suddenly idle. But without a considerable amount of leisure a man is cut off from many of the best things. There is no longer any reason why the bulk of the population should suffer this deprivation; only a foolish ascetism, usually vicarious, makes us continue to insist on work in excessive quantities now that the need no longer exists.[20]

The person whose life contains room for leisure, for the activities of the more complex type of flâneur and not just the random dashings of a whippet or the quick glance of the dilettante, can become the conduit to a future of ever-increasing possibility. He or she also enhances the present time. This is the promise of the browser.

The art critic Clive Bell wrote in a similar vein to Russell, just a few years before publication of Russell's essay:

> to be completely civilized, to experience the most intense and exquisite states of mind, manifestly a man must have security and leisure. He must have enough to eat and drink, and the assurance of it, he must have warmth, shelter, and some elbow-room, all the necessaries and some of the superfluidities of life. Also leisure is essential. He must have leisure to educate himself for the enjoyment of the best, and leisure to pursue it. Again he must have liberty: economic liberty which will put him above soul-destroying dominion of circumstance and permit him to live how and where he will, and spiritual liberty—liberty to think, to feel, to express and to experiment. He must be free to cultivate his receptivity, and to be putting it always in the way of adventure.[21]

Many people in postindustrial societies have yet to take this to heart but are stuck in the rut of unpleasant work and immediate reward. Yet, the leisurely flâneur, as something more than the aristocrat, has been around for a couple of centuries—and has contributed greatly to cultural development, not to mention to science and to technology. But the flâneur has yet to be fully accepted as a contributor to society though the digital age may be changing this.

A decade ago, Lev Manovich saw a limitation to the observation possible by the solo web surfer, making her or him something less than the better flâneur. He focused on the singularity of the internet experience of browsing, "on a single user navigating through Web sites rather than more communal experiences. . . And although different software solutions have been developed to make internet navigation more of a social experience—for instance, allowing remote users to navigate the same Web site together, simultaneously, or allowing the user to see who has already accessed a particular document—individual navigation through 'history-free' data was still the norm at the end of the 1990s."[22] Social networking has changed that; the rise of Facebook, Tumblr, and Twitter since the publication of Manovich's book has transformed (broadened, at the very least) the way most people, including the simpler type of flâneur, utilize the web and has moved much discussion to the crowd and away from the individual. Social networking adds a second layer to browsing— expanding and deepening the experience—making the totality even more like what Baudelaire's better flâneur experiences with art.

In his more expansive view of the flâneur, Baudelaire demands that one be "very sure that this man, such as I have depicted him—this solitary, gifted with an active imagination, ceaselessly journeying across the great human desert—has an aim loftier than that of a mere flaneur, an aim more general, something other than the fugitive pleasure of circumstance. . . . He makes it his business to extract from fashion whatever element it may contain of poetry within history, to distill the eternal from the transitory."[23] This is the flâneur as explorer and thinker, not simply observing, but processing. This is the flâneur as we now imagine the web surfer at his or her best to be: a contributor.

The flâneur of this newest sort combines information and content. This sounds oxymoronic, but in the eyes of information theorists, meaning is not itself part of information. Meaning lives in the receiver of information, not in the information itself—and becomes content only when the perceiver brings it to life. The thing is: it takes a great deal more than mere reception to make meaning of information gathered—which is the point Baudelaire makes in his distinction between flâneurs.

Again, the simpler sense of the flâneur relates to that cliché of the blogger in jammies in the basement, pretending contact with the world but speaking to no one, really: merely watching and ranting. But that's not the whole of the web experience, not even for that particular person. The other flâneur, the one who operates from knowledge and with the world is successful and effective in changing how the world is seen and *remains*. The one who simply watches and comments quickly passes by—or is passed by.

Manovich makes a distinction between the web surfer and the explorers of Cooper and Twain, but the two may be coming together, instead. Possibly (keeping with the analogy to American visions of its past), the pattern is the one that Wayne Franklin outlines, from discoverer to explorer to settler,[24] with the flâneur (of either type) being a creature of the settled age (one just beginning on the internet), where it is no longer just looking ahead or about what is important but looking back, looking at, and being a part of, as well.

There remains another related tendency, one running counter to the pajama'd narcissist, the tendency to romanticize the cyber-flâneur, making him or her akin to Natty Bumppo or Huck Finn, imagining that "there is neither map to depend upon nor end to reach for"[25] on the internet or, at least, in the eye of the flâneur. But the web *is* a map, and surfers rarely surf randomly. In fact, most web surfers are aiming for, if nothing more, just the sort of unity of vision, again, that Baudelaire says underlies any approach to real understanding of beauty; very few explore the web just to explore. Exactly: "the *flâneur* is not wandering aimlessly, but rather assembles 'raw materials' for the production of culture and identity. So, if early users of the initial incarnations of the web were more 'alienated' and passive, the active users of the Web 2.0 might reflect a desire to take control of the 'alienating space' by 'aestheticising' and 'colonising' it"[26] in much the same way, again, that Franklin's settlers might have been doing as they settled in groups and supplanted the lone explorers.

The flâneur, the person who browses (either as passive or active observer) continued to be of interest, of course, well past the time of Baudelaire. Following him by 70 years, Walter Benjamin adopted Baudelaire's conception for his study of 19th-century Paris (and of more), *The Arcades Project* (as it has since been named). Once again, the description of the flâneur bears resemblance to the simpler type of web surfer: "An intoxication comes over the man who walks long and aimlessly through the streets. With each step, the walk takes on greater momentum; ever weaker grow the temptations of shops, of bistros, of smiling women, even more irresistible the magnetism of the next streetcorner, of a distant mass of foliage, of a street name."[27] In many respects, it's not just the browser who can be found in the past; the internet of today, we see through Benjamin's *Project,* represents the arcades of 19th-century Paris brought forward in time and technology.

As is often the case with anything that seems revolutionary, we tend to forget that what we fancy as "the digital environment" is not new—not completely new, that is. In part, the internet is simply a newer and better postal service, and the post is traceable back to Cyrus the Great of Persia. In part, the internet is simply a more efficient library, and libraries are also ancient. In part, the internet is a diary or scrapbook gone mad through explosive and unplanned growth—and scrapbooks have also been around for centuries, at the very least. In part, the internet is a giant social club, with back rooms for whatever peculiarity an individual might exhibit—something as universal as it is old. In large part, it is simply a more convenient shopping mall—again, something that has been around at least since the arcades of Paris, but actually since the first space was cleared for trading at the center of a village. Still, though in each instance of web usage, a line can be drawn to it from something in the past; the totality is something completely new, an aggregation presenting possibilities never before imagined. This is what the best flâneurs are exploring and describing.

Fascination with something implying radical change—as the internet, even as it reflects the past, certainly does today—leads to flights of imagination, necessary parts of the evolving world: Baudelaire's fanci-ful flâneur of his own time can be seen as the herald of modernism and of pastiche as the postmodern idiom. Cyberspace, the idea of the internet as a new world, as something substantively different from the "bricks and mortar" reality around us, is perhaps the best known of these imag-inings by today's flâneur. But there are others: social networking as a way of interacting that will permanently change our social structures, making us interactive members of groups that can be mobilized for ac-tion, among other things, at a moment's notice; the wisdom of crowds as a new model for developing ideas into useable form; online global-ization, allowing everyone, anywhere onto a level playing field; and more. All of these, real or fanciful, assume that the internet is changing people, that we are creating a new and symbiotic relationship with our machines leading to what will be, effectively, a new form of human life. Yet all of these, like the web surfing flâneur and even the phoneur, can also be simply reflections of earlier ideas and times in mirrors jumped up with technology—until we look back and see how radically they have changed our lives.

Or haven't. At the same time that some wax poetic about cyber-possibilities, there are others who go to the opposite extreme—who see the internet simply as a tool, something to reach for and make use of as they see fit. The cultural impact has yet to impress them. These people don't wish to admit that they are, perhaps, being shaped by the tools they use—not on the basic level of *being,* at least. To them, the difference between a quill pen and the World Wide Web is simply one of degree, not of kind. Such people look askance at the starry-eyed believers in the unfolding new age. Such people don't understand the importance of the activities of flâ-neur, or of the web surfer when moving beyond mere idle watching, or the importance of the enhancement of activities today. Such people, perhaps, do not comprehend that a tool is rarely simply a tool.

In response to what he considers the overhyping of the role of social networking in the 2011 turmoil in Egypt, cultural critic Malcolm Gladwell wrote, "People with a grievance will always find ways to communicate with each other. How they choose to do it is less interesting, in the end, than why they were driven to do it in the first place."[28] The means, in his view, is much less important than the motivation. Gladwell doesn't see that the means—internet means—does more, in the contemporary world, than simply amplify what has been possible before. He argues that no one before the internet came into being was particularly concerned with the "how" of communications, conveniently forgetting that the "how" of the printed Bible completely changed Europe (though over a great deal of time) and has since been the focus of generations of scholars.

Neither of these extremes, the vision of a new world or dismissal of it as a pipe dream, can suffice, of course: not if one is going to intelligently interact with the possibilities and tools of the developing digital age. These present something of a false dichotomy anyway, though a useful one to our discussion here. On the one hand we have those who view the web with those starry eyes and imagine a new place and possibility. On the other are those who see simply wires and devices, who measure web expertise in terms of computer code and cables, not cultural possibilities. At first, when cyberspace was the realm of science fiction, the dreamers were in control. Then came the heyday of the techies, which lasted until the advent of Web 2.0 possibilities again relegated them to support status. Today, then, the pendulum has begun to swing back to the idealists—though it may, if we are lucky, be coming to rest in the middle.

The internet is built on language, both computer and human. Writing for the web has two meanings: one relating to code, the other to human interaction. Or, one related to the carrier and the information, the other to the carried and the utilization. This distinction is part of the logic behind the choice of the term *digital humanities* for the movement to integrate the foci of traditional humanities study with digital tools and possibilities. There's a lot to be said for the movement, as can be said for the early idealists who saw the web as something completely new and different. Like them, some digital humanists grow a bit misty eyed, imagining a great difference in what they do from what was done before. Stephen Ramsay, who teaches at the University of Nebraska-Lincoln and who is a Fellow at the Center for Digital Research in the Humanities there, makes a distinction between the work of the humanities *then* and now, seeing the digital humanists as being more active as contributors, as bringing something new to the world, than were the old humanists:

> Digital Humanities is about building things . . . and should include people who theorize about building, people who design so that others might build, and those who supervise building. . . . I'd even include people who are working to rebuild systems like our present, irretrievably broken system of scholarly publishing. But if you are not making anything, you are not—in my less-than-three-minute opinion—a digital humanist. You might be something else that is good and worthy—maybe you're a scholar of new media, or maybe a game theorist, or maybe a classicist with a blog (the latter being very good thing indeed)—but if you aren't building, you are not

engaged in the "methodologization" of the humanities, which, to me, is the hallmark of the discipline.[29]

That's from his blog, *literatura mundana*. In his next post, he explains a little further what he means:

As humanists, we are inclined to read maps (to pick one example) as texts, as instruments of cultural desire, as visualizations of imperial ideology, as records of the emergence of national identity, and so forth. This is all very good. In fact, I would say it's at the root of what it means to engage in humanistic inquiry. Almost everyone in Digital Humanities was taught to do this and loves to do this. But *making* a map (with a GIS system, say) is an entirely different experience. DH-ers insist—again and again—that this process of creation yields insights that are difficult to acquire otherwise. It's the thing I've been hearing for as I long as I've been in this. People who *mark up* texts say it, as do those who *build* software, *hack* social networks, *create* visualizations, and pursue the dozens of other forms of haptic engagement that bring DH-ers to the same table. Building is, for us, a new kind of hermeneutic—one that is quite a bit more radical than taking the traditional methods of humanistic inquiry and applying them to digital objects. Media studies, game studies, critical code studies, and various other disciplines have brought wonderful new things to humanistic study, but I will say (at my peril) that none of these represent as radical a shift as the move from reading to making.[30]

Though there is an important point here, this is the same type of hyperbole found earlier among those who extolled the virtue of cyberspace as a new world, "O brave new world, That has such people in't," as the naïve Miranda says in *The Tempest*. The desire for distinction, once again, has led to an eliding of parts of the past: in this case, of writing, one of the core tasks of the humanist, digital or otherwise. Writing is building, to use Ramsay's definition. It was so before digital possibilities, just as it is now. And all humanists write, be it about media studies, game studies, or anything else. As such, they *build*. That doesn't mean there isn't value in the digital-humanist approach: simply that it is not built on distinction or revolution—but on continuity—though an explosive one.

That said, the digital humanities are also about that more complex type of flâneur, as the definition provided by the University of Maryland's Matthew Kirschenbaum, read in light of our discussion here, certainly shows: "the digital humanities today is about a scholarship (and a pedagogy) that is publicly visible in ways to which we are generally unaccustomed, a scholarship and pedagogy that are bound up with infrastructure in ways that are deeper and more explicit than we are generally accustomed to, a scholarship and pedagogy that are collaborative and depend on networks of people and that live an active 24/7 life online."[31]

The digital humanities sees itself as having begun in something of a support role, only later catching the excitement of cyberspace. Swansea University's David Berry writes (following, he says, Katherine Hayles) that the name itself was chosen as a signal of a shift from service status to a new field with its own theoretical basis. "Ironically, as the projects became bigger, more complex, and developed computational techniques as an intrinsic part of the research process, technically proficient researchers increasingly saw the computational as part and parcel of what it is to do research in the humanities itself. That is, computational technology has become the very condition of possibility required in order to think about many of the questions raised in the humanities today."[32] Here again, we see the swing of a pendulum. Eventually, it should come to rest in a center where even a term like digital humanities will seem somewhat redundant: humanities encompassing all approaches, with the traditional embracing the digital, and vice versa, without even realizing a divide.

One of the arguments of the digital humanists today, however, points to a crying need unfilled in our current relations with our digital devices, a weakness even in Baudelaire's better flâneur. It is the argument behind the point Ramsay is trying to make with his focus on building. Being a flâneur of any sort isn't enough, ultimately: one must be a creator as well, if one is to fully participate in the world. The Paris arcades of Baudelaire's day, after all, did not just appear but were planned and constructed. Those who could get the most out of them were the people who were able to participate in the construction as well as in the browsing. It is recognition of this, even if generally unconscious, that leads people to characterize the modern flâneur as nothing more than a pajama'd parasite.

In part to meet the need to bring building to the web experience (making it more than simply browsing), there are now writing teachers arguing that writing should be expanded to include writing computer code. This forces a coupling of the action of writing to the action of the web—just the sort of melding that we would argue in favor of, between the digital and the humanities. Today, few understand the mechanics behind their writing—something that has become more important as the distance between input and output has increased. Not even familiarity with such things as Content Management Systems (CMS) would be enough to really provide knowledge for writing. At some point, it is going to be necessary for all of us to know something of Hyper Text Markup Language (HTML) and of the computer codes lying behind that—especially for those of us who hope to write (or build) using the web. Here, as everywhere, if we do not learn enough to understand the workings of our tools, we will always be commanded by them, rather than making them work for us. This, an understanding at the heart of digital humanities, will remain an important point until the melding of code and writing is complete—until writing implies code as well as communication. Or so the digital humanists argue.

Even if this is so (though it may prove an unnecessary yoking), there's a problem with the coupling of the mechanics of production and publication with the act of writing. In the early days of the American republic (and certainly during the colonial period), many writers were often also printers, well versed in the word from pen to published page. From the 1840s on, this began to change: the mechanics of printing began to require much greater specialization and attention. A printer could no longer stop in the middle of a print run to jot down a few lines or to talk to someone, but had to focus exclusively on the press—now producing upwards of 20,000 copies in an hour. The writer and the printer had begun to drift apart—and little reason was found for forcing them back together. Today, there may be as little reason to mix the mechanics and the message. We will see.

Compounding diverging demands on time and attention, the progress of technology as an aspect of production and publication forces increased specialization and creates obsolescence. Barlow spent much of his youth learning the skills of hot-type printing. By the time he was out of high school, he was also conversant in offset operation and had acquired what were, then, necessary darkroom skills. None of this proved much use to him later, for printing technology quickly moved beyond these technologies. The ability to set type and etch emulsion off of a negative are no longer building blocks to contemporary print production (and print production is itself becoming less central to our endeavors). By the same token, when we teach coding skills, we may be teaching something that will soon become as arcane as justifying lines of type by hand using hair spaces. Again, we will see.

There are positive aspects to concentrating, for the moment, on digital humanities rather than assuming the digital and the humanities have already melded into one—or *should* be melded into one. Without an emphasis on the digital, the humanities can find themselves mired in an outdated and less-and-less useful model for scholarly publishing, which remains rather backward-looking today, focusing on old models for publication and a peer-review process initially instituted as a necessary bottleneck in a milieu where it was not possible to publish everything or to quickly evaluate even that which *was* published. It can also waken scholars to the need for changing copyright conventions, at least as they apply to academic work. Because of attention drawn to the issue by digital humanists, "Scholarly publishing will presumably eventually make a transition from the present situation—in which the publishers own the copyright and are therefore able to restrict the group of people who can read your paper—to a model where publishers are funded not for the paper copy but for providing a refereeing service and a curated electronic journal archive with a permanent URL."[33] Furthermore, and also because of pressure from digital humanists:

> It seems just a question of time before scholarly publishing makes the "Harnad Switch"—the outcome that [Steve] Harnad has for a decade been describing as both optimal and inevitable. Authors actually want to maximize the impact and uptake of their research findings by making them accessible to as many would-be users as possible, rather than having them restricted, as they were in the paper era, to the minority of wealthy research libraries that can afford the access tolls. The Web has changed publishing forever and such a transition is inevitable. A similar transformation is likely to affect university libraries. The logical role for a university library in ten years will surely be to be the responsible organisation that hosts and curates (digitally) all the research papers produced by the university. It will be the university library that is responsible for maintaining the digital archive.[34]

Such changes will make it easier for the flâneur to cross the boundary of the glass window, to interact directly with the things she or he was simply watching, for the web surfer to become directly involved in the activities once simply observed. If this happens, if our online environment becomes more expansive and open (instead of becoming more restrictive, which is also possible), the *leisure* of the browser, so disdained, can become what Russell once envisioned, something of great power:

> In a world where no one is compelled to work more than four hours a day, every person possessed of scientific curiosity will be able to indulge it, and every painter will be able to paint without starving, however excellent his pictures may be. Young writers will not be obliged to draw attention to themselves by sensational pot-boilers, with a view to acquiring the economic independence needed for monumental works, for which, when the time at last comes, they will have lost the taste and the capacity. Men who, in their professional work, have become interested in some phase of economics or government, will be able to develop their ideas without the

academic detachment that makes the work of university economists often seem lacking in reality. Medical men will have time to learn about the progress of medicine, teachers will not be exasperatedly struggling to teach by routine methods things which they learnt in their youth, which may, kin the interval, have been proved to be untrue.[35]

The browser becomes not just browser but doer or, as Ramsay would call it, builder.

There are plenty of people who are trying to develop a carefully planned internet that leaves room for both exuberance and machines (and for understanding of both), though their voices are often lost in the hoopla of genuine revolution and its own inevitable backlash. Various groups of them address specific aspects and problems relating to the digital world. Among these are the people fighting for Net Neutrality or for other umbrella legal concepts governing internet use, those developing new copyright and intellectual property concepts appropriate to a digital age, those exploring and mapping information usage and placement, and more. Few people, however, are successful at trying to put all of this together—all of the problems and possibilities—in a form intelligible to the nonspecialist. Fewer still manage a coherent look at the dynamics of the new human/machine interactions—certainly not within their historical contexts. This, perhaps, is the job of the new flâneurs who, more even than the digital humanists, can stand back and assess the web—much as Baudelaire claimed their ancestors could understand beauty.

The people who are involved in crafting even a part of the internet generally speak only to politicians and legal scholars; to computer experts; to scholars in general and those involved in creative endeavors; or to the others directly involved in, say, information science. Perhaps the information explosion has become so huge that none of us can even imagine its entirety, let alone explain it. The Baudelairian flâneur, at least, might be able to put it into its contexts, to understand the beauty in what is and what comes to it from behind:

And so away he goes, hurrying, searching. But searching for what? Be very sure that this man, such as I have depicted him—this solitary, gifted with an active imagination, ceaselessly journeying across the great human desert—has an aim loftier than that of a mere flaneur, an aim more general, something other than the fugitive pleasure of circumstance. He is looking for that quality which you must allow me to call "modernity"; for I know of no better word to express the idea I have in mind. He makes it his business to extract from fashion whatever element it may contain of poetry within history, to distill the eternal from the transitory. Casting an eye over our exhibitions of modern pictures, we are struck by a general tendency among artists to dress all their subjects in the garments of the past. . . . This is clearly symptomatic of a great degree of laziness; for it is much easier to decide outright that everything about the garb of an age is absolutely ugly than to devote oneself to the task of distilling from it the mysterious element of beauty that it may contain, however slight or minimal that element may be. By "modernity" I mean the ephemeral, the fugitive, the contingent, the half of art whose other half is the eternal and the immutable.[36]

Even when they look to the past to bolster their arguments and hone their plans, the specialists generally examine narrow avenues of activity (or periods of time) and with specific ends already in mind.

Issues of copyright might be clear in law and philosophy, as might its changes, but how did people actually *use* books (and recorded music, etc.), and how did that use change as technology changed? Were (and are) these utilizations effective (and in what way, to what end)? Did law change to reflect usage or vice versa? Were new usages accepted and/or shrugged off? How was copyright viewed and used—not by the writer or publisher, but by the purchaser of the book—when the Statute of Anne became law in 1710? Did the nature of libraries change? The book itself, the physical object, fell outside of copyright law and was completely "owned" by its buyer—but its contents were not. Has that notion of the distinction between the physical object and its contents changed since then? In terms of actual usage, or in law? Sometimes these questions *are* explored today but usually in narrow form (generally relating to commercial concerns): copying of music or editing of movies on DVD for resale. For all the books and discussion of the last few years, there's a lot to this, culturally, that has not been adequately examined.

One way of learning about today's digital possibilities is to start with a look at the way information was organized and processed in the past—not simply in libraries, but in published works and in diaries, daybooks, occasion books, scrapbooks, and other individual works created for personal use and not for publication. All of these, of course, have come together in the internet. What were they like before—together, not individually? What was their impact on society? Before the electronic era, some people would act out scenes from favorite books in their living rooms. What impact did this have on drama? Harriet Beecher Stowe's *Uncle Tom's Cabin*, a popular novel throughout the second half of the nineteenth century, was often dramatized and often in excerpts. Was there a relation between this and scenes acted out at home? Finding and understanding pathways such as this (if they exist) will ultimately help us understand the pathways of the web, just as an understanding of the dual nature of beauty can. This task of the humanities will be enhanced by digital possibilities, answers and avenues becoming apparent that never before were seen, but it requires a disciplinary humanities that is both digital and analogue.

Before we continue trying to mold the internet to our best uses, then, it is perhaps worth pausing and imagining other attempts to organize information, for it is through these that we can start to have an idea of what we are actually up against in this digital age, rather than simply imagining what we would like or, as in some cases, what we fear.

There is, of course, a lot to fear growing from the inception of the new digital age. It is not that we have created something analogous to the monster in Mary Shelley's *Frankenstein,* but that our creation may have outstripped our understanding (which is, of course, one point of the discussions between Dr. Frankenstein and the monster). The digital age may be, at the very least, on the verge of moving beyond our ability to effectively make use of it without a careful restructuring of our approaches to the age and to information generally. Or of recognition of our own limitations.

The Argentinean writer Jorge Luis Borges, in one of his later (1974) stories, "The Book of Sand," managed to encapsulate some of the problems the internet would be posing two decades later. In an act very like random internet surfing (especially as it was imagined in the early days), his narrator describes his first attempt to look into the book of the title:

> I opened the book at random. The script was strange to me. The pages, which were worn and typographically poor, were laid out in double columns as in a Bible. . . . It also bore a small illustration, like the kind used in dictionaries—an anchor drawn with pen and ink, as if my a schoolboy's clumsy hand.
>
> It was at this point that the stranger said, "Look at the illustration closely. You'll never see it again."
>
> I noted my place and closed the book. At once, I reopened it. Page by page, in vain, I looked for the illustration of the anchor.[37]

The book of sand hasn't a Google engine with its algorithms making search possible and comprehensible. It doesn't even have access to the "Archie" FTP (File Transfer Protocol) archives search engine of pre-World Wide Web days (the first search engine widely used). Yet information, or latent information of some sort, *is* there, even if only accessible through chance. It just can't be used, not unless it is used *now* or transferred to another medium: "study the page well." In many ways, though pre-dating it, "the book of sand" *is* the internet, but without the possibility of organization, *is* information but with no system (or no discernible system), the centuries-old nightmare of the librarian and, today, of every serious researcher working through the web.

Our faith in Google and the other search engines we use, faith that they can return us to where we were, allowing us to find again a page once seen or producing the same results or lists of unseen pages, may be misplaced. Yes, there are bookmarks and marker program out there like Instapaper, but the pages themselves can change between views—so we're not even sure, always, that what we see is what we saw before. Yes, there is Google cache, but how many of us really know how to use that effectively? Yes, once something is on the web, it is there forever—but can we *find* it forever? Oh, and then there's the fact that most of us don't even know *how* Google decides what to show us. We take it on faith that we will see what we want in the first page or two of search results, ignoring those further back, never even thinking about what the sorting procedure might be or whether we're blindered by our unwillingness to look at every result of our own search.

No, Borges wasn't talking about the internet (though, unlike the World Wide Web it carries, a version of it, ARPANET, did exist at that time), but he was exploring knowledge and the way we approach it, exploring our limited possibilities and the ways in which we manage to avoid the issue of the constraints of our senses and minds. Eventually, the narrator of "The Book of Sand" finds himself addicted to this book, even without good search possibilities—just as many (especially the flâneurs of the more limited sort), in the nearly two decades since introduction of the World Wide Web, have become addicted to the internet, not to the tool or to possible utility but to the thing in and of itself:

> A prisoner of the book, I almost never went out anymore. After studying its frayed spine and covers with a magnifying glass, I rejected the possibility of a contrivance of any sort. . . . At night, in the meager intervals my insomnia granted, I dreamed of the book.
>
> Summer came and went, and I realized that the book was monstrous. What good did it do me to think that I, who looked upon the volume with my eyes, who held it in my hands, was less monstrous? I felt that the book was a nightmarish object, an obscene thing that affronted and tainted reality itself.
>
> I thought of fire, but I feared that the burning of an infinite book might likewise prove infinite and suffocate the planet with smoke. Somewhere

> I recalled reading that the best place to hide a leaf is in a forest. Before retirement, I worked on Mexico Street, at the Argentine National Library, which contains nine hundred thousand volumes. I knew that to the right of the entrance a curved staircase leads down to the basement, where books and maps and periodicals are kept. . . . I lost the Book of Sand on one of the basement's musty shelves.[38]

Were this story to appear today, we might read it quite differently (shades of Borges's earlier story, "Pierre Menard, Author of the *Quixote*"), passing it off as a reflection of extant oversaturation of information, as a commentary on a contemporary predicament. As it is, we are forced to recognize that there is something quite a bit more sophisticated going on here than simply observation of a cultural phenomenon, something that shows that all we see today isn't really new, and something that might actually help us organize our minds as we attempt to organize and even use the sand that the internet is piling up on our communal beach.

Borges's narrator hides the book toward where "maps and periodicals are kept" and not simply among the other books. Why? Periodicals, of course, change frequently . . . and maps are overlays of a sort (mostly metaphoric). In many senses, both are directly not anything in themselves, not really. Both periodicals and maps depend concretely and immediately on something outside, events and places. We don't read them as worlds of their own. In this regard, they aren't really things that belong in storage at all. Stored in libraries, they are no longer the living things of their popular and intended usage. Perhaps by hiding the book near them, the narrator hopes to kill the book, too, reducing it to static text.

The library can be the burial place of knowledge, even its death, in a cautionary tale such as this. Certainly, it is too much for the living. Imagine 900,000 books: a person reading a book per day over 50 years would only manage to read fewer than some 19,000 books. Even the best readers, realistically speaking, only get through maybe 5,000 in a lifetime . . . and that would be quite an achievement. Even were one simply dipping into a variety of books for a few pages each, one would never manage to read any part of more than a small percentage of the books in that library and would perforce become the lesser sort of flâneur, sampling but never delving or understanding. For the most part, for any individual, a library of close to a million books is simply a repository of the never used and never to be used. In fact, without its organizational principles, its card catalogs, etc., the library itself would be nothing more than a huge book of sand. Hiding a leaf in a forest, indeed!

What, then, is Borges's point? Clearly, he is exploring questions of information, but to what purpose, or to what conclusion? Why did he write the story? And how does it help us today?

Unlike most of us, who are confident in our knowledge, Borges recognized his inability, as a human being, to encompass all of knowledge within his own understanding, his own brain, his own ability to sustain organization. He doubted the possibility of books doing so either. Or even libraries filled with books, newspapers, and maps. If he had lived longer, he would even have doubted the capacity of the internet. In this story, as in much of his work, Borges explores the fact of human limitation, *especially* in terms of knowledge. We see, but not every possible wavelength on the electromagnetic spectrum. We hear, but not all the sounds that come to us through the air. We feel, but the discrimination of our touch is limited. Just so, our minds are limited, and in many other ways. So, in the case of the library and of the book of sand and the internet, even the creations of our minds outstrip us.

The point? Whatever we do with the information that surrounds us, it will never be enough, for we alone cannot handle the knowledge we amass. We must retain a certain level of humility in the face of information, never assuming that we have conquered it—or that we *can* conquer it. This, though, is not likely to happen anytime soon, given the nature of most of the human beings who use the internet. Given, also, is our faith that our devices can keep things in order for us, a faith that may soon prove unwarranted.

Though most people today will admit that there are limits to their knowledge, they still have confidence in what they know—or in what they believe they know. For, as Marcel Duchamp writes (quoted by Michel de Certeau), "In general, when one says 'I know,' one doesn't know, one believes."[39] People have confidence in themselves and in the tools they use. They operate on foundationalist assumptions even when they may claim a relativist view of the world—they have to. It's impossible to operate without confidence in at least a few things. Yet the distinction between the foundationalist and the relativist is quite real—and can be summed up in attitudes toward web searches. The foundationalists, looking for confirmation of beliefs already established, scan search results for sites agreeing with them. They exclude all others from their discourse arena. For them, the internet is a quick and useful tool, arming them with information they don't have to question and that bolsters their established positions. The relativists, on the other hand, will find themselves overwhelmed, on the internet, by the task of examining and evaluating information from myriad sources. For them, the web can become a trap instead of an aid, leading to too many possibilities with only minimal aid in distinguishing between the lead and the dross.

One, then, would be tempted to see "The Book of Sand" as a cautionary tale—but cautionary against what? Against books? Against libraries? Against the internet? Against seeking knowledge? That doesn't make any sense. Against arrogance? Well, if there had been any attempt to use the book of sand or the knowledge in it in any overstepping manner in the story, maybe so. But there is not. In fact, we soon discover that the story isn't against anything: it is simply a presentation of a decision, when faced with the addictive nature of information, to refuse. The story doesn't even show what the dangers of the addiction refused might be—aside from the single fact that it takes up way too much of the narrator's time. Still, the decision to step away from the book is a recognition of limitation, something akin to the first step of Alcoholics Anonymous, an admission (or recognition, really) of powerlessness.

A similar recognition should, perhaps, underlie any discussion of the internet and the massive amount of information it represents: Just as the narrator of Borges's story, who can't find the start or end of "the book of sand," we are powerless to control the information now surrounding us, though it may be of human creation. Even now, we cannot manage it effectively, though we do have the illusion of management through our search engines and a whole panoply of other devices and structures. Information has outstripped our abilities; the best we can do now is deal with small portions of what is available to use, recognizing that we do not have the whole picture, but understanding that we must wear blinders if we are to be able to operate at all. In this sense, we become the flâneur reduced back to simple onlooker, unable any longer to process enough of what we see to effectively analyze it or use it.

One problem is that we cannot yet stand back and look at the whole, drawing conclusions from a distance—and we may never be able to, for the same reason that we cannot judge a library by looking down the rows of books any more than we can by looking at individual volumes. We can't even use the number of books, for sheer size tells us nothing of quality or organization. The book and the library are a microcosm and a macrocosm—but they are also one and the same thing, a thing larger than any individual comprehension. And the internet is the same, too.

Looking today at the Borges story, we may conclude that the difference between the internet and the book of sand is more apparent than real. Both are bigger than we are, and we can never hope to tame them—and browsing in them without understanding leads to little. As long as we recognize this, we can, perhaps, begin to make limited sense—sense that works for our lives, at least—of the new universe of information the internet has opened up. At least, we can begin to see where we can get help outside of the book for our own explorations inside. We may even stop seeing what we are addressing now as revolutionary but may begin to look at it more realistically as expansionary—though expansionary to a degree that beggars our imagination. To a degree that becomes revolutionary.

Ultimately, the revolution of the digital age, we may find, is in us and in the way we try to organize and approach the vast new knowledge base, and not in our machines or in what they "do" to us. The real revolution may prove to be cultural, and not simply technological, just as it was in the centuries after Gutenberg. A real technological revolution may follow, but it is not here (or not obviously here) yet.

For that reason, we may not want to try to keep our focus to the narrow technological and legal debates that have dominated discussion of the internet over the past decade but try to open them up to place our discussions of information within the contexts of culture and use as well, considering implications that may seem far beyond either the World Wide Web or the information it houses. We may also want to look back at how the organization of information on the internet reflects—or changes—the ways we had organized information—and our lives—in the predigital world.

A remarkable analogy to the organizational structures of the internet— or lack thereof—can be found in that unfinished work of Benjamin's mentioned earlier, known today as *The Arcades Project* and written between 1927 and 1940 but focused (if focus can be legitimately applied) on 19th-century Paris. Its very status as incomplete (if completion is even a concept that should be considered in relation to it) reminds one of the ever-incomplete World Wide Web; its fragmentary structure (if structure is even a concept that should be considered in relation to its whole) does as well; the flâneur that Benjamin considers has, as we have seen, an obvious parallel to the web surfer; and the controversies about the organization of publication of *The Arcades Project* foreshadow such debates as that over Net Neutrality. And that's before we get to content.

In certain respects, what Benjamin was creating was (and is) no more than what a scrapbooker does, or a diarist who includes quotes and pictures and other items found during the day. And, in many respects, this is just what the internet is—though it doesn't have the single controlling intellect that Benjamin or a scrapbooker provides. The size and diffused structure of the internet makes it, of course, a completely different sort of creature but, here again, lessons from the one can certainly apply to the other.

So, one of the problems we are faced with as the internet grows both in size and diffusion is its lack of cohesion or any sort of parallel to the vision and purpose that someone like Benjamin (or even a scrapbooker) provides. One of the remarkable aspects of *The Arcades Project* is Benjamin's vision for it, which far outstripped the technological possibilities (for organization) of his time. Just so, one of the remarkable aspects of the internet, for both good and bad, is the lack of any overarching vision or unity beyond that provided by the technology itself and a structure initially envisioned (in part, at least) as a means for surviving attack or damage. For good or bad, there is currently no single controlling entity over the internet, and there probably could not be, save for an international agreement containing real possibilities of enforcement (cutting a noncomplying country from access, for example), something that is not likely to happen. More likely, the coalescing commercial forces now dominating the web will develop better and better internal controls for their sites and find new ways to limit and control access to their material on the web. This, too, has happened to *The Arcades Project*. It has been named, edited, organized, and published—making it a thing instead of a process or project. It has, through this, been removed from possible inclusion in the commons (though it was never really there, it could have been allowed to settle there) and now lives as property under copyright law. Though the road of the internet can run to it, *The Arcades Project* has become part of a gated community at its end.

Lawrence Lessig talks of the internet in terms of an end-to-end (e2e) network, where the network (or road) itself is neutral and accessible: "Because of e2e, no one need register an application with 'the Internet' before it will run; no permission to use the bandwidth is required. Instead, e2e means the network is designed to assure that the network cannot decide which innovations will run."[40] This means that the real power lies in the applications and not in the network—as does the real ability for self-protection. The facts of ownership of Benjamin's physical manuscript and (for those reading him in English) of its translation remove *The Arcades Project* from the open road and place it in a static, controlled "museum" where admission must be obtained if one would do more than peer through the gates.

Two of the biggest problems for the internet are security and confidence, related ones arising from the wide-open nature of the networks. There are two sides of this, one rarely acknowledged: the viability of the web itself and the reliability (and more—or less) of the user. The web, of course, is not a thing-in-itself, but part of a symbiotic relationship with each user— just as Borges's narrator is, saying in the passage quoted above, "no less monstrous was I, who perceived the book." Sometimes the relationship results in something larger and stronger than the two separately. At other times, however, it creates a reduction. This needs to be taken into account in any discussion of information in today's digital environment: are the users capable of making positive use of the possibilities before them? Borges's narrator in "The Book of Sand" quickly realizes he cannot; many people use the web today just as blindly, but without that understanding of their own limitations, without realizing they had best step back a bit, even if they don't need to reject it completely.

The limitations of the user confound any attempt to structure bodies of information. The problem isn't that "the book of sand" lacks tracking and useable organization: it's that the user hasn't the ability to construct a use-able schema on his own. Borges's user, fortunately for him, has enough sense to recognize that he cannot best the book, so he retreats from it. Most of us, not as self-perceptive, end up like Goethe's "sorcerer's apprentice." The water-carrying broom proving unstoppable, we react with anger and frustration but, by doing so, simply make the problem worse. Taking an ax to the broom doesn't stop it, but creates two:

> Both halves scurry
> In a hurry,
> Rise like towers
> There beside me.[41]

Not all of us are lucky enough to have the sorcerer return and save us—or even to recognize that we need saving. And there are few sorcerers behind the magic of the internet to save us, anyway.

One cannot concentrate just on the internet in examining its role as an information repository and source. People have access to it, with varying degrees of openness, but great access at a minimum. How they interact with what they find on the web, how they view what they discover, is as important a part of understanding just what the internet is as is com-prehension of the role of Google (and other search engines) in making information accessible. Like language, information is a dynamic, and not a thing—which is what Benjamin struggled with in the creation of his project. He struggled to bring flexibility and life to a project bound by the printed page, for he wanted it to interact with its user—be it himself as creator or any reader who might happen upon it. Benjamin's vision, though, was greater than the technological realities of the time could encompass.

Benjamin's project is known today not simply because it survived World War II hidden in a library (shades of "The Book of Sand"!). It is known, also, because it was written (or "collected," perhaps a better word) by a scholar whose reputation had been secured through other works, particularly "The Work of Art in the Age of Mechanical Reproduction," a seminal article on the place of the individual creation in an age of identical copies or originals, one that also has implications, often discussed, relevant to our topic here. Were *The Arcades Project* the product of a lesser-known scholar, it probably would not have been protected, let alone eventually published. This is the lesson that Arianna Huffington understood when she founded her blog, "The Huffington Post." She used her own prior name recognition as a base and invited well-known people to blog at her site, banking on their reputations to draw readers and not simply relying on what might be written and posted. This went against the then-prevailing attitude of egalitarianism that underlay many bloggers' views of their activities, but it proved prescient, leading to one of the greatest successes in blogging. Other blogs may have presented more accurate information and may have presented better writing on the subjects covered by The Huffington Post; but reputation, even amongst the blogs, generally triumphs—as it has for Benjamin.

One of the things that Benjamin clearly struggled with, just as his editors have struggled with it since, is organization of the material he had gathered. In some respects, Benjamin probably didn't want to control how his project was accessed—an attitude foreshadowing how many view the web—working to let the collection itself "speak" rather than it reflecting simply his own voice. The problem with this, of course, is that the very collection reflects Benjamin's "voice"—just as any website today reflects the attitudes of its creators.

In arranging his collection, Benjamin seems to have imagined interaction between its parts something like what we actually have managed to construct (or to amass) through the internet:

> the entire *Arcades* complex (without definitive title, to be sure) remained in the form of several hundred notes and reflections of varying length, which Benjamin revised and grouped in sheafs, or "convolutes," according to a host of topics. . . . These proliferating individual passages, extracted from their original context like collectibles, were eventually set up to communicate among themselves, often in a rather subterranean manner.[42]

The entire web, in its utilizations, is a similar process of extraction and communication . . . and there is also much about it that is subterranean, that is, unseen by the end user. Benjamin, his translators are saying in this passage, was just as manipulative as the creator of any contemporary website. Furthermore:

> The fact that Benjamin also transferred masses of quotations from actual notebooks to the manuscript of the convolutes, and the elaborate organiza-tion of these cited materials in the manuscript (including the use of numer-ous epigraphs), might likewise bespeak a compositional principle at work in the project, and not just an advanced stage of research. In fact, the montage form—with its philosophic play of distances, transitions, and intersections, its perpetually shifting contexts and ironic juxtapositions—had become a favorite device. . . . If we now were to regard this ostensible patchwork as, de facto, a determinate literary form, one that has effectively constructed itself (that is, fragmented itself),. . . then surely there would be signifi-cant repercussions for the direction and tempo of its reading, to say the least. . . .At any rate, it seems undeniable that despite the informal, episto-lary announcements of a "book" in the works,. . .the research project had become an end in itself.[43]

Just as the internet, to some minds, has become an end in itself.

Benjamin makes his project appear otherwise, though, by providing lit-tle in the way of readers' guides. The project has no index or table of con-tents. The organizing principles provide little help to the casual browser. Yet it can be seen as "the blueprint for an unimaginably massive and laby-rinthine architecture—a dream city, in effect. . . . In another of his let-ters. . . of this period, he speaks of the future construction of a literary form for this text."[44] Not "form," it turned out, but "formulation."

Benjamin's organizing principle, at its heart, is simply—as his editors say—an extension of montage (a mounting) or collage. This has much in common with the organization of the internet—except for one thing: a governing intellect, as mentioned before, such as Benjamin's. It may be that the accumulation of the internet becomes an intelligence, but that is of a different nature than what we are considering here. Collage and montage presuppose choice and consideration in placement (even in random place-ment), not simply chance or program or even the intelligence of the crowd. In a sense, of course, the web does what Benjamin envisioned while pre-senting the information *without* an organizing intelligence. In his file on methodology, Benjamin writes, "Method of this project: literary montage. I needn't say anything. Merely show. I shall purloin no valuables, appro-priate no ingenious formulations. But the rags, the refuse—these I will not inventory but allow, in the only way possible, to come into their own: by making use of them."[45] Today, we might smile at such a statement, at the naïve belief that it is possible to merely show—as if the venue we create for the showing doesn't affect the impact. The only way not to affect the viewing or reading is to re-create the original in every respect—but not even that can work, as Borges, again, shows in "Pierre Menard, Author of the *Quixote*."

The weakness of Benjamin's desire to use montage as a vehicle for merely showing can be understood through the montage/realism debate in film where Sergei Eisenstein posits montage as an essential skill of the filmmaker. In contrast, André Bazin argued for a realism of long shots, where the camera becomes a window on the world and not a manipulator of the world, as it becomes a vehicle for in montage filmmaking. In both, however, viewing is directed by a creative intelligence. Just so, "found art" is found by someone who then directs attention to it. Even the word *show* implies a guiding intelligence.

Eisenstein takes "montage" (which is the same word in the original French, in English, in the German of Benjamin, and in the Russian of Eisenstein) even further, arguing that montage is a tool for the construction of meaning: "As in Japanese hieroglyphics in which two independent ideographic characters ('shots') are juxtaposed and *explode* into a concept."[46] He has grasped the essential point that montage is not static but is the dynamic of the creation of meaning—hearkening back to Baudelaire's argument that beauty is understood through a number of juxtapositions acting in concert.

What seem almost random collections of information, added to by different agencies for different reasons at different times, are really no such thing. Not even in the digital age, where technology often appears to have taken on life of its own (quite literally, possibly, as Artificial Intelligence begins to seem more and more likely and as a hive mind possibly evolves). Plans, even if they do not unfold in expected manner, are still plans after all. Unexpected consequences are simply to be . . . expected. The internet may have grown so large that no one vision can encompass it, but it is still the result of a plan, even if one gone mad. Certainly, *The Arcades Project* consists of a plan in its attempt at non-plan, as Ester Leslie writes:

> The arcade was the *Ur-form,* the originary form, of modernity, for it in-
> cubated modes of behaviour—distraction, seduction by the commodity
> spectacle, shopping as leisure activity, self-display—that would come to
> figure more prominently as the century passed into the next. The Paris ar-
> cades sheltered the first modern consumerism. These covered walkways

with glass roofs had evolved out of the Galeries of the Palais Royal. With their jumble of diverse commodities from across the Empire, they turned shopping into an aesthetic event. They were perfect sites in which to linger and to learn how to window-shop and how to desire fantastic commodities. They were built, for the most part, in the decade and a half after 1822. A guide from 1852 describes each glass-roofed and marble-lined passageway as "a city, a world in miniature."[47]

Form, in this case, implies intent. Leslie couples Benjamin's concentration with modernism, but it extends well beyond that. Generally, "postmodernism," as a marker for cultural sensibility, as a name, simply equals sequence—after modernism. In this case, though, it perhaps also encompasses modernism into the digital age. "Commodity spectacle, shopping as leisure activity, self-display": these are at the heart of our digital culture, much more so even than in the modern period, where they were more for external presentation. In this sense, the internet has brought modernism home.

Let us emphasize: though the web has grown through the actions of humans, it has not grown through plan. There are plans within it, like the arcades of Benjamin's project, but there is no plan for the whole, not even if it becomes an intelligence. In some respects, this lack might be a good thing: plans can become restrictive, especially when the object of the planning is itself not fully known—or is knowable only as it grows (or unfolds). But it can also lead to the kind of tyranny Franz Kafka illustrated so well, a tyranny that can become one of man and machine interaction or synergy—and self-destruction—such as that shown in his story "In the Penal Colony." A synergy carried to an extreme far beyond that found in "The Book of Sand," where the very hint of its possibilities causes the character there to withdraw.

The Officer and the machine have a relationship almost of love, so much so that their purpose—and their victim—become something of an afterthought—shades of the simpler flâneur and the arcade. The Traveler, the hero of the story (if there is such a thing), observes this and questions the situation of the Condemned Man, who is the putative subject matter sparking the human/machine interaction:

"He doesn't know his own sentence?" "No," said the Officer once more. He then paused for a moment, as if he was asking the Traveler for a more detailed reason for his question, and said, "It would be useless to give him that information. He experiences it on his own body." . . . "But does he nonetheless have some general idea that he's been condemned?" "Not that either," said the Officer, and he smiled at the traveler, as if he was still waiting for some strange revelations from him. "No?" said the Traveler, wiping his forehead, "then does the man also not yet know how his defence was received?" "He has had no opportunity to defend himself."[48]

The Officer reflects the self-centeredness of the browser ("talking to himself") with no concern for the impact of what he does to others. This can become one metaphor for the internet user: the Condemned Man at mercy of machine and its tender, a tender who no longer understands the machine, having made something of a religion of it, and of the previous Commandant, now dead:

> ". . . I still use the diagrams of the previous Commandant. Here they are." He pulled some pages out of the leather folder. "Unfortunately I can't hand them to you. They are the most cherished thing I possess. Sit down, and I'll show you them from this distance. Then you'll be able to see it all well." He showed the first sheet. . . . These covered the paper so thickly that only with difficulty could one make out the white spaces in between. "Read it," said the Officer. "I can't," said the Traveler. "But it's clear," said the Officer." "It's very elaborate," said the Traveler evasively, "but I can't decipher it."
>
> "Yes," said the Officer, smiling and putting the folder back again, "it's not calligraphy for school children. One has to read it a long time. You too will finally understand it clearly. Of course, it has to be a script that isn't simple.[49]

If there is a weakness to the flâneur, even of the more complex type, of the web surfer, of the Traveler, it is that he or she has no real knowledge of the workings of machine or system but is merely a browser who is, in many senses, merely stopping by. And she or he has no real connection to the world beyond the connection to the machine. Someone else is always in control—as the ability of the Egyptian government to turn off the internet, as the ability of China's government to filter it, show so well. The Traveler could, conceivably, learn to use the machine—the Officer has explained how. But understand it? That is beyond him, just as, really, it is beyond the Officer.

Later in the story, the Officer once again tries to force the Traveler to understand his own documents:

> "Read that," he said. "I can't," said the Traveler. "I've already told you I can't read these pages." "But take a close look at the page," said the Officer, and moved up right next to the Traveler in order to read with him. When that didn't help, he raised his little finger high up over the paper, as if the page

must not be touched under any circumstances, so that using this he might make the task of reading easier for the Traveler. The Traveler also made an effort so that at least he could satisfy the Officer, but it was impossible for him. Then the Officer began to spell out the inscription and then read out once again the joined up letters. " 'Be just!' it states," he said. "Now you can read it." The Traveler bent so low over the paper that the Officer, afraid that he might touch it, moved it further away. The Traveler didn't say anything more, but it was clear that he was still unable to read anything. " 'Be just!' it says," the Officer remarked once again.[50]

Telling the Traveler what the page "says," of course, does not allow him to read it. He has to take it on belief, as he says, just as users of the internet, for the most part, do as they use the web. Few of us have any idea of what we are doing when we sit down to our computers, much less than when we drive our cars, where the relation between input and result are much more obvious (on most levels). In fact, few of us know much about even the destination our new machines are directing us to—the situation the Officer is in until his final "revelation."

The machine, the Officer, the penal colony itself—where the Traveler is visiting and the place he escapes at the end—can become an easy metaphor for our contemporary relations with our digital island, remote from our native land in some ways but reflecting it in others (the Traveler, however, is from another country completely). That the machine does not consume the Officer but destroys him as he used the machine to destroy others is extremely important to any understanding of the story as an unintentional allegory for our digital age—and can also help us understand why there is such distrust of our digital tools in some quarters.

Like the digital humanist, the Officer is caught up with the machine and what it can do. . . and becomes a warning to the digital humanist not to forget that the machine is ultimately only the servant up to the point where the user becomes too infatuated with the machine. The Traveler *is* the flâneur, but represents the weakness of the flâneur: a weakness the digital humanist, with his or her emphasis on building, tries to alleviate.

THREE

Intellectual Property in a Digital Age

Would Emily Dickinson's poetry be the same had it moldered in a locked chest? The physical relic, after all, does not change when taken out, read, or copied. There is no change at all, not even when it is shared with the world—so certainly no change in the aspects and rights of ownership. As Henry Mitchell, an intellectual property (IP) scholar, writes, "The author has full liberal ownership of his unpublished manuscripts: this ownership is the same as his ownership of his shoes or his furniture."[1] The fact of making them public shouldn't change that, any more than it does when one wears one's shoes in public. Someone makes off with them, or makes use of them, without the owner's permission? Should be illegal. Case closed.

Journalist and professor Marcus Boon, who is actually an advocate of copying, details how we tend to think of what people do when they take something that an author has created without paying for it:

> We have a word for such activities: "stealing." And stealing is punishable by law. Don't the store owners, musicians, writers, and software programmers whose work is suddenly made available . . . deserve to be compensated? How would you like it if someone came and stole your stuff, or . . . made copies of all your work and sold them or distributed them for free without your permission? In terms of the current legal, economic, and social regime, these questions are all valid.[2]

Yet it is not quite so simple: when someone steals your shoes, they have shoes and you do not. When someone copies something that you wrote and posted on the internet, on the other hand, you both then have it. Is there a loss? Even if there is, it is not the same loss as when someone takes your shoes—or your Corvette.

Many people ignore the difference, including Sherman Frederick, president and CEO of Stephens Media and a founder of Righthaven, a company dedicated to vigorous copyright protection. He writes in the *Las Vegas Review-Journal* (which his company owns):

> Say I owned a beautiful 1967 Corvette and kept it parked in my front yard.
>
> And you, being a Corvette enthusiast, saw my Vette from the street. You stopped and stood on the sidewalk admiring it. . . .
>
> There'd be nothing wrong with that. I like my '67 Vette and I keep in the front yard because I like people to see it.
>
> But then, you entered my front yard, climbed into the front seat and drove it away.
>
> I'm absolutely, 100% not OK with that. In fact, I'm calling the police and reporting that you stole my car.
>
> Every jury in the land would convict you.
>
> Yet, when it comes to copyrighted material—news that my company spends money to gather and constitutes the essence of what we are as a business—some people think they can not only look at it, but also steal it. And they do. They essentially step into the front yard and drive that content away.[3]

But, again, the two are not the same. The Corvette may be his, but you can still take a picture of it and could even, in most cases, replicate it exactly without his having any recourse in law. Furthermore, Frederick didn't design the Corvette in the first place but is displaying the creative work of someone else. Finally, the Corvette would have to be both driven away and still there, if this were a case of copyright theft. The analogy Frederick makes does not hold: there's a difference between copying and stealing. Judge Richard Posner, who sits on the United States Court of Appeals for the Seventh Circuit and who teaches at the University of Chicago Law School, explains:

> Someone who steals my car deprives me of valuable property that cost me money to acquire, and he pays nothing; he free rides on my purchase, my investment. Likewise if he copies the novel, or software, or new molecular entity for the treatment of disease, that I created at what may have been considerable cost in money, time, and risk. But the analogy to theft is imperfect. The car thief deprives me of my property; the copier does not—I

retain it and remain free to license or sell it. And while the copying may reduce my income from the work because I have lost the *exclusive* use of my property, though not the use, the reduction may not be great. It may even be zero, if for example the person who "pirated" my software did so only for his personal use, and not to resell it, and if in addition he could not have afforded my price, so that I do not lose even a single sale as a result of the "piracy."[4]

Posner goes on to say that "IP law is economically distinct from that involved in the theft of tangibles."[5] Yet there can be loss through copying, and the creator does need some level of protection from that loss. James Boyle, a lawyer and professor specializing in IP, argues that:

We should not be indifferent to this kind of loss; it is a serious concern. But the fact that a new technology brings economic benefits as well as economic harm to the creation, distribution, and sale of intellectual property products means that we should pause before increasing the level of rights, changing the architecture of our communications networks, creating new crimes, and so on.[6]

He's right: we do need to be careful if we are going to change our IP protections. And we also need to recognize that the conceptions we've used in the past, particularly concerning ownership of intangibles and of the easily copied, might need reexamining. It won't work to leave things as they are. Technology has been (and is) changing not only our physical relationships to things but to our cultural assumptions about them as well.

We can't leave our laws and our conceptions of ownership the way they are, in part, because they are going to change anyhow. As Boon writes:

below the surface of contemporary consumer culture, there is a collective dream of free access to an infinity of things. It is one of the principal themes which advertising manipulates, except that "free access" has been replaced by the promise of access via the purchase of a product—say, a soda or a pair of sneakers. . . . [R]adical shifts are taking place. . . . And the word "copy," a ubiquitous but poorly understood word, is playing an active role in these shifts. This word cannot be restricted to the particular set of definitions that we currently give it—any more than the appropriations . . . of digital file-sharing . . . can simply be dismissed as a crime.[7]

The laws and economic models in use today do not reflect these and other changing realities of either IP or of the possibilities for copying. At some point, in law at least, we are going to have to play catch-up by reexamining just what we mean when we say ownership. Our current assumptions and legal structures will no longer suffice.

The case *isn't* closed: Questions of ownership—and more—of IP (creations having no distinct and necessary unique physical presence) change as soon as any particular work becomes public (or is utilized discretely but for public purpose), if for no other reason than it is then covered by copyright, patent, trademark, or trade-secret laws. It loses its simple property status and becomes part of the intellectual commons, though with a great deal of restriction.

Kembrew McLeod, a communications professor and the media activist who once as a prank registered the phrase "freedom of expression" as a trademark, describes one aspect of this change in status through an experience of his own: "I've had my own work, a documentary, excerpted and shown in a context that made me squirm, but I didn't prevent it from happening. After all, I had already put it out into the world. Perhaps if someone took unpublished excerpts from my diary I would have objected, but works that have already been published are quite a different matter, both legally and ethically."[8] Again, the creator has complete power over an unpublished work, but once it is offered by the creator to the public (or used in a fashion affecting the public), the situation changes. McLeod lost some control over his work, clearly, but he still might have had legal recourse should he have chosen to use it. His phrase, "I didn't prevent it," shows awareness of this possibility and points to the fact that he, himself, sees ownership in a greater framework of sharing, no matter the consequence to his own rights, and is not willing to see it as simply a means of protecting what is his.

Similarly, in the 1990s, Barlow offered his doctoral dissertation to a website dedicated to the work of its subject, the science fiction writer Philip K. Dick. A few years later, someone in Spain emailed him, asking permission to translate one chapter and publish it in a journal there— permission that was granted. Some time after that, Barlow received an email from another person in Spain asking if he knew that his entire dissertation had been translated and published as a book. He did not. After some exploration, Barlow found that his initial permission had been somehow expanded and without further consultation with him. He did finally manage to track down the highly embarrassed publisher and get a couple of free copies of the book, but he never asked for recompense or that publication be halted. Like McLeod, Barlow probably had more recourse in law but, again like McLeod, he did not choose to pursue it. After all, the incident had worked in his favor, for it had led to a certain reputation in

Spain, a good story, and an invitation to contribute to a volume put out by another Spanish publisher.

Barlow had believed, since first allowing his work to be posted on the internet, that by offering the dissertation on the web he was relinquishing a certain sense of ownership over it; whatever happened after was beyond his control, so he might as well just sit back and watch. He had never expected money from the dissertation anyway and was pleased that it gained readers rather than languishing forgotten—the fate of most dissertations.

Still, the argument for absolute and perpetual and unchanging ownership of IP remains persuasive to many and continues to underlie a portion of creator rights in law. It is based on that "actual" lack of a change in physical status, about ownership with absolutely no consideration of publication as an act of alteration. However, as we see through McLeod's short description of his own case and through Barlow's experience, in the event of publication (including offering it on the web), things pertaining to the status of work really do change—and, counterintuitively, *they even change the original*. Its status is no longer what once it was—even in legal terms. Sale (or any public offering) of the work carries implications quite unlike sale (or the wearing) of shoes.

In American law, according to Mitchell: "Once the manuscript has been published or registered for copyright, the author's rights are determined by a completely different legal regime" than that governing a private document or other property.[9] Why? Because that first view of ownership (simply as physical property) does not take into account the meaning of reproduction or of cultural prerogatives, or of the further question of where value resides in the public sphere—or of how it is created. That view of ownership rests on origin and distinction, as well as on a simplified view of creation. Yet, though the law sees things somewhat differently, this remains the most common and most easily accepted view of ownership today—even of IP. The belief is that the owner of *anything* (generally the author, in terms of IP) has exclusive rights to his or her work.

In section 1, article 8, paragraph 8 of the United States Constitution, one finds that Congress is granted the power "To promote the Progress of Science and useful Arts, by securing for limited Times to Authors and Inventors the exclusive Right to their respective Writings and Discoveries." This bothers promoters of absolute ownership of IP. Mary Bono Mack, the widow of entertainer and member of Congress Sonny Bono (and herself succeeding him in Congress), spoke in the House of Representatives in favor of the Sonny Bono Copyright Term Extension Act in 1998, stating that "Actually, Sonny wanted the term of copyright protection to last forever. I am informed by staff that such a change would violate the Constitution. I invite all of you to work with me to strengthen our copyright laws in all of the ways available to us. As you know, there is also Jack Valenti's proposal for term to last forever less one day."[10] Valenti, longtime head of the Motion Picture Association of America, had been a tireless promoter of increased corporate protection for creative products. Of course, the suggestion of getting around the constitutional mandate of a time limit by making it "forever less one day" would never stand in court—forever less one day being the same as forever itself.

In terms of copyright, passion for protection can lead people to take things to extremes. A case in point may be seen in the legal dispute between the Directors Guild of America and a company called CleanFlicks that, with a couple of other companies, edited digital versions of movies they had purchased on video or DVD and then resold or rented the edited versions (with the originals) to people concerned about levels of sex and violence. The filmmakers, with reason, deplored the alterations of their work, especially as the movies continued to be represented as the movies they had created—which they no longer really were. The filmmakers were further incensed by the attempt to skirt the law by reselling or renting the legally purchased movie coupled with the altered version—as if that made altering the art of someone else legitimate. The film "sanitizers,"[11] on the other hand, argued that they paid full price for each copy before adding the edited version and reselling the two together—therefore never depriving the filmmakers of any profit (helping them, if anything, with sales to people who would not otherwise buy or rent the movies). Judge Posner, speaking on misappropriation of IP has argued that the

difference between theft properly so-called and copying is that while theft is very rarely productive, unauthorized copying of inventions and expressive works often is. The fact that copying does not necessarily deprive the owner of the original work of all or even any of the value of his work creates room for trade-offs—for asking whether social welfare as a whole might be increased by allowing some copying because the gain to the copier might exceed the cost to the owner of the original (sometimes both would gain).[12]

In this case, the sanitizers had argued, both would gain. But they argued unsuccessfully.

The sanitizers also believed that, through purchase, they had complete ownership rights to the purchased copies, so they could do anything they liked with them (exercising the right of second sale). In the last ruling of the case (CleanFlicks and the others said they hadn't the money to pursue it to a higher level), Judge Richard Matsch wrote, "What is protected are the creator's rights to protect its creation in the form in which it was created."[13] With this ruling, the Directors Guild of America had succeeded in pushing to *expand* protection rights for filmmakers—while CleanFlicks failed in similarly trying to expand the rights of film buyers and users.

In his comments, even if they did take the law a step beyond where it had been before, Judge Matsch was reflecting on American copyright law that, today, provides broad protection for creators, much broader than was envisioned in early American (and English) copyright law—and that provides much less protection for the user and the public domain. The current version of copyright law reads:

> "Copies" are material objects, other than phonorecords, in which a work is fixed by any method now known or later developed, and from which the work can be perceived, reproduced, or otherwise communicated, either directly or with the aid of a machine or device. The term "copies" includes the material object, other than a phonorecord, in which a work is first fixed.[14]

This is proving to be a rather simplistic and restrictive definition for a digital age where copies can be made quickly and almost for nothing. It would make subject to copyright, for example, the postcard of the Mona Lisa that Marcel Duchamp's "readymade" "L.H.O.O.Q." is an alteration of, were it to be produced today. That is, Duchamp's changes of a copy could contravene copyright—were it not that the Mona Lisa is in the public domain (the postcard itself might be copyrighted, so the status of the original might not even matter). Conceivably, if one were to buy a postcard of a copyrighted work of art (or a copyrighted postcard of a work of art) and were then to alter it after the manner of Duchamp, reproduce it, and offer it for sale, that person would be contravening copyright law.

In a sense, in the law, there isn't even an original—not as a necessary physical object. Yet, quite clearly, the power over the original and its copies by the copyright holder has become extensive and not simply in duration. The implications of that power in digital environments, where copying (again) is quick, easy, and cheap—and when the original is no different from a copy and so might not (necessarily) exist at all—are enormous and can be quite restrictive.

Contrary to Frederick's implied assertion that creating a copy is no different than stealing an original, most people believe (though generally without ever having thought about it) that where there is no harm (that is, no loss), there is no wrong. That the possibility of gain may be erased by copying concerns very few: copying machines have produced millions of acres of copies of copyrighted material; people have been taping music— off the radio and off commercial recordings—for generations. Homemade videotapes were made with no sense of ripping off the filmmakers. However, all of this in law is supposed to be for private use. When copies enter into the public arena or can be publicly traced, things begin to change—for the copying can then be proved and used in a court of law as examples of copyright contravention.

Righthaven, the company that Frederick funded to go after copyright offenders, has developed a process of suing without warning (normally, one might expect a cease and desist order first), of asking for an exorbitant ($150,000) recompense, and of settling privately. Righthaven, "says its lawsuits . . . are necessary to crack down on rampant online infringement of newspaper stories, columns, editorials, photos and graphics."[15] Its detractors, however, call it a copyright troll, a company trying to make money off of the collision between outdated legal frameworks and modern digital possibilities. In response to its actions:

> Some attorneys are advising bloggers to simply follow the rule laid down by the *Las Vegas Review-Journal*'s parent company [Stephens Media] and refrain from quoting anything more than the headline and first paragraph of news articles. Following this advice essentially allows a newspaper to decide what constitutes fair use, a term they are motivated to construe as narrowly as possible. Still others suggest that "the easiest way to avoid copyright infringement claims is to avoid copying," which is true only in the sense that the easiest way to avoid getting robbed is to have no possessions. Quoting, linking, aggregating all involve "copying" and all are integral to any number of perfectly legal creative, often non-commercial, uses of copyrighted works. Indeed, these uses are what makes the internet such a remarkable tool for fostering innovation.[16]

The rationale behind Righthaven comes completely from an ownership (as opposed to creator or user) viewpoint. " 'We believe it's the best solution out there,' [Steve] Gibson says [CEO of Righthaven]. 'Media companies' assets are very much their copyrights. These companies need to understand and appreciate that those assets have value more than merely the present advertising revenues.' "[17] However:

> [Kelly] McBride [of the Poynter Institute] . . . expressed skepticism that the Righthaven's actions are intended primarily to protect newspaper

copyrights. "This may just be meant to make money, because when you look at the individuals that Righthaven has sued, a lot of them pose no threat to the newspaper's financial viability."

"I just think it's a red herring. I don't think they're after deterrence," she said.

McBride pointed to one of the most controversial of Righthaven's practices—the filing of an infringement lawsuit as the first action against an alleged infringer, with no takedown request or cease-and-desist letter submitted prior to litigation.

"In theory, if they wanted to solve the problem rather than make money, they would offer the opportunity to take the content down, and figure out a way to partner with the defendant," she said. Instead, Righthaven is filing lawsuits and demanding settlements, "which is hostile at best . . . and I don't know that it will in the long run [benefit their clients] because there's so many users out there that are creating and aggregating and reposting content."[18]

What is happening through these cases isn't new but is part of an ongoing struggle between copiers and copyright holders that has been going on at least since *Sony v. Universal City Studios* (which was settled in Sony's favor in 1984, allowing home copying of television shows):

Righthaven's lawsuits come on the heels of similar campaigns targeting music and movie infringers. The Recording Industry Association of America sued about 20,000 thousand file sharers over five years, before recently winding down its campaign. And a coalition of independent film producers called the U.S. Copyright Group was formed this year, already unleashing as many as 20,000 federal lawsuits against BitTorrent users accused of unlawfully sharing movies.[19]

Two cases brought by Righthaven are of especial interest, one because of the irony it carries and the question following of who owns what; and the other because of involvement by the Electronic Frontier Foundation (EFF), a major defender of online freedom in the United States. The first suit was brought against blogger Anthony Curtis for a posting on his blog, the second against the group-blog site Democratic Underground and David Allen, its founder.

According to Wendy Davis, writing in *The Daily Online Examiner* in June 2010:

Copyright enforcement outfit Righthaven has filed some questionable lawsuits in the past, but really outdid itself in a case against Anthony Curtis, publisher of the *Las Vegas Advisor*.

That lawsuit, one of several filed on Friday, alleges that Curtis infringed copyright by reposting an article from the *Las Vegas Review-Journal*. Problem is, that article was itself based on an annual survey conducted by Curtis of ticket prices for entertainment shows.

Yes, Curtis went to the trouble of fielding a survey and then shared his findings with the newspaper, only to find himself sued for posting portions of the ensuing article on his own blog.[20]

The conundrum here reflects that of the Duchamp Mona Lisa postcard. Who owns what? A postcard could be copyrighted although it is something of a copy itself. Just so, information collected by Curtis and the interview with Curtis are not owned by Curtis but by the newspaper that presented and conducted it.

This isn't the only instance where ownership and creation are now presented as distinct, even without formal transfer of ownership from the creator. It has long been the case that works created for an employer are owned by that employer, though credit for creation is often given to an individual or team. It is also common for the name of a ghostwriter to be omitted (though the courtesy "with" in attribution has become prevalent over the past generation) when acting as a paid creator in another's name for a print product (for a speech this is almost always the case, of course). In all of these cases, there's an implied distinction between creator and owner, though a certain privilege is generally given to the creator regarding future use of the product. In the past, this courtesy would have been granted to Curtis, with the newspaper allowing him to reprint much more than he actually did.

On January 28, 2011, *Gawker* posted a story by Maureen O'Connor entitled *"Men's Health* Editor Plagiarizes His Own Writers." Dave "Zinczenko—whose cult of personality includes books, regular TV appearances, and a restaurant in partnership with 'wingman' Dan Abrams— routinely rips his writers' bylines off their articles, slaps his byline on, and republishes the material as though he wrote it himself."[21] Rodale, Inc., the publisher of *Men's Health* responded, saying:

> The byline doesn't take credit for the work, but serves as an overarching tag used in conjunction with the logo to indicate that the material has been written, assigned or edited by the brand (i.e. Dave and his team) at some point. That is why the *Men's Health* logo appears on this particular blog. Much of Dave's work is original for this blog, but in addition to generating new content, Dave—and many editors in general—also edit existing content that the company owns to connect with readers. A number of the articles you

cite that simply carry the *Men's Health* byline are indeed stories by Dave that he wrote for his books that were then adapted by *Men's Health* staffers to later appear in the magazine.[22]

Not only does the circularity of this make one dizzy, but it makes creation simply an aspect of ownership—as though Frederick, by virtue of ownership of that Corvette, could claim to have designed or built it. It denies the validity or status of prior ownership, concentrating into the work ownership rights to those things incorporated from elsewhere.

In the other Righthaven case, according to Kurt Opsahl, a lawyer working with EFF:

> Democratic Underground, a political message forum, refused to be intimidated by Righthaven's action. They retained counsel and responded with a counterclaim that joined Righthaven'[s] affiliate and funder, Stephens Media, LLC (publisher of the Review-Journal), and laid bare the numerous defects not only in Righthaven's claims, but in its business model itself. Not surprisingly, Righthaven now wants out—so badly, in fact, that it has moved to voluntarily dismiss its claim with prejudice in order to avoid a decision on the merits. However, Righthaven pleads to be let off the hook for Democratic Underground's fees and costs defending the lawsuit.[23]

On December 7, 2010, the lawyers for Democratic Underground filed a motion against Righthaven's own motion for voluntary dismissal of the case (which, as Opsahl says, would have left Democratic Underground responsible for its legal fees, creating a warning for others who might try to fight Righthaven: a warning that doing so would not be cheap). The Democratic Underground motion explains a great deal about the case, though certainly from the defendant's viewpoint: "This was a meritless lawsuit from the beginning, launched as part of a well-publicized business model in which Righthaven acquires interests in copyrights for the sole purpose of suing unsuspecting alleged infringers, and then seeks to leverage the cost of defending (and its own purported right to attorneys' fees and domain name seizures) to coerce settlements."[24]

The motion goes on to argue why Righthaven should not be allowed to simply drop the suit and walk away, leaving the defendant with what amounts to punitive legal bills:

> Defendants cannot be liable on this Complaint under at least two grounds (among others not briefed here): (i) as the mere host of a discussion forum to which a third party posted an excerpt of an article, and having taken down

the excerpt promptly when first informed of Plaintiff's objections to it, Defendants committed no "volitional act" of copying or distribution giving rise to copyright liability; and (ii) in all events, fair use provides a complete defense to the infringement claimed.[25]

The suit was sparked by a posting in May 2010 by an anonymous contributor using the name "Pampango." On the Nevada U.S. Senate race, the posting used five sentences from a 50-sentence story in the *Las Vegas Review-Journal* and included a link to the original story. This is well within the standards of fair use as generally practiced on the internet today, but it did not satisfy Righthaven.

Eventually, as we have seen, Righthaven attempted to drop its case. This was the result of a counterclaim that could undercut many of its suits if the counterclaim should prove successful:

> The Counterclaim named Stephens Media, as well as Righthaven, as Counter-Defendants, based on the former's creation of, control of, financial interest in, and collusion with the latter to pursue meritless claims of infringement. The 196 paragraph Counterclaim spelled out in detail the facts supporting its requests for declaratory relief, including at least the following dispositive issues: 1) that Defendants did not infringe Righthaven's copyright based on a lack of a volitional act; 2) that Defendants did not infringe Righthaven's copyright because it made a fair use of the Excerpt; 3) that Righthaven does not rightfully own the copyright in question, in that the assignment was a sham designed solely to pursue litigation with rights being retained by Stephens Media; 4) that Righthaven and/or Stephens Media have, by their invitation to copy and share the Article, granted Defendants a license to post the Excerpt; 5) that Righthaven failed to mitigate its damages, in that it gave no notice or opportunity to remove the allegedly infringing work; 6) that any harm was not actionable as *de minimis* [too small to be brought to law]; and 7) that Righthaven and Stephens Media are engaged in barretry, champetry and maintenance [a legal phrase meaning, essentially, the bringing of frivolous or vexatious lawsuits when one is not even directly involved] by spawning transactions designed for no purpose other than to pursue litigation.[26]

If the counterclaim were to be upheld, Righthaven could find itself liable for legal fees for a great many of the defendants in suits it has brought.

The jealous, closely held copyright concept championed by Righthaven has a great deal of support in an America that has put property rights above almost all others. But it doesn't have to be this way. We could be experiencing a much more open vision of copyright that still protects creators, perhaps something like that crafted by Creative Commons, an organization providing an alternative to restrictive copyright by presenting its own licenses allowing much greater public use of a work. Creative Commons recognizes the fact that, as McLeod describes it, "in an environment where copies are being shared with the world, it's hard to defend the position that an author can (or should) have *total* control over his or her creation. Even though Congress has regularly created compromises that address how copyrighted materials can be used by others, there are also philosophical and moral principles that can't be ignored."[27] Creative Commons, recognizing that copyright laws, strongly backed by America's largest corporations, are not going to be loosened, provides a way of giving blanket permissions without conflicting with the law. Yet, for the most part, many of McLeod's philosophical and moral principles continue to be ignored or twisted (as the implications of the CleanFlicks ruling have made more likely and as the number of predator copyright trolls grows), especially as copyright continues to be extended into new areas of the digital environment and becomes a much more important aspect of corporate profitability.

If the CleanFlicks folk had been willing to work only with films outside of copyright, they would have had no problem. Unfortunately, most everything made since the advent of sound movies is still in copyright as of 2011, thanks to copyright extensions in 1976 and 1998 that include retroactive extensions of duration. There is little room for someone to work with extant movies, someone who wants to take movies and make them into something else, into parts of new works of art. One could claim that there is also a tremendous loss now guaranteed by the structure of contemporary American copyright law, and not through ownership, but through lack of clear parentage:

> Companies have gone out of business. Records are incomplete or absent. In some cases, it is even more complicated. A film, for example, might have one copyright over the sound track, another over the movie footage, and another over the script. You get the idea. These works—which are commercially unavailable and also have no identifiable copyright holder—are called "orphan works."[28]

Even had CleanFlicks wanted to make deals to use particular films, in plenty of cases it would have had a hard time establishing who the owners are—who to make deals with. These orphan works, as Boyle says in the passage above, remain in a legal limbo, dropping away from the historical/cultural continuum, changing our knowledge of the past through the resulting reduced accessibility, providing an unintended consequence of copyright extension and expansion.

In addition to that, creations such as Mike J. Nichols' *The Phantom Edit,* a reworking of the George Lucas film *Star Wars Episode I: The Phantom Menace,* would be much more likely to appear today were copyright still at its earlier limitations. Were that the case, the public domain would be huge and wide open for incorporation into new art. We don't know what might have been created, of course, for the law has left little room for it and few have pushed it, and what people have done privately may never be seen.

Contemporary copyright laws have also severely restricted the "sampling" that was so much more important to hip hop music before rapper Biz Markie lost a copyright infringement case in 1991 over his sampling of the Gilbert O'Sullivan song "Alone Again (Naturally)" on his album *I Need a Haircut.* Biz Markie's recording was withdrawn from the market, casting a pall over sampling, which has since become a much more limited aspect of hip hop, producers having to negotiate—and pay for—rights, so sampling less and less. In this instant, copyright actually changed art. Today, mashup and sampling artists, such as Gregg Gillis ("Girl Talk") and Brian Burton ("Danger Mouse"), operate outside of the mainstream of the music industry (though with considerable influence) in part because their work contains constant possible copyright violation, given the current configuration of the law. The legal status of their work, like the concept of fair use itself, has yet to be clearly established by the courts.

In movies, in music, and in other areas, copyright has limited the intellectual commons, and the "intellectual commons contains the raw materials that people use to create works."[29] When it is constrained, creation is restrained, which is doubly unfortunate, given the fact that there is no scarcity when the raw material is—or should be—infinitely reproducible. What copyright has done is to create boundaries where none existed or, as some would argue, need to exist. Though there may be justification for boundaries of some nature, the fact remains: copyright as practiced today, whether it is meant to or not, constrains creativity. Many owners of copyright may argue otherwise, that copyright enables creativity, but the evidence says otherwise. Certainly, the beneficiaries of copyright are rarely the actual creators.

All four of the primary aspects of legal protection for IP: copyright, patents, trademarks, and trade secrets, have impact on the new digital environment, but it is copyright that is proving to be the most important currently, and most contentious, with patent following somewhat behind. After all, the word is the prime carrier of information on the internet; and the word itself, in reproduction, is at the heart of copyright. In addition, just about all of the other means for conveying information on the web, primarily video, photo, and sound applications, had also come under the same copyright protection by the time the internet came into wide use.

In the United States, debate over copyright "is driven by the interaction of three conceptions: a pragmatic or economic point of view, a view that focuses on the property rights of creators, and a view that focuses on the uncircumscribed nature of ideas and the inherently communal nature of the creative process."[30] The tension between these has led to the development of four ways by which copyright law attempts to ensure that the user, and not just the creator, can make maximum creative use of the original work. These are (1) the fair use doctrine, (2) the distinction between the expression itself and the ideas carried, (3) the right of unimpeded resale, and (4) the limited duration of copyright itself.

Fair use "allows anyone to copy, quote, and publish parts of a copyrighted work for purposes of commentary, criticism, news reports, scholarship, caricature, or even . . . recording and time-shifting of television programs."[31] According to that defense motion in the Democratic Underground case:

> The fair use doctrine "creates a limited privilege in those other than the owner of a copyright to use the copyrighted material in a reasonable manner without the owner's consent." *Fisher v. Dees*, 794 F.2d 432, 435 (9th Cir. 1986). It permits and requires courts "to avoid rigid application of the copyright statute when, on occasion, it would stifle the very creativity which that law is designed to foster."[32]

Current American copyright law is rather vague on fair use, and its limits have not been clearly established by the courts. The law itself reads:

§ 107. LIMITATIONS ON EXCLUSIVE RIGHTS: FAIR USE

> Notwithstanding the provisions of sections 106 and 106A, the fair use of a copyrighted work, including such use by reproduction in copies or phonorecords or by any other means specified by that section, for purposes such as criticism, comment, news reporting, teaching (including multiple copies for classroom use), scholarship, or research, is not an infringement of copyright. In determining whether the use made of a work in any particular case is a fair use the factors to be considered shall include—

(1) the purpose and character of the use, including whether such use is of a commercial nature or is for nonprofit educational purposes;

(2) the nature of the copyrighted work;

(3) the amount and substantiality of the portion used in relation to the copy-righted work as a whole; and

(4) the effect of the use upon the potential market for or value of the copy-righted work.

The fact that a work is unpublished shall not itself bar a finding of fair use if such finding is made upon consideration of all the above factors.[33]

These four factors are all rather vague, allowing groups like Righthaven the room to interpret them as narrowly as possible and for other groups to see them as granting a great deal of leeway. Only the passage of time, with new determinations by the courts or through new laws, will tell how fair use will ultimately be defined.

The distinction between the specific expression covered by copyright and the ideas that expression carries, which are not covered (though they may be protected under patent or trademark or trade-secret laws) by copy-right, always proves difficult to define, for changing phrasing here and there (for example) is not enough for claiming that ideas are being used and not expression: but where's the line? Fair use aside, just how much of something needs to be changed for the work to be distinct enough to evade copyright challenge?

The unimpeded resale concept is, among other things, what makes lend-ing libraries and the old video rental stores possible, for the work (in its physical and particular manifestation) is owned completely and may be dealt with in any manner the owner wishes. It is this concept that Clean-Flicks was utilizing when it resold (or rented) the originals along with the edited versions of the movies.

The last of the four, time limitation for copyright, has been the most thoroughly emasculated, rising from 14 years (renewable once) to the au-thor's life plus 70 years. For copyright owned by a corporation, the terms, for the most part, are now 120 years after creation or 95 after publication, whichever is shorter. It is this last number, ultimately, that determines the duration of almost all copyright, for it is corporations (publishers among them, but copyrights are owned by every major corporation) who most influence the laws. As Mitchell writes, "an exclusive focus on the author as the source of IP rights would be misleading. The vast majority of wealth created by authorship flows to publishers, not authors. Most authors are either employees who have no property rights in their work or independent contractors who sell their rights to their employers or publishers."[34]

So, it is corporations who have become the greatest promoters of copyright extension, both in time and in coverage, for corporations see their copyrights in ownership terms only and, quite naturally, see loss of copyright as a reduction of corporate assets. Because of the corporations and their influence, Lawrence Lessig claimed in his Melville Nimmer Lecture in 2001 that almost everyone today has come to see copyright in property-metaphor terms (we even refer to Intellectual Property as, well, property), and few manage to see it in other fashions or in terms of something less than absolute ownership: "This view of the naturalness of intellectual property is not simply the construction of overly eager Hollywood lobbyists. . . . The reality is that it reflects the understanding of ordinary people, too. The ordinary person believes, as Disney's Michael Eisner does, that Mickey Mouse should be Disney's for time immemorial."[35] Lessig goes on to point out the irony of the Disney Corporation being so protective and yet so damaging to the public domain, for Disney itself is one of the greatest users of stories in that public domain, including Victor Hugo's hunchback, Pocahontas, and numerous others. Sometimes, Disney comes close to crossing the line into infringement. Disney's *Alladin* (Ron Clements and John Musker, 1992), for example, owes a great deal to a much older movie, *The Thief of Bagdad* (Ludwig Berger and Michael Powell et al., 1940), itself a remake of a silent film.

Because of its value to corporations, copyright is now on the verge of becoming a permanent right (if it isn't already, in practice if not in concept)—something that entities like Righthaven are trying to force into reality. The duration of copyright has been extended to the point where any further extension might as well make it perpetual, though that flies in the face of the U.S. Constitution. Yet, it will certainly be extended again and, just as certainly, this will happen by 2023, when Mickey Mouse will turn 95. Disney is not about to allow its signature product to enter into the public domain—and its power to influence lawmakers is countered, in this case, only by a few lonely Don Quixotes, for the public domain that copyright extension encroaches upon does not produce the concentrated revenue stream that would motivate concerted opposition.

An example of the complex nature of works and value within the public sphere can be found in the experience of the rock band the Grateful Dead. Founded in the 1960s, its most successful years (financially) were in the 1970s and 1980s. Never a particularly popular band in terms of record sales or radio play, the Dead, early on, staked its reputation and income on its live concerts. By the early 1970s, it was encouraging fans to tape its shows and then to trade the tapes. Soon, fans had collections of shows that could reach into the hundreds, all copyrightable but unenforced. Soon, also, and partly as a result, the band had become (and remained, for well more than a decade) one of the top-grossing live acts in the United States.

Rather than protecting recordings of their music through copyright, the Dead encouraged free distribution. Instead of making a little money on the recordings themselves (the record companies always gain the lion's share), the band became rich through live performance, a much more lucrative arena, generally speaking, for musicians.

Significantly, this model has become important to the development of careers in popular music in the early 21st century for a number of musicians, building name recognition through the giving away of digital copies of their music—especially since the advent of YouTube and other means of distribution through the internet. The pop duo Pomplamoose (Jack Conte and "Nataly Dawn" Knutson) turned YouTube into a venue leading to financial rewards—specifically through participation in ads for both Toyota and Hyundai.

A growing body of entrepreneurs and artists within the music business are beginning to recognize the value of "unauthorized acts, because it's free advertising. Instead of attacking these bastard pop confections—fruitlessly trying to track down the anonymous infringers—some record companies are appropriating the appropriations. They also realize that they can capitalize on these active audiences, expropriate this creative labor and make it theirs."[36] Ironically, this has come on the heels of attempts by others to protect music, particularly on the internet, from copying that does not immediately financially benefit the performer or her or his label. Even Lessig, the prime promoter of alternatives to the standard vision of copyright, agrees that music should be protected. "The passion for Napster [a file-sharing website eventually stopped by the record industry] is wrong if it means that artists should not be paid. I realize there are those on the other side . . . but I'm not on the side of free music if free music means that artists don't get paid. In my view the issue is not whether artists get paid; the issue is how."[37] But, as in the case of the Grateful Dead and some of the musicians, like Pomplamoose, of the new digital era, it is not simply a question of how one gets paid, but for what. The recorded music given away becomes bait, leading to financial reward through other means. By not getting paid, sometimes the artist can actually make more. At the same time, the costs associated with music production are going down as much and as quickly as the costs of copying—and the marketplace is growing, increasing potential profits through volume. Boyle asks, adding nuance to his earlier comments on protection:

> Is the net result a loss to rights holders such that we need to increase pro-
> tection and control in order to maintain a constant level of incentives? A
> large, leaky market may actually provide more revenue than a small one
> over which one's control is much stronger. What's more, the same tech-
> nologies that allow for cheap copying also allow for swift and encyclopedic
> search engines—the best devices ever invented for detecting illicit copying.
> What the Net takes away with one hand, it often gives back with the other.
> Cheaper copying does not merely mean loss, it also means opportunity.[38]

Unfortunately, this opportunity is exactly what the evolving IP laws seem to be trying to prevent. Sometimes it appears as though the intent is to "make this technology of the internet, which was hailed as the great 'technology of freedom,' into a technology of control and surveillance. The possibility of individuals circulating costless perfect digital copies requires it."[39]

The result of all of this, Boyle believes, may be the emergence of a new business model that will encourage rather than stopping copying, yet that will remain profitable, Looking at this in terms of possibilities for book publishers, he writes:

> Why might free digital availability make sense for parts of the publishing
> industry? First, most people hate reading a book on a screen, but like finding
> out if it is worth buying. I am sure I have lost some sales, but my guess
> is that I have gained more new readers who otherwise would be unaware
> of my work, and who treat the digital version as a "sampler," to which they
> then introduce others. This is a leap of faith but not an unreasonable one.
> Second, even professional authors make money in multiple ways other than
> by royalties—ranging from options on film production to commissions for
> magazine articles to consulting, teaching and speaker fees. Most are aided
> by wider exposure. As [science-fiction writer Cory] Doctorow says, "my
> biggest fear as an author isn't illicit copying, it is obscurity." Third, digital
> distribution is almost free. The "cost" is the gamble over lost sales, not re-
> maindered books with their covers torn off. Some publishers are willing to
> take the risk to build current and future demand.[40]

Like Lessig, Boyle was one of the early supporters of Creative Commons. The new model would be like that of the Grateful Dead, based on the idea that public awareness sparked by easy and free availability is worth more, ultimately, than whatever might be gained through restrictive first sale.

Perhaps because musical performances, before electronics, could not be reproduced and were, therefore, not subject to copyright, it has been easier for the Grateful Dead to experiment with alternatives to the ownership system that had grown so powerful over the previous half century. In publishing, with a much longer copyright tradition, a similar mindset may take more time in developing. Instead, according to Boyle, we now have that zero-sum argument claiming that the strength of copyright protection must balance the ease of copying. Expensive copying provides its own protection for the original: not many will be willing to pay for it. Cheap copying, on the other hand, provides no protection in and of itself for the copyright holder, so something else is needed. A look at the history of copying provides an explanation:

> To deal with the monk-copyist, we need no copyright because physical control of the manuscript is enough. What does it matter if I say I will copy your manuscript, if I must do it by hand? How will this present a threat to you? There is no need to create a legal right to exclude others from copying, no need for a "copy right." As copying costs fall, however, the need to exclude increases.
>
> But then comes the Internet. To deal with the Internet, we need the Digital Millennium Copyright Act, 13 the No Electronic Theft Act, the Sonny Bono Copyright Term Extension Act, and perhaps even the Collections of Information Antipiracy Act. As copying costs approach zero, intellectual property rights must approach perfect control.[41]

At the beginning of copyright in the early 18th century, it was the value of the word that was of concern, and that value of the word hadn't even started to become apparent until quite recently, then, when manuscripts began to be reproduced relatively cheaply and quickly, completely changing the relationship between knowledge and information, leading to a growing demand for education—for literacy, in particular, and for the new books. As Neil Postman reminds us:

> There was a time when information was a resource that helped human beings to solve specific and urgent problems of their environment. It is true enough that in the Middle Ages, there was a scarcity of information but its very scarcity made it both important and usable. This began to change, as everyone knows, in the late 15th century when a goldsmith named Gutenberg, from Mainz, converted an old wine press into a printing machine, and in so doing, created what we now call an information explosion. Forty years after the invention of the press, there were printing machines in 110 cities

in six different countries; 50 years after, more than eight million books had been printed, almost all of them filled with information that had previously not been available to the average person. Nothing could be more misleading than the idea that computer technology introduced the age of information. The printing press began that age, and we have not been free of it since.[42]

Before Gutenberg printed his Bibles in 1455, manuscripts in Europe *were* laboriously copied one at a time, costing a great deal and making each individual copy valuable as a physical item in its own right (a result of the effort put into creation of the individual copy). "Printing fostered the modern idea of individuality but it destroyed the medieval sense of community and social integration. Printing created prose but made poetry into an exotic and elitist form of expression. Printing made modern science possible but transformed religious sensibility into an exercise in superstition."[43] In addition, with printing, the value of the individual item went way down, but profit in the aggregate for the new replacement of the copied manuscript, the printed page, began to rise. "Imagine a line. At one end sits a monk painstakingly transcribing Aristotle's *Poetics*. In the middle lies the Gutenberg printing press. Three-quarters of the way along the line is a photocopying machine. At the far end lies the internet and the online version of the human genome. At each stage, copying costs are lowered and goods become both less rival and less excludable."[44]

Even with print, as would happen later with the Grateful Dead and which had also been the rationale behind radio play of songs sold as single records from early in broadcast history, giving away a product could help make sales stronger, a case in point being Thomas Paine's *Common Sense*. The pamphlet was read aloud (given away) in taverns and coffeehouses throughout the American colonies. Having heard it, people wanted to own it, just as those who heard the amateur live recordings of Dead shows soon wanted to experience the real thing themselves. Before long, Paine's pamphlet had attained a greater penetration into the American colonial public than almost any other publication, excepting the Bible. Experiencing something (reading it or hearing it) did not necessarily lessen demand for it but, as Boyle claims, could increase it.

From our vantage point in the 21st century, the impact of the change Gutenberg sparked is hard to overestimate, for we see it every day as we struggle with new change away from a culture built over centuries and imbued with assumptions sparked by the primacy of the printed word. Walter Ong, in *Orality and Literacy,* traces the growth of the impact of print on culture over the five-and-a-half centuries since the start of European emergence from an orality-based culture. In his Introduction, he writes, "Our understanding of the differences between orality and literacy developed only in the electronic age, not earlier. Contrasts between electronic media and print have sensitized us to the earlier contrast between writing and orality. The electronic age is also an age of 'secondary orality,' the orality of telephones, radio and television, which depends on writing and print for its existence."[45] Though he was writing a decade before the start of the digital revolution (which began with the advent of the World Wide Web) that we are experiencing today, Ong put his finger on something quite relevant to our studies of the differences between our post-"secondary orality" and literacy: we cannot see what is happening now as well as the future will—but we can get a better sense of the present if we look back—in this case, taking into account the changes in culture that occurred as Ong's literacy culture developed along with concepts of ownership of the new published works.

These changes had been recognized before Ong, of course. Marshall McLuhan, perhaps the most famous media investigator of the 1960s, commented in 1954 on the importance of what Gutenberg had started:

> The printed page was itself a highly specialized (and spatialized) form of communication. In 1500 A.D. it was revolutionary. . . . The printed book soon liquidated two thousand years of manuscript culture. It created the solitary student. It set up the rules of private interpretation against public disputation. It established the divorce between "literature and life." It created a new and highly abstract culture because it was itself a mechanized form of culture.[46]

But that wasn't the half of it, as we are now seeing. Today, recognition of the types of changes McLuhan points toward is particularly significant for the understanding of contemporary information and culture even as both are changing. Though he was able to look back from a vantage of almost half a millennium, a perspective that won't be possible relating to our current information revolution for quite some time, his comments (like Ong's) still provide analogies to current events; and these are useful to attempts at understanding our revolution as we experience it. From the midst of it, we have a difficult time seeing the whole; looking back for analogies makes things easier.

McLuhan and Ong both note the impact of technology on the act of reading itself, an impact that has also changed how we view ownership of—and the value of—the written word and its successors. McLuhan writes:

Before printing, a reader was one who discerned and probed riddles. After printing, it meant one who scanned, who skipped along the macadamized surfaces of print. Today at the end of that process we have come to equate reading skill with speed and distraction rather than wisdom. But print, the mechanization of writing, was succeeded in the nineteenth century by photography and then by the mechanization of human gesture in the movie. This was followed by the mechanization of speech in telephone, phonograph and radio. In the talkies, and finally with TV, came the mechanization of the totality of human expression, of voice, gesture, and human figure in action.

Each of these steps in the mechanization of human expression was comparable in its scope to the revolution brought about by the mechanization of writing itself. The changes in the ways of human association, social and political, were telescoped in time and so hidden from casual observers.

If there is a truism in the history of human communication it is that any innovation in the external means of communication brings in its train shock on shock of social change.[47]

If the introductions of the telephone, radio, the talkies, and TV were revolutionary, what we are experiencing now is beyond revolution—and, again, we don't know what the outcome will be. The act of reading is changing (and changing us), as it changed with print—and so is our relationship with the written word—which also changed with print.

Though we are struggling to adapt to the complex changes brought about by advances in communications technology, and to understand their impact on our ways of reading and writing and on our cultures, our laws of copyright have merely been amplified, not adapted, to a changing world. They still reflect the culture, the "literacy" culture, of the 18th century. A wind-up Victrola record player from the 1920s could be amplified and its crank replaced with an electric cord, but it will never be adapted to digital technology without a complete overhaul, right down to the records played themselves. It would be better just to replace it. Just so, copyright needs more than a complete overhaul if it is going to be useful in the digital age. It too needs replacement.

Our ideas on copyright, we find, were developed for and by an emerging literacy culture based on print reproduction and a simplified vision of IP ownership. They reflect the needs of authors and publishers of a bygone era, as well as those of a reading public now largely superseded. In other words, they have no foundation other than in cultural conventions of the past and in the laws that still reflect them. Furthermore, there's no moral basis to copyright, simply a series of compromises between a number of competing needs with no natural law behind it, not even in the libertarian sense of property. IP, says Mitchell, "can never be mine in the sense that the shirt on my back or the change in my pocket is mine. There is no intellectual property in the state of nature, even if there is property in acorns and apples. The rights, obligations, and sanctions of an IP regime only make sense in the context of a broader political system."[48]

Legal grapplings with questions of ownership of ideas, methods, and product designs (essentially of information or IP) can be traced back, in English law, at least to the Statute of Monopolies enacted under King James I in 1624. Legal protection of invention was slow to cover authors, but the idea grew—and was expanded to include them specifically under Queen Anne, when the first English copyright law, the Statute of Anne, was enacted in 1710. Both statutes limited protection to 14 years, a recognition that neither invention nor creation conveys permanent ownership, but that they are, in part at least, rights granted simply to provide economic incentive for invention and creation and not for permanent ownership. The newer statute added a renewal clause: "after the expiration of the said term of fourteen years the sole right of printing or disposing of copies shall return to the Authors thereof if they are then living for another Term of fourteen years."[49] Significantly, this right is given explicitly to living authors only and not to their proxies or to their estates, for it is living writers who produce, not their heirs. The implication, also, is that rights shall revert (return) to the author at that time, though they may have been ceded earlier. From this and other items of the statute, we see that "the Statute of Anne was primarily concerned with establishing and securing a 'property,' "[50] but within a framework of public rights.

The "return" of the property as a part of the creator's rights is a particularly interesting point in light of the ways copyright has been extended over the centuries since, in Britain and also in America. Apparently authors themselves did not at once take full advantage of their new right of reversion, and so it atrophied even as other aspects of copyright expanded. Lionel Bently and Jane Ginsberg write:

> In part, this can be explained by reference to the fact that few works would have had a substantial market fourteen years after first publication, and, in a good number of those that did attract continued demand, the author may well not have survived the first fourteen year term. But, in the few cases in which the reversion right related to works for which there remained continuing demand, the right would only have had value if a writer were

conscious of his or her legal rights and able to interest other publishers in such rights.[51]

Imagine what the situation would be today, were rights to necessarily revert to the author (or other creator) after a specified period of time! The position of the author in relation to the publisher (or other corporate copyright holder) would be quite different than it is now. As it is, the reversion right disappeared in the Literary Copyright Act of 1814, where the duration of the first term was doubled and extended (without reversion) only if the author were living, and only for the rest of the author's life. In the United States, the right never really existed at all: the first copyright law in 1790 providing coverage for a duration of 14 years, with an extension for an additional 14 if the author were still living. Even if there were implied reversion, this disappeared with the Copyright Act of 1831, which doubled the first term to 28 years and removed the necessity of a living author for extension—thereby removing possibility of reversion.

The tension between the rights of creation and the rights of the commons were apparently recognized by the British lawmakers of 1710, as provision for each was built into the Statute of Anne. The law was, in part, a means of breaking the power of the Stationers' Company, which controlled much of the printing in England. The parallel with the rights granted under the Statute of Monopolies was made explicit through identical duration; implicit was the idea, carried forward from the earlier statute, that these rights were an encouragement to creativity, not rights of ownership. But it was also, as the reversion provision shows, a reaction to and affirmation of the growing sense of proprietorship felt by authors who, more and more, relied on the sale of their works (and not on patronage) for their livelihood and who felt they were not receiving fair recompense for their work:

> Under the regime of printing privileges that preceded the Statute of Anne, authors generally received from publisher-booksellers a one-time payment, made when the authors surrendered their manuscripts for publication. Authors whose works enjoyed particularly high demand might negotiate additional payments for new editions or for new printings of a work that had done well, or they might extract a higher price per sheet for their next work, but neither law nor custom generally assured authors remuneration reflective of their works' sales. As a result, few authors participated in the continued success of their works.[52]

Daniel Defoe, a supporter of the new law, took the property analogy a step further, likening his writing to property just as (in his view) a man's wife and children were property: "A book is the Author's Property, 'tis the Child of his Inventions, the Brat of his Brain; if he sells his Property, it then becomes the Right of the Purchaser; if not, 'tis as much his own, as his Wife and Children are his own."[53] He wasn't the first to have seen his work as his children: more than a generation earlier, in 1666, Anne Bradstreet had penned "The Author to Her Book," utilizing what, even then, was not a new conceit:

> Thou ill-formed offspring of my feeble brain,
>
> Who after birth did'st by my side remain,
>
> Till snatcht from thence by friends, less wise than true,
>
> Who thee abroad exposed to public view,
>
> Made thee in rags, halting to th' press to trudge,
>
> Where errors were not lessened (all may judge).
>
> At thy return my blushing was not small,
>
> My rambling brat (in print) should mother call.[54]

Her book, *The Tenth Muse Lately Sprung Up in America, By a Gentlewoman of Those Parts,* had been published without her knowledge (though without ill intent) a decade and a half earlier. The gentle metaphor she uses to apologize for what she felt was a flawed presentation of her poetry was certainly commonly heard by the time of Defoe, though perhaps it was not as thoroughly considered as it might have been. Outside of slavery, for example, one does not offer wives and children for sale to others, something that didn't seem to have entered into Defoe's thought when he argued just this as his right concerning his book children. As Mark Rose asks, "If pirates are faithless child-stealers, what are fathers who sell their children for profit? One's family is one's own, but does it follow that children are therefore freely vendible commodities, mere property like any other?"[55] There are other weaknesses to this argument for ownership: "the paternity metaphor renders invisible the fact that literary generation is an ongoing, serial process."[56] It also

> obscures the fact that literary works are the products of complex collaborations in which many individuals are involved, including authors, editors, colleagues, friends, and previous authors, and that literary works are produced through acts of generation that involve the adaptation and transformation of materials from the literary gene pool rather than creation out of nothingness.[57]

Defoe, like others who use the paternity metaphor, ignored the fact that it takes more than a single author to create a child. Yet it has become common to view the author as a creator ex nihilo. This, in turn, as Mitchell points out, has proved both good and bad for those espousing authorial rights:

> Making the author the original source of copyright proved to be a very effective weapon indeed. It also has at least one surprising consequence: the creation of a "public domain." If ownership of IP originates solely in authors, then existing works whose authors are long dead or unknown are not owned by anyone. IP ownership is also further circumscribed by imposing a limited term on ownership.[58]

Though there have been positive results from the focus on the author as unique source, the conception is flawed—as is the other great argument justifying ownership of IP: the idea that it is, simply, property. Both paternity and property are, Rose argues, metaphors of limited viability:

> Of course, like all tropes, the paternity and real estate metaphors are fictions. The writing of a book is not really like fathering a child. A literary work is not really like a parcel of real estate. Indeed, copyrights have never been aptly characterized as real estate because copyright has never been perpetual. The real estate metaphor more nearly represents wishful thinking than it does reality. Again and again in the last three hundred years, perpetual copyright has been rejected. But again and again the term of copyright has been extended. The fact that the real estate metaphor forms part of the unconscious of copyright, and is built into the way we think about copyright, will surely contribute to further extensions in the future.[59]

Rose manages to turn the paternity metaphor against those who use it to claim ownership:

> Implicit in the original copyright term, then, was the notion that, like a child, a protected work would eventually be emancipated. What has happened over the years, however, is that the copyright term has been extended again and again until now, under the Sonny Bono Act, it may extend for a hundred and twenty years or even more. This is no longer apprenticeship but slavery.[60]

So the metaphor of paternity, taken to extremes, works for both sides of the debate over the limits of copyright and of the public sphere of the emancipated work. It also can be used to further understanding of another aspect of creativity, its genesis. Claims of authors notwithstanding, no work is created out of thin air. As we said above, all have ancestry, and aspects of that ancestry can be seen in the works, just as a person might have her grandmother's eyes. As fewer and fewer older works are emancipated, it becomes more and more difficult to create new works that don't, somehow, infringe on the ownership of those still under the control of their creators. Fewer new works can honestly claim originality, if any can at all (every one having parentage).

The question of originality remains pertinent to discussions of copyright even though all works are derivative (as are all children). To defend originality, an argument is made distinguishing creativity and facts, the expression/idea distinction mentioned earlier. Supreme Court Justice Sandra Day O'Connor, writing for the majority in *Feist Publications, Inc. v Rural Telephone Service Co.*, made just such a point:

> The key to resolving the tension lies in understanding why facts are not copyrightable. The sine qua non of copyright is originality. To qualify for copyright protection, a work must be original to the author. . . . Original, as the term is used in copyright, means only that the work was independently created by the author (as opposed to copied from other works), and that it possesses at least some minimal degree of creativity. . . . To be sure, the requisite level of creativity is extremely low; even a slight amount will suffice. The vast majority of works make the grade quite easily, as they possess some creative spark, "no matter how crude, humble or obvious" it might be. . . . Originality does not signify novelty; a work may be original even though it closely resembles other works, so long as the similarity is fortuitous, not the result of copying. To illustrate, assume that two poets, each ignorant of the other, compose identical poems. Neither work is novel, yet both are original and, hence, copyrightable.[61]

Though logical in terms of the progress of copyright law as it has developed over the past two centuries, O'Connor's perspective is nonsensical: you cannot have two distinct copyrights on what becomes, in all aspects except authorship, one work.

Initially, copyright was an option that authors and publishers could take advantage of, not an automatic right, as it later became. Most did not bother to register their works, so the vast majority of publications fell immediately into the public domain. This was an important consideration for newspapers of the late 18th and early 19th centuries. Wanting material to fill their pages, editors were constantly seeking stories from other papers and could generally reprint them without reprisal. In fact, as newspapers were most often the vehicles of political parties and partisans, the originators were glad to see this happen. In the United States, foreign works weren't covered by copyright at all (nor were foreign copyrights re-spected) until 1891, so all were fair game for any printer wanting to bring out editions of works originating outside of the country.

Encroachment on the idea that creative works should be soon emanci-pated, to go back to the parentage metaphor, began almost as soon as the passage of the first copyright law in the United States in 1790. The law reflected the English Statue of Anne's 14 years with an equal renewal. Within a generation, authors were agitating for a longer term, again taking the British model (where the duration of copyright was doubled in 1814) as example.

Today, cultural thinking on copyright for the digital age, in legal terms, has a ways to go before any sort of comprehensive and workable copyright system could be instituted—something Lessig has long recog-nized. In conjunction with Creative Commons, he has helped to establish that alternative to traditional copyright which, with its emphasis on the property-rights metaphor and extrapolation from ownership of physical items, is now providing as much impediment as asset to the digital age. Creative Commons, however, is little more than a release valve for pres-sures that current copyright laws and concepts cannot contain.

It won't be sufficient to simply change our laws if we are to make copy-right into a concept that will work in today's information environment. Among other things, we will have to come to a new understanding of the very concept of "copy." Scholars like Boon are already trying to do so but, so far, their impact has been minimal on public or cultural understanding of the term. Boon recognizes the key question, one that many of us miss, though it should be obvious:

> when original and copy begin to overlap to the extent that they do today (and the struggle to maintain the distinction between these two things, "original" and "copy," is precisely what constitutes the crisis, to my mind); when original and copy are produced together in the same factory, at dif-ferent moments; when a copy is actually self-consciously preferred to the original, we must ask again: What do we mean when we say "copy"?[62]

Few of us, even when we consider this question seriously and completely, can answer it adequately. Where is the dividing line, for example, between a copy and a new work derived from the original? In the case of that post-card Duchamp drew on, the original is itself a copy . . .or is it? No one would mistake a postcard of the Mona Lisa for the Mona Lisa painting, so the postcard is original in its specific existence as a postcard.

Compounding the problem are the numerous ways the word copy has been used. When Barlow was in college in the early 1970s, he worked for a summer as a copyboy at the *New York Times*. His job was to pick up copy from one place and deposit it in another. What was that copy? In some cases, it was original stories that had been pounded out by reporters at the rows of typewritered desks off to the side of the newsroom. In others, it was wire copy that had been ripped from teletype machines and that had been distributed to newsrooms all over the world. Many of these copies, edited or bounced to rewrite reporters for revision before being edited once more, eventually went upstairs to "composing," where they were set in type. Soon they were in the paper itself, rolling off the presses downstairs to be sold as copies of the *New York Times*. From copy to copies was the nature of news production.

Taking another use of copy from that era (specifically from the process of composing for photo-offset printing), we all now use the terms *copy, cut,* and *paste* in our daily computer usage. This now causes teachers problems, for copy-and-paste has not only become an important part of the process of writing with digital tools, but it is also the process for plagiarism. It has, then, both a necessary attribute and a somewhat scandalous connotation, and the distinction between the two is often poorly understood, especially by students.

If we really want to confuse the issue of copy, we can go back to Plato, who saw all that we experience as copies of an ideal, copies that don't quite (at best) measure up to that ideal. This leads to a general sense of the copy as not as good as the "The Real Thing," something Henry James plays with in his story of that name, where an artists finds that the models he considers to sit as royalty would never do—though, unbeknownst to him, they are royalty. The artists find other models, people who can copy the look of royalty, to pose for him. Still, in the sense put forward by Plato, and most popular in the Western tradition, copies always lack some aspect of the original, never being quite as good, for all they may sometimes seem so—or be so, as they are, in digital environments. "But suppose copying is what makes us human—what then? More than that, what if copying, rather than being an aberration or a mistake or a crime, is a fundamental condition or requirement for anything, human or not, to exist at all?"[63] asks Boon. If his supposition is correct, then a copy isn't a corruption but something partaking of the essence. Yet, as Boon later writes:

> While the idea itself exists in a realm beyond the human realm, the expression belongs to this world, and to the person who, receiving the idea as

author, inventor, or owner, fixes it materially as self-expression through his or her labor and turns it into property. This is called "originality." Others who fix it materially via access to the this-worldly original expression, rather than receiving the idea, are said to be making a copy. The law protects the rights of the former, but not the latter—unless the expression is a fact, a generic term, etc., in which case it belongs in the public domain.[64]

This is what Justice O'Connor was arguing.

We have become satisfied with the idea that copies are things worth having, even if they are debased things. And satisfied that they have a reality in their own right even though they remain connected to the original. This has become the basis of IP protections, especially in its distinction between things (which can be measured and, therefore, protected) and ideas (which cannot be so easily pinned down). According to Boon:

> IP law's three constituent parts—copyright, trademark, and patent law—are each built around the paradox that you cannot protect an idea itself, but can protect only a fixed, material expression of an idea. One claims an idea as property by materially fixing it through describing a process for realizing it (patent law), by inscribing or figuring it materially in the form of a picture, text, notated music, film sequence (copyright law), or by developing some method of inscription that one uses to mark otherwise generic objects as one's own (trademark law). What is the ontology of intellectual property? Ideas cannot be owned, because they are intangible, but the original expression of an idea can be owned when it is tangible, material, fixed.[65]

This, of course, is the reason the metaphors Rose describes as attempts at justifying copyright were created: it's impossible to pin down ideas themselves, but their expression can be counted and described in detail. Also, the act of creation becomes deified, after a fashion, making it and its immediate output the form and all the rest copies. In fact, though, "the concept of an original could not exist without that of a copy, and, in practice, 'originality' was not an objective fact but a historically specific style of presentation—a recognizable roughness, spontaneity, or naturalness, for example."[66]

One of the fears of the framers of the U.S. Constitution was state-sanctioned monopoly, something they'd seen enough of prior to the revolution. They wanted to provide some protection for authors but did not want it to reach that level. The result, says Lessig, was that:

> Unlike every other power-granting clause, this [the copyright clause] was the only power-granting clause that specified the means and purpose to

which the power was devoted. Congress was not given the power simply to enact copyrights. Nor was it simply given the power to enact copyrights for limited times. Congress was given the power "to promote the Progress of Science" by granting, not to publishers, but to authors, "exclusive Rights" "for limited Times."[67]

This gave the people who were doing the actual creative work control over their creations but only for time enough for them to make initial gains from it, not perpetual income, giving incentive but not absolute ownership. This protected the creator, the commons, creativity now, and creativity in the future. Limited in scope, it was probably a sensible concept, though it did need to be expanded in type as technology progressed and copies became something more than just printed documents. What was not needed, however, were the expansions of duration and of automatic reach that ensued. Unfortunately, as Lessig says, this "tiny regulation of a tiny proportion of the extraordinary range of creative work in 1790 has morphed into this massive regulation of everyone who has any connection to the most trivial of creative authorship."[68]

When everything is copyrighted automatically, as is pretty much the case today, everyone ends up breaking the law at some point or another. Most of these instances are trivial, but even these can turn into something else, into lawsuits brought as intimidation (or as warnings to others), as efforts by the Recording Industry Association of America (RIAA) against file sharing of music files have demonstrated in the past and as firms like Righthaven are showing today.

In 1826, newly arrived from England, where he had become acquainted with the British copyright laws, Noah Webster, about to turn 68 and extremely concerned with the weakness of his financial affairs, wrote to his cousin, Massachusetts Congressman (soon-to-be Senator) Daniel Webster:

Since the celebrated decision, respecting copy-right, in the highest British tribunal [Donaldson v. Beckett, decided in the House of Lords in 1774], it seems to have been generally admitted that an author has not a permanent & exclusive right to the publication of his original works, at common law; & that he must depend wholly on statutes for his enjoyment of that right. As I firmly believe this decision to be contrary to all our best established principles of *right & property*, & as I have reason to think such a decision would not now be sanctioned by the authorities of this country, I sincerely desire that while you are a member of the House of Representatives in Congress, your talents may be exerted in placing this species of property, on the same footing, as all other property, as to exclusive right & permanence of possession.[69]

Clearly, as a writer, Webster was not happy with a situation where American copyright had half the duration of the British, but he wanted more: the same control and rights as the owner of any other property. In this letter, he goes on to argue that, if "any thing can justly give a man an exclusive right to the occupancy & enjoyment of a thing, it must be the fact that he has *made* it." Creation, in his mind, implies absolute ownership; he doesn't stoop to the paternity metaphor but runs full tilt with the real estate one with all the fervor of a passionate libertarian. In response to his cousin's letter, Daniel Webster demurred from advocating unrestricted ownership under copyright (without explaining himself) but agreed that the period of protection should be extended,[70] as it soon was, in an 1831 law that matched the term of the British law but also added rights for the estate of a deceased author.

Noah Webster wanted what many authors, artists, and other creators of IP want: control over what they have produced. For a number of reasons, few today would argue with that—and copyright and intellectual property laws have grown in power and length, reflecting the general contemporary attitude toward IP, reaching the point where, as we will see below, even something simply identified in nature for the first time can conceivably be covered by copyright and patent law. However, though we have a developed cultural attitude toward the products of creative endeavor (as property), it is not necessarily the most advantageous attitude for anyone trying to array a useful digital environment. And the idea of the author that it rests on also may be outliving its usefulness.

It was only recently that our contemporary idea of the author, the one espoused by Defoe and Webster, emerged:

> In early eighteenth-century England, the notion of the author was still an unstable marriage of two different concepts inherited from the Renaissance: a "craftsman" who followed rules, manipulating words and grammar to satisfy tradition for patrons in the court, or, in some cases, the author might produce something "higher," more "transcendent." That "something" was attributed to a muse or to God.[71]

As God and external forces began to be played down, as individualism (as we know it today) became more and more central to the way both the

British and the American colonists viewed their existences and action, the image of the author began to change. Compounding and furthering the change was the fact that the printing industry had advanced enough to allow authors to survive on income from the sale of their works alone, something not previously possible, and something increasingly common after the Statute of Anne was enacted.

The romantic vision of the author himself or herself had become quite popular by the time Webster wrote his cousin, stemming, in part, from claims like those of William Wordsworth in the 1800 Preface to his and Samuel Taylor Coleridge's *Lyrical Ballads*:

> For all good poetry is the spontaneous overflow of powerful feelings: and though this be true, Poems to which any value can be attached were never produced on any variety of subjects but by a man who, being possessed of more than usual organic sensibility, had also thought long and deeply. For our continued influxes of feeling are modified and directed by our thoughts, which are indeed the representatives of all our past feelings; and, as by contemplating the relation of these general representatives to each other, we discover what is really important to men, so, by the repetition and continuance of this act, our feelings will be connected with important subjects, till at length, if we be originally possessed of much sensibility, such habits of mind will be produced, that, by obeying blindly and mechanically the impulses of those habits, we shall describe objects, and utter sentiments, of such a nature, and in such connexion with each other, that the understanding of the Reader must necessarily be in some degree enlightened, and his affections strengthened and purified.[72]

The act of authorship, in this vision, is tied absolutely to the individual and exalts the process of creation within that person, making that the highest and most important—and most original—aspect of art. "A more modest approach," writes Mitchell, "is to describe creation as a process of taking pre-existing materials and 'stamping' them with the unique perspective of the writer."[73] This approach makes much more practical sense today, but the romantic vision of originality continues to have great influence. It is sustained, in part, by practical considerations, particularly concerning plagiarism within our educational institutions, where students are expected to have done the work of writing themselves to further their learning, not having lifted passages wholesale from other sources. Claiming primacy for originality makes the dangers of plagiarism easier to explain.

In fact, the impact that schools have on the contemporary stress on originality is difficult to underestimate. Writing teachers (in particular but certainly not exclusively) have to emphasize the importance of doing one's own work to the extent that this becomes conflated with the idea of originality in authorship, creating an atmosphere where the writing product becomes connected to the writer on an exclusive one-to-one basis.

The generalized contemporary attitude toward authorship, then, is based on a false premise—a misunderstanding of the place of creation within an intellectual environment. Within any environment for that matter. The misunderstanding comes from the assumption, discussed earlier, that ex nihilo originality is, in fact, possible. In this view, creation stems not from what others have done—building on their accomplishments—but comes exclusively from the individual, the genius. To put it bluntly, we have reached a state where we deliberately mistake disguised plagiarism (reworking what others have done) for originality and attempt to make this originality into ownership.

The misunderstanding is also a result of a misapprehension of means toward greatest return on a creative project. We believe, as we have seen, that we own our creative works and feel we should share in any immediate profit—or possibility of profit—in their use. But because these works are not, in fact, real property in the way a building or a briefcase is, or even a rental car is, they cannot be expected to operate in an analogous fashion— yet, as we have seen, this is just what we often expect. Compounded by the fact that no one ever really creates anything out of nothing, though laws may assume they do, this has allowed a skewed and shortsighted vision of copyright to dominate in American law and society, one that is miserly and, in a sense, dishonest.

Noah Webster is a case in point. Though dictionaries with his name on them have been selling in America since 1806, when he first published *A Compendious Dictionary of the English Language,* Webster made relatively little money from his work until late in his life, once *An American Dictionary of the English Language* was published. Soon after his death, his rights were sold to George and Charles Merriam (leading to Merriam-Webster). Members of Webster's family continued to be involved with the ongoing and increasingly profitable project.

Today, "Webster's" has become a generic term for *dictionary,* a pattern that would be followed later by such diverse terms as *thermos, zipper,* and *aspirin.* There's a bit of irony in this, for Webster, after his letter to his politician cousin, became one of the major and most outspoken proponents of copyright protection. It was his own lobbying, in fact, that assured the passage of that 1831 copyright extension. That his very name became so generally attached to the concept of dictionary that it could no longer be claimed as protected under copyright (or trademark) would certainly have frustrated him greatly. As would the fact that most of the money made off of Webster's has gone to others besides Webster and his family, though they certainly did profit.

The case of Noah Webster also provides an example that can help clarify that rather peculiar status that has been granted the creator of IP over the past centuries, making information into property. Even though he regularized spellings and contributed in other ways to the American language, Webster's greatest contribution was collection and presentation of the words used and created by others. A dictionary, more than all but a few other written works, can never be said to come from nothing, to spring from the creativity of a solitary genius. Its success comes from the accuracy of its reflection of usage by others much more than from any originality on the part of its creator.

Though Webster himself never became a celebrity able to trade on his name for monetary gain, his name certainly did become valuable over the generations. Had Webster been born 100 years later, he might have been better able to take advantage of the development of a new aspect of celebrity, its commercialization and commodification—and the ownership of image. McLeod writes:

> Mass-produced celebrity images flourished throughout the nineteenth century, but it wasn't until the twentieth century that famous people began to think of themselves as legally protected commodities. It would have been inconceivable for Martin Luther to see to regulate the reproduction of his image in the same way that the estate of Martin Luther King Jr. does. Phillip Jones, president of the firm that manages the King estate, reminds us, "King may belong to the public spiritually, but King's family is entitled to control the use of his image and words."[74]

Entitled. Certainly, the King family deserves respect for the loss of a member willing to endanger himself for the public good. But why *entitled*? Apparently, nobody belongs to history any more but to the estate and its survivors.

One paradox of copyright, the one at the heart of the CleanFlicks case and the major flaw in the paternity metaphor as an argument for restrictive copyright, is that the idea of expression as property conflicts with the idea of sale of the vehicles for that expression, the copies—or even of the originals. The artists (or the owners of copyright) want to sell but not to sell completely. If we sell you a table we've made, all we can do afterward is watch helplessly as you destroy it with a sledgehammer. Furthermore, we would have no legal leg to stand on if we were to demand a share in the profits from the movie you made of the destruction.

In the world or art, it's not so simple—emotionally, at least. The difference between the sale of creative works—one-of-a-kind artworks—and the sale of other items also shows the difference between copyrightable items and other types of property. Gulley Jimson, narrator and hero of Joyce Cary's 1944 novel *The Horse's Mouth,* resents that a collector stands to profit from works he sold cheaply and early in his career, before he had reached the point where he had a picture in the Tate Gallery. The collector has created nothing but would be the one to gain from any sale. "Here am I, I said, Gulley Jimson, whose pictures have been bought by the nation, or sold at Christie's by millionaires for hundreds of pounds, pictures that were practically stolen from me."[75] The idea that another could benefit from one's art still causes artists pain, and many would like to be able to extend their control past the act of sale. In fact, one of the major problems for copyright in the digital age is this desire for control in a milieu where copies, again, are almost costless to make and nigh on impossible to stop.

The provocative title of his essay "The Death of the Author" aside, Roland Barthes puts the real position of the author, the creator, in a more reasonable and accurate context than the one provided by that romanticized vision of the artist presented by Wordsworth:

> We know now that a text is not a line of words releasing a single "theological" meaning (the "message" of the Author-God) but a multi-dimensional space in which a variety of writings, none of them original, blend and clash. The text is a tissue of quotations drawn from the innumerable centres of culture. Similar to Bouvard and Pecuchet [Gustav Flaubert's fictional clerk-copyists and obtuse seekers of knowledge], those eternal copyists, at once sublime and comic and whose profound ridiculousness indicates precisely the truth of writing, the writer can only imitate a gesture that is always anterior, never original. His only power is to mix writings, to counter the ones with the others, in such a way as never to rest on any one of them. Did he wish to express himself, he ought at least to know that the inner "thing" he thinks to "translate" is itself only a ready-formed dictionary, its words only explainable through other words, and so on indefinitely.[76]

Shades of Noah Webster! Barthes, not really trying to "kill" the author, recognizes the overblown image that had been developing at least since the time of the Romantic poets and tries to puncture it or, at least, reduce it (or the author's ego) to manageable size. Law has not followed suit.

According to Boon, copy in the sense of textual duplication was used as far back as the 14th century, with the sense of imitation arising a couple of centuries later. It was at that time, he claims, that the concept took "on a pejorative meaning: the copy as a degraded version of an original."[77] The original/copy ontology, with its Platonic roots, has come down to us pretty much unchanged since then, though it will be changing. It will have to change; our contemporary digital milieu provides little place for original documents or works of any sort, not if they are created in a digital environment. In a sense, we have replaced copy with duplicate and have erased the idea of a privileged original completely—in digital terms, that is. Yet, we still are trying to protect some idea of originality or, at least, individuality on the web with "the use of copyright, patents, and trademarks to control mimetic transformations. These laws are backed up by the omnipresent codes and passwords which function as ritualized protectors of identities in places where transformation is rapid, such as the banking system, the airport, the supermarket checkout, and the Internet."[78] Our passion for privacy, individuality, and ownership marks the internet more deeply that just about any other factors outside of the powers of capitalism (which they are also a part of) and its marketplace.

The internet is providing means for IP enforcement to a degree never before possible, as the Righthaven lawsuits demonstrate, and is reaching into areas where violation had gone unchallenged for decades. For example, "As high school sports have become more prevalent on television and the internet, potential infringements have become more visible to licensing companies, universities and whistle-blowing college fans."[79] Now, high schools, which might have felt their logo was a tribute to a popular state college, are finding themselves forced to change to something that has no possibility of infringement, a process that can cost money—not only in making the physical changes but in the research into each proposed new logo. The colleges probably gain very little, certainly no more than they lose in community relations. The high schools only lose.

As with Righthaven, stopping such violations may only be happening because it *can* happen (though some will make the claim that they are simply making sure that more egregious violations don't happen elsewhere), not because it is in anyone's interest that they be stopped. Still, the colleges might actually do better to see the imitation as flattery and drop it at that.

In 1933, Walter Benjamin wrote that "Nature produces similarities; one need only think of mimicry. Human beings, however, possess the very highest capability to produce similarities. Indeed, there may not be a single one of the higher human functions which is not decisively co-determined by the mimetic faculty."[80] Boon calls Benjamin's discussion in this essay, "Doctrine of the Similar," and in the slightly later and related "On the Mimetic Faculty," the "most elegant and concise formulation of sameness in the Western tradition."[81] Benjamin writes of two types of similarity, one of appearance (sensuous) and one of correspondence (nonsensuous), as that between the written word and the spoken word. A transcription of a speech, then, would be a nonsensuous copy. It is this general concept (though not stemming from Benjamin; he was simply identifying something that was already around) that has guided certain types of expansion of copyright, making it possible for movies made from novels, for example, to be covered by the novelists' copyrights.

The nonsensuous similarity extends right down to the digital sequences behind all of our computers and the internet. It is how creations become information and how they become valuable. A manuscript becomes a book through nonsensuous similarity, and it's the same for a song that becomes a record, though the sound produced may develop a new sensuous similarity. Oddly enough, it is sensuous similarity that is at the heart of the internet and the information it carries. The transformation into nonsensuous copies is no longer necessary nor, as with a phonograph record, is the nonsensuous copy a necessary vehicle for a reconstructed sensuous copy.

As a social construct (at least in part), information falls victim to the constraints of culture as rapidly and easily as any other manipulable. It follows, as we see with IP protections, that information is never strictly free but bound to structures of law and custom, structures that try to make it as much a product, even, as the automobile, say, or a DVD. As we've also seen, information is associated (in terms of ownership) with the one (a single person or a group or a corporate entity) who ordered or identified the particular block of information. We make the assumption that such activity amounts to creation and assign a special legal ownership relation with the product of such creation to the creator.

All of this can lead us down Alice's rabbit hole. Jeff Jarvis, a professor at CUNY's Graduate School of Journalism, points to a "difficult line-drawing between proprietary facts and those in the public domain."[82] He reacts: "*Proprietary facts?* Is it starting down a road of trying to enable someone to own a fact the way the patent office lets someone own a method or our DNA? Good God, that's dangerous."[83] Though what is generally meant by proprietary facts might better be called proprietary information, the phrase certainly blurs the concept and even expands it, as Jarvis says, making it possible for it to cover information that is not a part of creation—after all, facts *are*; they are not creations.

Recently, courts in the United States have been faced by the question of who owns genes—or, at least, who owns information developed about genes. In one such case, a patent held by a company called Myriad Genetics was challenged by the American Civil Liberties Union representing breast cancer victims. United States District Court for the Southern District of New York Judge Robert Sweet decided that the patents are invalid because they "are directed to a law of nature and were therefore improperly granted."[84] In other words, identifying a previously unknown aspect of existence does not convey ownership, though many do want to extend authorship prerogatives all the way to that level. This case, however, has not made its way completely through the legal system; it may end up that the decision is made that such identification *is* ownership, taking nonsensuous similarity to extremes.

One way or another, nonsensuous similarity possibilities have exploded ever the past century—even more so as time has passed. McLeod writes that the "images produced by television, comics, and motion pictures created a new kind of vocabulary that artists used to comment upon the world"[85] in the period after World War II. This has also created new kinds of infringement. McLeod goes on to claim that artists like Andy Warhol and Roy Lichtenstein, who blur the line between the sensuous and the nonsensuous similarity, "became the first copyright criminals."[86] In a sense he is right—and his point about law is an important one. However, just that sort of activity had been going on since the advent of language. There may have been "a new kind of vocabulary" ripe for the picking, but borrowing to create art (as McLeod makes clear elsewhere and as Barthes also argues) has been around as long as language.

In fact, again as Barthes says, borrowing, in many respects, *is* language and is what makes possible the collection and utilization of information. This is exactly where Noah Webster's position on copyright comes right into conflict with the necessity of maintaining a commons of knowledge, a public sphere where all within it is fair game for the creator of tomorrow. With too much restraint, progress would soon come to a halt: no one able to present anything new for fear of infringement.

The most famous case of the past generation concerning forward intellectual and technological motion that could have been stymied by patent and copyright concerns Xerox Corporation's Palo Alto Research Center (PARC), the lab that developed much of what is now standard on our computer screens. Both Bill Gates of Microsoft and Steve Jobs of Apple built on PARC concepts for their Windows and Macintosh systems. When Apple sued Microsoft for infringing on the Mac, the company lost after Microsoft was able to show that the technologies had begun at PARC, not Apple. Had Xerox protected the developments at PARC, today's internet would have been delayed, for the desktop computers so integral to it would not have appeared so quickly (Xerox, apparently, had no idea of what to do with what its lab had developed).

Today's concerns for IP have turned away from systems such as those of Microsoft and Apple (they have developed internal safeguards making copying expensive enough to restore the balance Boyle talks of) and has moved to content whose copying has never been protected by cost, something Righthaven is trying to address through its financially punitive lawsuits. This raises new questions and concerns, especially in view of the anarchic qualities the web does carry:

> The question is not whether the Internet should be an intellectual property-free zone; it should not be, is not, and never was. The question is whether, when the content industries come asking for *additional* or *new* rights, for *new* penalties, for the criminalization of certain types of technology, we should take into account the gains that the Internet has brought them, as well as the costs, before we accede to their requests.[87]

The question goes far beyond this, we are discovering, for content industries are not simply businesses but are governments as well. When governments become involved in providing content—either voluntarily or, as in the case of WikiLeaks, involuntarily—an entirely different set of problems needs to be considered, especially when national security and government secrecy in general come under consideration.

Established in 2006, WikiLeaks became world famous in 2010 with the release of hundreds of thousands of documents, some relating to the Iraq War and including thousands of diplomatic cables. Compounding its notoriety were the antics and unrelated legal troubles of its leader, Julian Assange, and the activities of a group called "Anonymous" that tried to retaliate for what its members saw as attempts to shut WikiLeaks down. The real significance, however, came not in the information released, the Assange soap opera, or in the threatened cyberwar by hackers. The real significance was in the various ways responsibility for information was taken or denied, from governments to news media entities to web service providers to WikiLeaks itself to the users of the web.

Without government prodding, a number of major businesses providing online services decided to move against WikiLeaks, sparking the ire of "Anonymous" and attempts at retaliation by overloading and crashing websites associated by the businesses. Significantly for the future of freedom of expression on the web, the businesses used the excuse of violation of terms of service by WikiLeaks. Terms-of-service are the agreements customers must accept to establish an account utilizing the company's services. Very few people actually read those terms of services, but they can be used as a means of legally denying services, which is what Amazon Web Services, among others, tried to do to its services with WikiLeaks. Eugene Robinson describes what probably happened:

> Before using practically any Internet service or software for the first time, you have to accede to a long, dense agreement. Actually taking the time to read one of these documents—rather than just clicking the "accept" button—is headache-inducing but revelatory. Essentially, you agree that the company providing the service or the software can do anything it wants to your account, at any time, for any reason, and you have no recourse.
>
> In this case, WikiLeaks violated Amazon's requirements that the user "own or otherwise control all of the rights to the content" posted on the Amazon web servers and that the content "will not cause injury to any person or entity."[88]

Though WikiLeaks' released documents certainly could cause injury, the same is probably true of thousands of accounts. Amazon clearly decided not to suspend WikiLeaks because of violation of terms of service but because of concern for its own interactions with governments. Robinson puts his finger on the question this raises: "So who gives executives of private companies the right to decide that some unapproved speech will be encouraged and some will be suppressed? Do we want the people who run Amazon, PayPal, Facebook, Twitter or perhaps even—shudder—Microsoft, Apple or Google making political decisions on our behalf?"[89] The very idea that commercial enterprises have the wherewithal to stop the actions of particular groups sits poorly with most internet users and raises questions of what might be called the privatization of censorship.

Writing for *SFGate,* Caille Millner identified two sides that she sees in conflict in the WikiLeaks case, seeing internet culture as "changing rapidly from a free-wheeling, anything-goes space into a place that's more reflective of society as a whole—society with all of its rigidities, indignities, inequalities, and yes, securities. The fight over WikiLeaks—a fight with hackers and computers activists on one side and governments, established companies, and everyday computer users on another—is really a culture war."[90] This could be the fault line of an earthquake that may shake the structure of the internet, at least in terms of control over information. Instead of copyright being the issue, questions of ownership of information become questions of control: Who can do what? Who has the *right* to do what?

In addition to Amazon, MasterCard, eBay, and PayPal all distanced themselves from WikiLeaks, using the same basic strategy. " 'None of those companies want to be singled out for helping undermine American national security,' said Jeff Chester, the executive director of the Center for Digital Democracy in Washington, an organization that aims to promote democratic expression and human rights on the Internet. 'It shows a lack of independence and an attempt to curry favor.' "[91] It shows a renewal (or a reaffirmation, at least) of the confluence of business and government put so well by GM head Charles Erwin Wilson at his confirmation hearing for his new position as Secretary of Defense in the Eisenhower administration when he said, "I thought what was good for the country was good for General Motors and vice versa."

In many respects, these businesses are moving into a position vis-à-vis information much akin to that of the news media—but without the arms-length friction that has developed through competing needs of newspapers and governments going back for more than a century. They are moving blindly, unfortunately, into an entirely new arena: one of information control—not simply one where they provide platforms for information. They are also moving into a new dance with the government, one different from the old ones of influence and regulation, for this one concerns, also, regulating *government*.

On the face of it, all of the companies involved appear to be acting within their rights, particularly as defined through those rather untested terms-of-service agreements. The options for WikiLeaks do not include fighting them for restoration of service. That would be expensive and probably fruitless. Plus, the organization has managed to find alternatives and has continued its activities. The government, however, is unlikely to step in to defend WikiLeaks and not simply because the organization has broached government secrecy. The private sector, acting as government proxy by acting against WikiLeaks, has a great deal more latitude. Freedom of speech, after all, only exists in terms of government. The First Amendment to the U.S. Constitution commands that "Congress shall make no law respecting an establishment of religion, or prohibiting the free exercise thereof; or abridging the freedom of speech, or of the press." It says nothing about how private individuals or corporations might or might not act. So, private entities are free to act where government might feel more constrained. "The Supreme Court has stated. . . . that the question remains open whether the publication of unlawfully obtained information by the media can be punished consistent with the First Amendment. Thus, although unlawful acquisition of information might be subject to criminal prosecution with few First Amendment implications, the publication of that information remains protected."[92] This inability on the part of government has been compensated for by the companies that have moved against WikiLeaks: companies, significantly, that include no members of the traditional news media—even though a number of these, including *The New York Times,* have been directly involved in the WikiLeaks releases.

Concerns over IP have, and will continue to have, an impact on how information is organized, transmitted, and used on the web, guiding not only our methods but also our access. Even in as narrow an area as scholarly publishing, copyright has (and will) guide not only what is published, but where and how and who has access to it. As Tony Hey and Anne Trefethen write, "Scholarly publishing will presumably eventually make a transition from the present situation—in which the publishers own the copyright and are therefore able to restrict the group of people who can read your paper—to a model where publishers are funded not for the paper copy but for providing a refereeing service and a curated electronic journal archive with a permanent URL."[93] This will be something of a circumvention of standard copyright in order to meet changing needs, returning ownership to the scholar and separating it from the publisher's immediate financial considerations. Were a different copyright model in place, publication of scholarship would already look different than it does and would probably be moving vigorously into a commons-based model.

Change is occurring, however, in spite of copyright laws and concepts more appropriate to a different age, as new economic models for gain through IP are emerging through the web. Creators of IP, rarely themselves the primary economic beneficiaries of their work, are beginning to find ways of bypassing the old publishing entities that once controlled their work, keeping them within a narrow framework of generally immediate gain. Today, they are able to balance personal immediate and long-term possibilities, sometimes deciding that it is worth waiting for return, giving IP away to increase eventual profit. They can make such decisions because, thanks to the internet, they don't have to share IP ownership with corporations in order to find success but can explore alternate avenues.

As corporations, in turn, find themselves less dependent on IP for their own profits, they will also turn to other avenues. This will make them less dependent on copyright protection as a basic part of their business models. It will reduce the pressure on legislatures to continue to expand copyright protections, for there will be less reason for the companies to lobby for them. As a result, in this optimistic model, copyright will eventually be able to be restructured in a way that can be more useful to future IP creation and to the information age in general.

FOUR

Smart Mobs or Mobs Rule?

Today's internet has power one could only dream of yesterday. No longer is it limited by file size, bandwidth, memory, storage capacity, or processing speed. We now have more access to information, news, and media of all kinds than ever before. Not only is the web able to efficiently process terabyte upon terabyte of information, but Web 2.0 platforms allow users to interact with and share, distribute, organize, and manage the content they themselves create *and* the content created by others. These new possibilities are grounded not only upon the ability to manipulate data but upon the ability to connect; it is this latter ability that defines the intelligence of the internet today.

Best-selling authors Howard Rheingold (*Smart Mobs*), Clay Shirky (*Here Comes Everybody*), James Surowiecki (*The Wisdom of Crowds*), and Steven Berlin Johnson (*Emergence, Everything Bad is Good For You*) have all argued that contrary to popular belief, groups, crowds, and mobs exhibit a wisdom and intelligence that defies so-called individual genius. The general premise that there is an intelligence inherent in a group or herd surpassing the intelligence of its smartest member is an argument that stands in stark opposition to the notions considered to be the backbone of American society. As we discussed earlier, the genius of the US Constitution has always been its ability to leverage the power of the many to ensure the liberties of the individual.

As crowd intelligence grows in importance, shaping not only the ways we produce, consume, play, and work but also the ways we think and theorize these activities, we—and by "we" we mean anyone who uses the computer on a regular basis—will need to face directly the fact that the pioneer spirit of individualism is itself facing a new challenge. Indeed, many of us may find that the backbone of American culture may soon be in need of chiropractic services.

For some time, writers from a variety of quarters have argued that there is a special intelligence to the crowd. The rise of the blog and Web 2.0 resulted in an explosion of books in the first decade of the new millennium, drawing our attention to the idea that we now have an unprecedented ability to communicate on a massive multidirectional scale, and that the emerging technologies were finally bringing people together in ways and with an ease never before imagined. These writers implored us to recognize the good that lies with these developments, maintaining that the benefits clearly outweigh the costs. Our societal and cultural fabric continues to change as a result of these developments, and for these authors, it is finally time to recognize that there is an intelligence in our collective wisdom, one that we have failed to recognize while we have been absorbed in our concerns with the individual.

Not surprisingly, after this initial wave celebrating the power of the many, the pendulum swung back, and a new breed of writers pointed out that Web 2.0 wasn't all that it was cracked up to be. Sherry Turkle argued that the web was causing us to lose our ability to empathize. Jaron Lanier could not stand that the web encouraged herd-like behavior. Evgeny Morozov argued against the democratizing power of information communication technologies. The list goes on. A key moment came in 2008, with publication of Nicholas Carr's galvanizing article in the July *Atlantic Monthly* titled "Is Google Making Us Stupid?" With it, the flood of Web 2.0 celebrators began to recede and the old landscape of individualism could be seen again on the horizon.

While it is true that we've seen similar patterns of ebb and flow in the past, each time a new possibility presents itself, it seems just different enough to make things interesting. The dynamic keeps movement in check, assuring that we will not be overwhelmed by a rush in one direction. With the glaring exception of the Civil War, the United States has managed, throughout its history for the most part, to survive, even if recent economic developments shake our faith in a foundation. In this sense, America may be able to successfully negotiate the movement into a digital age without losing its basic conception of itself.

Even beyond America, this is far from the first time that there have been those who celebrate the development of a new technology and those who worry about the kinds of damage to ways of living and being. Writers frequently remind us that for each new technological development there have always been portents of both glory and disaster. Plato famously feared writing because it would cause one to lose the power of natural memory. Today's IBM Watson computer, which illustrated its perspicuity by playing—and winning—the television show Jeopardy in 2011, is an example of Plato's fears being taken to their logical outcome. Watson won because it was able to interpret questions posed in natural language, search databases of reference works, articles, and literature, and retrieve the correct answers faster than its human opponents could. Watson didn't use natural memory. It used information. Memory isn't in our heads any longer. It's in the network. We are moving from a culture of natural memory to a memory of the database. Just Google it.

Older than Plato, the story of Icarus taking his father's invention too close to the sun, of course, is a cautionary tale of expecting too much from technology too fast. On the other hand, the Industrial Revolution could never have occurred if there hadn't been enough willingness to risk failure and disaster to reach riches and knowledge. Nor could American success in World War II, culminating in that disaster-in-riches, atomic power.

There is another group between the social media apologists and the traditionalists—those who try to take a more measured look at how the web is changing us and attempt to find a compromise between the two. Too often, however, those who fall into this camp assume, along with Tim Wu (discussed in chapter 1), that the internet is not something all that new. They argue that one can find particular patterns each time a new technological development is introduced—that the technologies themselves follow pathways predictable from the past, as the poet William Butler Yeats did, with his widening and narrowing gyre. That may be true, but while the patterns may reveal something about the ways we respond to the new technology, the technologies themselves are, in each case today, major and life changing.

We may have responded to the birth of various technologies in the past similarly to the way we are now responding to the birth of the internet (it is very much still a baby), but what we are responding *to* is unprecedented; and so our particular responses, concerns, fears, and celebrations are specific to this moment. Those who seem to claim the middle are not really staking out a middle ground, for people don't live in the swing of history but in the now. Unlike those who attempt to find a middle ground that tries to compromise between two warring groups, we ask a question of a different kind. If the internet is creating the conditions for collective intelligence to emerge, do these conditions apply to human beings? Are we becoming smarter on the internet? Are crowds intelligent? And, if so, what conditions need to be present for that intelligence to be manifest? This chapter investigates the collective wisdom of the crowd and just how that wisdom, if it exists, configures itself on the internet. If we are right in our assumption that recent recognition of the power of crowds is challenging the notion of the pioneering individualism as the root of Western liberalism and American society, in particular, then the conditions for this change need to be unearthed.

In *Everything Bad is Good For You,* a book that its author Steven Berlin Johnson calls an old-fashioned work of rhetorical persuasion, he argues against critics who bemoan the loss of a highly literate culture and in favor of one hooked on watching television and playing video games. He puts forth the unlikely argument that television and video games are actually making us smarter or at least teaching us to be more visually and digitally literate.

Perhaps Johnson's most influential book is his earlier *Emergence: The Connected Lives of Ants, Brains, Cities, and Software.* For us, what makes Johnson's book scintillating is a simple thought: how is it possible that something like human consciousness can form from the collection of cells in a human brain, especially when you think that each individual cell has no intelligence by itself? Johnson undertook the study to discover just how and why a community filled with dumb individuals (such as ants, cells, routines, and bytes) can actually create an intelligence that transcends the smartest of any of its individuals.

If it's possible to take the example of cells forming together to make an intelligent brain, increase the scale and you'll notice a similar kind of emergent behavior taking place at the individual members form together to make a cooperative intelligence that supersedes the smartest of its members. Is it possible to increase the scale once again and to view humans in the same way? Is there an emergent intelligence that occurs from human organizations and/or from human creations that is greater than the individual of its members, and does the internet specifically demonstrate this intelligence?

As mentioned in chapter 1, Kevin Kelly writes of what he calls the technium—the composite, connected mass of technology that surrounds all human activity. He refuses to consider it as different in growth or possibility from a biological mass or even from the human brain:

The technium contains 170 quadrillion computer chips up into one mega-scale computing platform. The total number of transistors in this global network is now approximately the same number of neurons in you brain. And the number of links among files in this network (think of all the links among all the web pages of the world) is about equal to the number of synapse links in your brain. Thus, this growing planetary electronic membrane is already comparable to the complexity of a human brain. It has three billion artificial eyes (phone and webcams) plugged in, it processes keyword searches at the humming rate of 14 kilohertz (a barely audible high-pitched whine), and it is so large a contraption that it now consumes 5 percent of the world's electricity. When computer scientists dissect the massive rivers of traffic flowing through it, they cannot account for the source of all the bits. Every now and then a bit is transmitted incorrectly, and while most of those mutations can be attributed to identifiable causes such as hacking, machine error, or line damage, the researchers are left with a few percent that somehow changed themselves. In other words, a small fraction of what the technium communicates originates not from any of its known human-made nodes but from the system at large. The technium is whispering to itself.[1]

Kelly writes that "a superorganism is emerging from the cloak of wires, radio waves, and electronic nodes wrapping the surface of our planet."[2] Do humans act the same way as such a being—or vice versa? Is it possible to pool together human thought where, if taken together, the collective thought of humans will be greater than the smartest of any one of its individual members? If the technium whispers to itself, will this human aggregation do so also?

Before we get to these questions, let's first look at the principles behind the idea that intelligence can spring from the bringing together of dumb individuals, the notion of *emergence*. Consider the following:

- Under water, herring school together as they migrate to their breeding grounds. They turn instantly and collectively, split into two halves around an obstacle, and reform in perfect harmony. They each travel at exactly the same speed, keeping their distance from the other herring around them exactly. Yet they do not appear to follow the movements of each other; rather, they all move at the same instant in perfect coordination, exhibiting a collective intelligence that emerges from the collective behavior of the whole and not simply from individuals cooperating or imitating each other.

- In the sky, a flock of auklets forms an almost perfect V of over several hundred members. It begins to break apart, one of the wings of the V shattering and becoming disorganized. A wind current has hit that portion of the flock. The members continue to fly, adapt to the wind current, regain their course, and come back together to form the perfect structure once more.

- In an ant colony, workers cart off dead members and deposit them in a common area, in what amounts to an ant burial ground. This burial ground is located at the furthest distance possible from the colony's food source.

- Several bees from a hive set out in different directions in search of food. When they find their sources, they return and communicate to the other bees that they have found nectar, communicating by dance. The better the food source, the more spirited the dance. The other bees follow the most spirited of the dancers, ensuring the greatest amount of nectar for feeding the hive.

All of these examples come from the social behavior of animals, a branch of science known as sociobiology; researchers have been fascinated by them for years. One reason for this interest is the influence of Edward O. Wilson's *Sociobiology: The New Synthesis,* which catapulted Wilson to intellectual stardom by initiating the latest phase of the 20th century's vitriolic nature vs. nurture debate, a debate that continues to this day.

Aside from being a key influence in this debate, Wilson's book brought renewed attention to the role that insects play in developing a productive understanding of social organization. About ants, Wilson wrote: "It is fair to say that as an ecological strategy, eusociality has been overwhelmingly successful. It is useful to think of an insect colony as a diffuse organism, weighing anywhere from less than a gram to as much as a kilogram and possessing from about a hundred to a million or more tiny mouths."[3] Wilson would later come to call this phenomenon a superorganism, a label he used in the title to his 2010 book *The Superorganism: The Beauty, Elegance, and Strangeness of Insect Societies* and the basis for Kelly's use of the term. Here, Wilson and co-author Bert Hölldobler used the image of a colony of African driver ants to paint a picture in the reader's mind:

Viewed from afar, the huge raiding column of a driver ant colony seems like a single living entity. It spreads like the pseudopodium of a giant amoeba across 70 meters or so of ground. A closer look reveals it to comprise a mass of several million workers running in concert from the subterranean nest, an irregular network of tunnels and chambers dug into the soil. As the column emerges, it first resembles an expanding sheet and then metamorphoses into a tree like formation, with the trunk growing from the nest, the crown an advancing front the width of a small house, and numerous branches connecting the two. The swarm is leaderless. The workers rush back and forth near the front. Those in the vanguard press forward for a short distance and then turn back into the tumbling mass to give way to other advancing runners. These predatory feeder columns are rivers of ants coming and going. The frontal swarm, advancing at 20 meters an hour, engulfs all the ground and low vegetation in its path, gathering and killing all the insects and even snakes and other larger animals unable to escape. After a few hours, the direction of the flow is reversed, and the column drains backward into the nest holes.[4]

What it must be like to see this phenomenon in process!

Wilson and Hölldobler use the term *superorganism* to describe an entity/phenomenon that exists between the level of an organism and an ecology. Does the internet exhibit traits of a superorganism? Though Kelly says yes, the answer to that question may border on whether we consider the internet to be a form of artificial intelligence—and on whether or not "artificial" starts to merge into something we might call self-awareness (that whispering Kelly mentions). Mark Millonas, a researcher from the Complex Systems Group at the Center for Nonlinear Studies, explains that "swarms provide the inspiration for many recent studies of the evolution of cooperative behavior, but the action of the swarm on a scale of days, hours, or even minutes manifests a nearly constant flow of emergent phenomena of many different types. . . . The notion that complex behavior, from the molecular to the ecological, can be the result of parallel local interactions of many simpler elements is one of the fundamental themes of artificial life."[5] As we will see, Kelly is not the only one who has been suggesting that the internet follows this pattern of becoming an intelligence of its own.

As Mark Taylor writes, "swarms of bees, flocks of birds, schools of fish, and colonies of ants fascinate researchers who attempt to understand complexity" because "the same rules and principles operating in cellular automata seem to be at work in these natural phenomena."[6] Taylor's observation is that the principles that are at work when intelligence emerges from the firing of brain neurons are the same as when groups of animals or insects exhibit collective intelligence. A superorganism is an example of what researchers call a complex adaptive system, one that occurs at the level of insects; but it also can be any system that exhibits the traits of being able to evolve, adapt, and make an intelligence that exceeds the smartest of its members.

The key to understanding a complex adaptive system is that collective intelligence is able to emerge from just a few central principles. Understanding what these are helps us to answer the question of what we mean by group intelligence:

1. The system exhibits a level of intelligence that is beyond the sum of its parts and the smartest individual in the system. This is the notion that something like intelligence in the brain can *emerge* from individual cells that have no intelligence on their own. As Taylor explains it, there is a very fine line between emergent systems and nonemergent systems, one that walks a line between order and chaos and that generally is closer to chaos than to order. Those that emerge with intelligence, however, are those that manage not to collapse into chaos.

2. The system is *open* and *adaptive*. Over time, it evolves to accommodate changes within the system so that it can continue to survive and adapt. In addition, if it stops evolving, the system collapses into disorder.

3. It displays spontaneous organization. This means that there is discernible macrobehavoir that can be observed that takes place beyond the sum of its parts. The actions of the aggregate are beyond, in perception and even in decision making, what could be expected from an individual.

4. Emergence spontaneously occurs from the culmination of local actions and members or constituents in the system taking cues from their neighbors. Jean-Louis Deneubourg calls this allelo-mimesis, or literally imitating one's neighbors, a key notion to understanding how such systems organize—and, in the case of many human systems, why they fail.[7]

5. The final principle is feedback. Feedback is communication that takes place within the system, the sending out of signals that can be both useful in increasing the health of the system and, paradoxically, in causing the system to deteriorate. Signals that have a deleterious effect upon the system are necessary for the system's ability to strengthen and adapt, but too much deleterious feedback will cause the system's death. Signals that have a positive effect on the system's health will allow the system to operate and function. The majority of feedback allows the system to continue its operations. This hearkens back, of course, to the first of the principles and that line between order and chaos.

A superorganism is much the same as the individual—the brain—even though there may seem to be no possible comparison between the two. No matter how we try to differentiate individual human consciousness from what we see forming in the world, either biologically or technologically, the individual shares traits with the superorganism. Whether or not the significant differences are of a very particular level of specificity, preventing intelligence to emerge, has yet to be determined.

Emergence takes place at the space between chaos and order in a very particular way. Of course, there is an obvious difference between groups of human beings and a colony of ants, but there remains a particular resemblance between the colonies of microorganisms that comprise a human body and an ant colony. In fact, individual humans, in their complexity, are more kin to superorganisms than are human societies and civilizations. This has long been recognized. Some writers, like Kevin Kelly, Howard Rheingold, and Henry Jenkins are trying to establish that the onset of the internet and networked computing may be having effects that should be causing us to think about the emergent properties that could be taking place in the network. Is the internet developing something we might call a mind, not a *human* mind but a *computer* mind? And what would the difference be? At this stage, it is a difficult case to make, that the internet exhibits the signs of a complex adaptive system or a super organism, without slipping into an extended analogy, saying that the internet is *like* one rather than being able to say it is so, definitely. From this perspective, we simply put on a pair of glasses and choose to see the internet in a particular way, but complex adaptive systems have been studied. They exhibit rules, and while they may give us a model for thinking about the internet today, it is worth proceeding cautiously.

While it is hard, so far, to make the case for the internet actually being a superorganism, we can effectively argue that there are similarities between the internet and superorganisms: that the internet exhibits an intelligence that emerges from the local interactions that take place on the web. Less concerned with technology per se, James Surowiecki's *The Wisdom of Crowds* presents a more measured and more effective picture when attempting to narrow down the focus on how group intelligence might occur across large groups of humans. Some subtle connections certainly do exist between the principles underlying complex adaptive systems and the ones that show intelligent group behavior. In both cases, a specific set of narrowly defined conditions are required in order for intelligence to occur. Surowiecki puts forth a variety of examples and three key principles for how groups of humans might act intelligently. While these conditions show affinity to complex adaptive systems, they are in practice fundamentally different. After all, when thinking about intelligent group behavior, we do find that small differences have significant effects. The conditions for wisdom are in fact the opposite of the kind of behavior most often observed in the dumbest of human crowds.

The foundational rule for a complex adaptive system is allelo-mimesis. An ant follows the chemical trails left by other ants, chemicals that serve as a form of communication. The stronger the scent, the more likely the ant will choose one scent over another. The ant chooses an activity based on the strength and frequency of the pheromone it encounters and duplicates that activity. If the pheromone is "follow me for food," then that is what the ant will do. The strength of the message determines that the members in the colony will duplicate a particular activity. This form of imitation is central and foundational to the success of the colony.

Surowiecki opens his third chapter with an example that shows a breakdown in the communication system in a superorganism like an ant colony. The image is that of what sociobiologists call a circular mill. In 1921, an American naturalist, William Bebe, happened to be in the Guyana jungle when he witnessed a collection of ants, 1,200 feet in diameter, moving around and around in an enormous circle. This phenomenon occurs, it was determined, when a group of ants has been separated from its colony. The mill was so large that it took each ant 2.5 hours to make one revolution. After two days of doing nothing but following pheromones that said "follow me," the ants died.

The contrast between a circular mill and the swarm discussed by Wilson illustrates how a different set of environmental and contextual conditions can cause the same set of underlying principles to have radically different outcomes. Why, we might ask, is it easy to think about the circular mill in human terms but difficult to think about the swarm in the same terms? Is it because humans are not insects? Perhaps. Circular mills, a phenomenon of "monkey see monkey do," may perhaps be what Western liberalism has thought of by giving so much firm belief into the autonomy of the human subject—the ability to act individually and decisively and not simply in pattern. Western liberalism teaches us that we each have the capacity for intelligent individual thought; this idea is so deeply ingrained in American culture that it becomes very difficult to make an argument counter to it or to have a reasonable discussion of its merits. Many of us, if not most, accept this notion as an undeniable truth, without regard to recognition that it is an idea that each one of us inherited from the culture at large and not from some foundational truth. So, when we say that humans are not ants, that humans don't follow each other around blindly, we say this because we Americans, at least, have been raised on a steady diet of Individualism.

One of the points raised in this chapter is that network culture is changing and challenging this notion of the autonomous individual. Whether we like it or not, individual control of action is less than the libertarian ideal. Even our knowledge is limited and circumscribed by the network, by the greater whole of which each individual is a part.

For ant colonies, one reason the circular mill does not often occur is the sheer number of ants in the colony. The increased numbers mixed with a different environment leads to *diversity* in the signals that the individual members receive. In the ant world, diversity means diversity of communication. As different ants receive different signals of different intensities from different sources, the colony comes alive. Not surprisingly, then, diversity is also a key principle in the possibility of showing how the intelligence of groups of humans can be harnessed. Certainly, the worst of human behavior, the kind most analogous to the circular mill, often comes from lack of diversity, from insular and isolated thought and action.

Diversity is not the only factor, however. Surowiecki lists two others: independence and decentralization. None of these principles in themselves are good enough for the potential intelligence in crowds to be harnessed, so we will add a fourth: one that Surowiecki mentions but downplays—the ability to aggregate information.

First of all, let us look at how a large number of humans can, in fact, function together as a unit to make intelligence. Surowiecki offers several interesting examples, one of them being the case of the U.S. submarine *Scorpion* that he gleans from Sherry Sontag's and Christopher Drew's bestseller *Blind Man's Bluff*. In it, Sontag and Drew try to explain what occurred in May 1968 when the USS *Scorpion* sank in the North Atlantic. The total knowledge of what happened to the ship amounted to the location of the sub at its last identified radio transmission and a few other scraps of information. Consequently, the Navy had to begin its search in an area that was "a circle twenty miles wide and many thousands of feet deep." "You could not imagine," Surowiecki writes, "a more hopeless task."[8] How to find this needle in the haystack? The navy did not know what had caused the vessel to sink, what speed it had been traveling, how quickly it descended, or any other of the many bits of information that could have helped.

Surowiecki reasons that the most usual response in attempts to solve this problem, especially in an American culture that has traditionally valued the role of the expert, would be the gathering of several experts in the area, having them collaborate, and having them offer their best guesses. Fortunately, however, the officer in charge of locating the sunken ship had a different plan. John P Craven, the chief scientist on the U.S. Navy's search and recovery team, who has written his own account of these events in his book *The Silent War,* had his crew—a collection of mathematicians, submarine specialists, and salvage men—place bets on where they thought the ship had gone down.

The crew had scraps of data to go on, bits of hydrophonic recordings, and Craven's own assumptions of runaway torpedoes.[9] As Craven himself recalls the story, he employed a mathematical formula known as Bayes Theoem to create a grid of the area where the ship could have sunk and, based on the bits of evidence he had gathered, created seven scenarios to explain how the ship had sunk.[10] He then asked his crew to place bets on the likelihood of any one of these scenarios and to submit their best guess as to where the ship might be. Oh, and just to make sure his crew would try their best, he offered bottles of scotch to the winners. Meanwhile, the navy had already begun a separate search mission and was not open to another one based on Craven's hypotheses. They believed the ship was probably sunk by a runaway torpedo and so continued on without Craven's input. When the search ran dry, they finally decided to search the coordinates that Craven had already provided them, coordinates stemming from the bets. The ship was found within 220 yards of the coordinates.

Important for our purposes is the method by which Craven and his team were able to locate the ship. Craven explains that several weeks before the sinking of the USS *Scorpion,* he had attended a lecture by Harvard mathematician Howard Raiffa on "the esoteric subject of Bayes's subjective probability."[11] Craven explains that Raiffa was more interested in discussing horse betting than esoteric math. Raiffa revealed in his lecture that the crowds of people betting on horse races were accurately able to predict the odds of the winning horses. After much research and application, Raiffa explained that the crowds at the tracks collectively and correctly determined the chances that a particular horse would win. With odds determined before the start of the race, a horse with 6:1 odds would win one-sixth of the time. A horse with 100:1 odds would win one one-hundreth of the time. Even odds would win half the time. The crowd was able to consistently and accurately predict the odds. Craven writes that Raiffa determined that "he could successfully predict the correct odds not only for win but for place and show . . . through the mathematics of probability."[12] These equations of probability originated with Thomas Bayes, a mathematician of the 18th century, a founding mathematician in the areas of subjective probability and later, game theory.

And so, just as Raiffa could predict the winners of horse races, Craven was able to use Bayes's Theorem and his collection of specialists to formulate a collective guess of where the ship had sunk. Because Craven's collection of experts was relatively small, nowhere near the 45,000 people attending the Belmont Stakes, presumably a larger group of experts predicting the location would have come closer than 220 yards from the exact spot, but it was still accurate enough for a successful search.

Locating a sunken submarine or predicting which horses will win are just two examples of collective intelligence. Consider the following examples, all gleaned from Surowiecki's first chapter:

- In the television show *Who Wants to be a Millionaire,* the audience picked the correct answers 91 percent of the time.
- In the early 1920s, Colombia sociologist Hazel Knight established interest in the field among her students by asking her class to predict the temperature in the room. Collectively, the class predicted 72.4 degrees. The temperature was 72 degrees.
- In one experiment, 200 students were asked to rank items by weight. The group was correct 94 percent of the time.
- In another experiment, students we asked to look at 10 different piles of buckshot and rank each according to size (they appeared to be of similar sizes). The group guessed with 94.5 percent accuracy.
- In a different kind of experiment, this time using a computer program to simulate individuals, a physicist constructed a maze that was built so that it could calculate the distance and time it would take an individual to find the exit. The group's collective work found the shortest possible exit after the first round.
- Within 30 minutes of the 1986 Space Shuttle Challenger explosion, the stock market accurately determined the company at fault for the space shuttle's malfunction and explosion by selling off 12 percent of its stock by the end of the day. Other potential companies in the explosion saw only a 3 percent drop in stock. It took six months for the Presidential Commission on the Challenger to release its findings as to the company responsible for the crash.
- The public consistently predicts the odds for sports betting across all sports. This is not to say it predicts the individual games correctly, but it does consistently predict the odds.
- The internet search engine Google use PageRank algorithm to query pages by using the web's links structure to determine the number of links to pages; it also looks at the number of links that pages that link to the searched page have, as well as the number of links linking to the linking pages. As a result, Google aggregates the total number of links

that the pages and the pages linking to them contain to display its results. The total number of links suggests votes for a particular page. Typically, desired results are found within the first 10 "hits" of a search and often within the first three.

- A number of "decision markets" have recently sprung up using the collective wisdom of crowds to predict election results and other types of unknowns, such as Oscar award winners. Two of these markets are the Iowa Electronic Market (election results) and the Hollywood Exchanged Markets (Oscars). In both cases, these markets are highly accurate, consistently performing in the 90th percentile in their predictions.

As Surowiecki makes clear, a few fundamental principles are at work in accurately predicting the wisdom of crowds. While humans alone do not aggregate as a superorganism, particular situations can be created that allow the power of the collective to be harnessed. Of course, anyone investigating these relationships should be careful not to suggest that the intelligence exhibited in Surowiecki's examples is the same as a complex adaptive system, although some similar rules are indeed at work. The difference of course, is that large groups of people do not exhibit properties of emergence, the so-called phase transitions where a new order of intelligence is achieved once the system reaches a liminal point, such as the quality of consciousness that emerges out of the brain's cells and firing neurons or the dream of a self-intelligent internet.

As mentioned earlier, Surowiecki observes three constants at work in intelligent organization and mentions what we consider to be an essential fourth. In order for a group of humans to exhibit an intelligence that is beyond the grasp of the best of its individual members, there must be independence, diversity, and decentralization (along with the ability to aggregate information) in place. While all three of these principles share and overlap characteristics, there is enough distinction in each term to make these descriptions independently discrete and meaningful:*

---

* For example, members of a group may enter the group exhibiting diverse characteristics (they are unlike other members of the group) but fail to act independently once they are a part of the group, effectively cancelling out their diversity. Conversely, if a nondiverse member is part of a group and it acts independently, the fact that it acts independently will not have much benefit (if any at all) because it will already be inherently duplicating the influences of other members of the group since it wasn't different from them to begin with.

- Independence: Members in a group function independently from the influences of other members in the group. One of the powers of human collective intelligence when applied to the kinds of cases mentioned above is that the intelligence is an effect of a large number of people acting according to their own ideas, independent of those of each of the others. If you have a group of 100 people, for example, and they all say the earth is square, then the crowd exhibits no intelligence. Even if they all say it is round, they still fail to exhibit any intelligence (although they may just happen to be right). But if another group of 100 people are left to answer using their own backgrounds and individual knowledge, and they all guess based on that (and not on what the others think), the chances dramatically increase that the collective choice will be close to the accurate answer. It is this last fact that leads to recognition of the importance of the next principle.

- Diversity: Groups must be sufficiently diverse in order to exhibit intelligence. Otherwise, their members are not able to maintain the necessary independence, each from the other members. A diverse cross section, where people have been exposed to a wide range of ideas, languages, philosophies, backgrounds, politics, religions, and ways of seeing, thinking, and experiencing avoids the risk of duplicating the same information. This makes the group as a whole even more diverse, providing a broader range of possible perspectives on any one problem. Diversity of this nature, of course, has been one contributing factor to the success of the United States.

- Decentralization: This principle is the most unlike the others two. Proponents of decentralization argue that local actions are generally better actions than those that take place at a distance. A teacher, advocates of decentralization convincingly argue, knows better what a particular child needs than do distanced administrators who have no regular contact with the individual student. As Surowiecki puts it, "the closer a person is to a problem, the more likely he or she is to have a good solution to it."[13] Decentralization of decision forming allows people to focus their efforts on the problems closest to them. It also allows them the freedom to share their results with others. In addition, it is more effective at identifying which problems should be addressed and in what order.

Whether it is a group or a crowd attempting to locate a sunken ship or a group trying to guess the numbers of jelly beans in a jar, groups that are successful consistently exhibit these principles. But in order for them to work, the fourth factor is absolutely essential: aggregation—the ability to gather and assess the information.

At the core of Surowiecki's analysis is that the first three principles work together to ensure one particular outstanding quality that must be present in order for groups to act in an intelligent way. They must, at all costs, be co-decisive and immediate. They must avoid covering an extended period of time where it would be possible for one member of a group to make decisions based on the opinions of the other members of the group. In these cases, consensus or consensus building is unhelpful, even counterproductive. While consensus may be beneficial sometimes for a variety of reasons and in many other circumstances, it is not a useful goal in these particular types of situations.

Each one of the principles—that an individual member makes decisions without being influenced by the group at large (independence), that the members in the group are unlike the other members of the group (diversity), and that members are permitted to use their own local environments as resources for their knowledge (decentralization)—helps make possible the elimination of the most common problem that exists with group decision forming: the cascade.

The cascade is like a true/false problem. There's a 50/50 shot of getting it right. The cascade for humans has the same effect as a circular mill for ants. If your neighbors happen to be right and you do what they do, then no problem. But if they are wrong, watch out. Because of the influence (to be distinguished from the intelligence) of a group, the implications of following your neighbors can be devastating. The groupthink of the cascade can lead to a closed society with no toleration for deviance of any kind. On the other hand, in January of 2011, the world witnessed an unprecedented cascade event in the Middle East. In a matter of days, the people of Tunisia demanded the removal of President Zine El Abidine Ben Ali, who himself had taken power in 1987 in a bloodless coup d'état from then-President Habib Bourguiba. The method for this revolution, peaceful street protests unprecedented in the Middle East, began to spread with phenomenal speed. On January 14, Ali relinquished power and fled to Saudi Arabia. The protests jumped across cultures and countries. In Egypt, the protests persisted and grew in intensity, and 11 days later (on January 25), President Hosni Mubarak resigned and fled Cairo. The mass protests took on the name, in the media, of the *Jasmine Revolution* or the Arab Spring, affecting Iraq, Syria, Yemen, Bahrain in the Middle East; and further into the Maghreb, into Algeria. Of course, the loudest of these took place in Libya where peaceful protests against an openly and internationally recognized malevolent dictator Muammar Gaddafi escalated. Eventually, the unsuccessful protesters took up arms in what became a full-blown revolution that ousted Gaddafi from power.

Each one of the situations is independent in its own right, but the fact that all of these uprisings occurred within days and hours of each other cannot be ignored. There is a great deal of anecdotal evidence about the role of social media sites, backing the argument that Facebook and Twitter played a role in the downfall of the old leaders of Egypt and Tunisia. Indeed, the differences that such websites may have played when compared to what was possible in Libya are significant.

Jillian York of the Berkman Center for the Internet and Society wants to make sure that a strong distinction between the role that the internet played and the role that mobile technologies *may* have played in Libya is made clear. York cites the International Telecommunications Union (ITU), an organization that tracks global communications statistics in various media. The ITU reveals that where only 5 percent of Libyans have internet access, 150 percent of them have mobile phones (many have more than one phone). York's point is that 5 percent is a very low number to make a revolution. She sent, via Twitter, this comment aimed at those who advocate what she calls "cyberutopian bullshit":

> Please spare me the "Internet/free/flow of info/Libya" meme. 5% Internet penetration, friends, does not a "net revolution" make.

The role that social media sites such as Facebook and Twitter played in the Arab Spring deserve full analysis, something that will come once time has passed and information is more fully available; but we raise the issue here because it is significant to any discussion of the general intelligence of crowds and the influence of cascades. For our purposes, in discussing the intelligence of crowds and whether the internet can be said to exude such an intelligence, it doesn't matter whether the Libyan people were spurred on by each other through mobiles, Facebook, or Twitter. What matters is that they were spurred on by *each other*. They followed their neighbors; they did what they neighbors were doing.

A cascade is, simply, paying attention to your neighbors and doing what they do *because* they are doing it. The cascade of the toppling of multiple leaders and a restructuring of governments is the kind of thing that rarely happens, and so, from a first glance, it can appear that cascades are extremely powerful and beneficial phenomena. When America was searching for weapons of mass destruction after September 11, 2001, one of the stated reasons for entering Iraq was to help the people become democratic. Years, lives, and trillions of dollars later, the people in Iraq finally broke out in their own protests. Both the internet and mobile phones allow the possibility of exponentially increasing the connections one has with the many; but, in a cascade, if everyone is turning against the government then you do too.

If, in recent phenomena, cascades were central to unseating of dictators in the Middle East, the Holocaust provides ample evidence of cascades working in the opposite direction. When Hitler was elected Fuhrer in 1934, he had an approval rating of 90 percent with the German people. When Nazi troops invaded and annexed Austria in 1938 without firing a single shot, the Austrian approval rating of Hitler was 98 percent. These are extreme examples of cascades, but history is rife with similar ones where scientists, philosophers, and experts of all kinds have followed the crowd to devastating effects. If everyone is jumping off a bridge, then so will you. That's the nature of cascades.

It's also the nature of economic bubbles, the results of which the world experienced when the American and European housing-derivatives market burst in 2008. Similar things have happened over and over for centuries—perhaps starting with the Dutch tulip mania of the 1630s—but we still have not found a way to stop them. There were certainly plenty of warnings about the housing bubble over the years leading up to its bursting, but the cascade effect proved too strong and the warnings were ignored.

At the other end of the spectrum, we see that independence, decentralization, and diversity actually make groups smart because these conditions typically work to ensure that each smaller set of data that gets put into the total set is distinct from the rest of the data entered into the set. The information or knowledge of the group is the result of a large cross section of knowledge from many independent sources. When this information is taken together, that is, aggregated and analyzed in some way, then the results of that information, of all those independent inputs, can be assessed and the knowledge can be implemented for a useful purpose.

As we mentioned earlier, this is not a process of consensus, of convincing all of the members of a group that a particular result is correct, but of stepping back from intact and unaltered individual views without changing or challenging them—of seeing instead what the percentages found in the aggregate may tell us. Quaker consensus may work for a small group seeking a route to communal endeavor, but it is no means of ensuring that the decision reached will be the best, not even if made by seemingly well-meaning individuals, as the cascade effect shows.

Aside from avoiding the cascade or circular mill, the last necessary condition for human crowds to act intelligently is to have a method of aggregating the data; for humans, the heart of crowd intelligence is the ability to organize and make meaning from collective actions. So long as the data are being collected and organized in some manner *with the intention of using the collective wisdom concerning the data,* that information will be useful. This is a step in the process that does not come from the crowd itself but from an independent actor existing independently from the crowd who is looking for patterns in the information—and this is what scares many about this method of decision making, for it necessitates at least the illusion of hierarchy, of decision-making beyond the crowd. Without some method of aggregating data, however, the information or knowledge exhibited by the crowd will have no significant effect; it will remain dormant and without consequence.

Bureaucracies are strong examples of the failure to aggregate information. New York City, a place that provides residence and work to some of the world's most interesting and intelligent people, regularly acts counter to the potential of those very people, often inhibiting the potential for creativity and growth. Anyone native to the city understands the difficulties of the government and agencies as part of the city's way of life, but anyone who has moved to the city from a more, shall we say, "efficient" municipality or state will recognize that, from renting an apartment to doing laundry to obtaining a driver's license or buying a house, New York can sometimes be a place where people spend entire days off from work lining up to line up for other lines for the chance they *may* (or may *not*) be helped.

In her State of the City address in February 2011, city council speaker Christine Quinn told a sad-but-true story of one of the failures of the city's agencies to aggregate, a story featuring small business owner Oliver Strumm. Here are her words:

> Oliver owns a small restaurant called Café Select. Last year he wanted to turn a space behind his kitchen into a private dining room. The Department of Buildings told him all he had to do was build a partial wall to enclose the kitchen—it's what's referred to as an open kitchen design. He hired an architect to draw up plans, and got them approved by DOB [Department of Buildings].
>
> Then the Health Department came to inspect. The first inspector told Oliver that an open kitchen was in fact illegal, and he'd have to build a wall from floor to ceiling. The next inspector said an open kitchen was OK, but the wall had to be five feet high. A third inspector said the wall had to be six

and a half feet high. A fourth said it had to be eight feet—and when asked why, he said—"Do you know how tall some people are these days?"

So how does this ridiculous story end? Six months and thousands of dollars later, Oliver still doesn't have final approval.

It sounds crazy, but sadly it's far from unique. We hear stories like this from small business owners every day. City Agencies just aren't communicating with each other—they aren't even communicating with their own employees.[14]

Similar kinds of bureaucratic headaches, where agencies fail to communicate with each other, occur every day across America, most notoriously in government, leading to a great deal of the current American dissatisfaction with government (just as it did in 19th-century Russia, among many other places, providing a goldmine of material for writers like Nikolai Gogol). In this case, the Department of Buildings that gave Strumm clearance to build the dining room; and the Department of Health apparently did not have the same information, so there was a breakdown in the information aggregation and communication between the two departments. In addition, the health department seems to have had its own internal communication problems, since all of its own inspectors are acting in an extremely independent way. Yes, this is a classic example of a failure to communicate, but do not overlook the fact that it is also a classic example of how "opening lines of communication" does not necessarily result in an increased intelligence.

If we run down the list of the conditions that are necessary for making a group intelligent, it appears that government bureaucracies oftentimes do actually satisfy several of the requirements. The situation outlined by council speaker Quinn meets the need for diversity, independence, and decentralization. The different agencies are acting independently from each other and are not being influence by the other (independence and diversity); they also are using their local knowledge and environments to assess and determine what is appropriate in the situation (decentralization). The conditions to avoid a cascade are in place. And yet their collective behavior has the result of being chaotic for the unfortunate Mr. Strumm, who is forced to keep changing the height of his walls even to accommodate people who are eight feet tall.

The failure of these agencies to help Strumm provides a snapshot of what is often overlooked when we think about what makes groups smart. For the past 20 years, scientists, humanists, business people, and technologists have been preoccupied with the power of decentralization. They have seen the combination of information communication technologies and bottom-up systems as essential to solving problems and being more creative. In decentralized systems, the power lies in allowing those involved in the system to make collective decisions without the influence of a centralized authority. Newer technological developments have increased the speed, scope, and breadth of the network and our ability to connect. As time goes by, the network gets more sophisticated and the number of potential connections multiplies.

One of the alleged powers of the network, as we have seen, is that the opening of communication channels allows people to easily find the solutions to problems without top-down coordination. Behind this idea, of course, is the model of complex adaptive systems—the suggestion that says that if a colony of ants, a school of fish, or a swarm of bees can act intelligently in a nondirected, spontaneous way, then so can humans. If this is true, all we need to do is open the floodgates of multidirectional communication so that we're connected to the network all the time and let the swarm do its dance of collective intelligence.

But the case of Oliver Strumm provides an example working counter to this ideal. There is little reason to suggest that the two different departments might be effectively coordinating with each other, given that they have very different histories and goals. It is one thing if Strumm hears one thing from one agency and another thing from another, but it is quite a different matter for him to hear a completely different thing from multiple inspectors in the same agency. In this case, employees in the same agency are hired to do the same jobs. They share the same offices. They go to the same meetings, receive the same memos and emails, go to the same office parties, and know the same people. Their network reaches far beyond Facebook and Twitter; their network is a significant part of their daily 9 to 5 life. Nobody in this scenario is expecting the employees to solve a problem; the expectation is much lower. It is simply that Strumm, Quinn, and any New Yorker would expect that employees with the same job description doing the same job in a single agency should be able to agree with each other and to give Oliver the same information. Because they are in the same department, the answer is not increasing the lines of communication, for every mode of communication is already open. There is every opportunity for them to act in an intelligent, decentralized way without top-down coordination, and yet they do not.

What happened to Strumm is not even unusual. Barlow, who closed his own New York City café in 2001 (but kept the nonfood aspects of his business open), received a final inspection by the Department of Health twice. The second inspector, who had no idea that the first had been there, tried to cover the mistake by then claiming he had arrived to look for a secret restaurant hidden in the basement. He proceeded to peer behind boilers and piles of old building material, seeking something he knew wasn't there, and wasted both his and Barlow's time.

Whatever the *reasons* are for the workers at the Department of Health to fail to coordinate with one another, doing so would apparently be doing something more than what they are now doing. Perhaps the city council recognizes this. According to Quinn, the city has implemented a new program for small business owners called Business Link. With this new program, business owners call 311 and connect to a link coordinator. Link coordinators work on behalf of the business owner as an advocate to help with every department and agency in the city. As Quinn notes, the idea is to help the business owner get "every permit, every license, every inspection—everything short of a date for Saturday night." While potentially adding another layer of bureaucracy to the city's already bloated system, if effective, these positions actually appear to function as purposeful aggregators of information missing from Strumm's scenario. Certainly, they would have saved Barlow the aggravation of having to follow on a pointless, face-saving search. With the links coordinator, there is an outside party looking into a collection of data and looking for answers and patterns in the data. By aggregating and selecting the relevant information and using it for the business owner, the work that takes place across the agencies is neither being ignored nor being contradicted, and the aggregator effectively puts it to use, saving time and effort for all involved.

What's refreshing about this move by the city council is that the link coordinators are interested in a particular kind of information. Health inspectors, for whatever reason that they might feel is central to their jobs, may not have an inherent interest or need to coordinate with each other or to send the same message to all parties; in other words, their own local situations, as they are currently defined, do not require that they aggregate the information that would have been valuable to Strumm or Barlow, impeding rather than helping business. The creation of the Business Link effectively asks a third party to become interested in this kind of information and to set to work the work of using the available information in an effective manner.

Open lines of communication may help, but there is no guarantee that they will. In each one of the cases taken from Surowiecki and mentioned above, from guessing temperatures to finding web pages via Google to predicting election results, an outside and *purposeful* aggregator has been present. But the purposeful aggregator must be an outside party who is specifically interested in what the information yields. It is necessary for such an aggregator to be present (but not within) for crowd intelligence to function.

The work of aggregation is a key difference between human group intelligence and the kind of smarts that can be witnessed in complex adaptive systems. Work that has taken place in areas of collective intelligence, complex adaptive systems and their links to the rise of social media, mobile technologies, and participatory culture has resulted in what might be called a cottage industry of folks claiming that a social media revolution is afoot and that changes in our ability to connect are giving us an intelligence that we would not have been able to imagine before. Emergent behavior among humans is not easily observable, but it does occur. Anyone who has been part of (as listener or player) an improvisational jam session has experienced the delight that occurs when an instrument responds to its neighbors. The sense of joy resulting from instruments is close synchrony with the group is an effect of the "intelligence" that happens in the jam. Perhaps there are now more similarities than ever between how group intelligence works in nature and how human intelligence works in culture, and it appears as though these similarities are enough to suggest that emergent behavior is at work in internet culture.

In *Smart Mobs,* Howard Rheingold draws specifically on this tradition. After a discussion based upon research coming from the Los Alamos research laboratory on complex adaptive systems and inquiries into human-centered swarm logic, Rheingold writes:

> The Internet is what happened when a lot of computers started communicating. The computer and the Internet were designed, but the ways people used them were not designed into the technology, nor were these tools anticipated by their designers or vendors. Word processing and virtual communities, eBay and e-commerce, Google and weblogs and reputations systems *emerged.*[15]

In this view, the internet is not a thing but an event—and a continuing event, at that.

So far we have been discussing how intelligence works in emergent systems and how it works when groups of people are coordinated in a specific way to exhibit a form of collective intelligence. At this stage, we'll draw some distinctions between the two. Research tells us that complex adaptive systems exhibit both emergent behavior and intelligence, both of which surpass the intelligence of any single group member. Our research also tells us that humans can exhibit collective intelligence under particular conditions. Consider Chart 4.1:

Chart 4.1 Comparison of the conditions necessary for collective intelligence for human groups and complex adaptive systems.

Conditions for intelligence in complex adaptive systems and in human groups		Applies to complex adaptive systems	Applies to human groups
1.	System is open and adaptive	☑	☒
2.	Members in the system work together	☑	☒
3.	The system spontaneously organizes itself	☑	☒
4.	Allelo-mimesis (doing what your neighbors do)	☑	☒
5.	Regulation of the system through feedback	☑	☒
6.	Requirement that the members of the group be diverse	☒	☑
7.	Requirement that the *actions* of the group be diverse (more is different)	☑	☑
8.	Requirement that the members of the group act independently	☒	☑
9.	Requirement of decentralization	☑	☑
10.	Requirement that cascades be avoided	☑	☑
11.	Requires a method of purposeful aggregation	☒	☑

Both adaptive systems and human groups exhibit intelligences that are beyond any single member, but the conditions under which this intelligence occurs in both cases is very different. Human groups do not organize themselves to act as complex adaptive systems because humans act with agency and purpose, an assumption that often remains consistent when it relates to the internet. It is much easier for ants to exhibit signs of emergent behavior because they have no thought, being genetically programmed to act as they do. Cells within a body also exhibit emergence behavior, but humans have historically had a difficult time in keeping themselves from being disengaged in the choices of how to act. Unlike primal societies that recognized the equilibriums that need to be maintained so that a colony or an ecology might survive, the self-interest of Westerners has typically been at odds with the balance necessary to keep an ecology functioning harmoniously. Different rules are necessary for something like collective intelligence to emerge concerning humans. This difference is largely based on the quality or principle of allelo-mimesis. In order for intelligence to occur spontaneously, allelo-mimesis is essential, but with humans it can often result in a cascade (groupthink) or chaos (a mob or riots). Cascades do not always have negative effects, but they often times do, leaving the possibilities to chance.

Emergent behavior requires that local interactions perform without knowledge of the global system. They solve small, specific problems, such as connecting two points with a tunnel. In order for emergence to occur, in order for consciousness to spring from the firing of neurons in the brain, the elements must self-organize into a pattern without knowledge of the greater whole and walk a fine line between chaos and order, always on the tipping point before order becomes chaotic. It could be true that the internet exhibits signs of emergent behavior, but no discernible patterns can be recognized in itself at this point. This is not to say that we cannot locate complex adaptive systems on the internet, but the internet as a system itself, as put forth by people like Michael Chorost in *World Wide Mind,* would need to undergo a phase transition, a jump in complexity where a new level of consciousness is attained. Various writers have speculated on the day that such an intelligence might occur. Vernor Vinge, for instance, was one of the earliest thinkers to discuss the oncoming singularity, the moment when humans create a computer intelligent enough to create a computer more intelligent than itself. Following the pattern of Moore's law that says technological progress becomes more complex and more efficient at increasing rates and at cheaper costs, the day we create a computer that can create more intelligent computers will be the beginning of the singularity where the human ecology will be dominated by a machine ecology. For Vinge, that day is inevitable, and he predicts that it will happen before 2050. Ray Kurzweil has made a similar prediction. Since they deal with the future, these predictions cannot be validated, but Moore's law can, and we can be quite sure that computational processing power will continue to increase at incredible rates. For Paul Virilio, "one day the day will come when the day will not come." We'll just have to wait and see.

FIVE

Getting Savvy, or Draining the Information Swamps

Digital resources are never simply pliant and receptive, only awaiting an actor to manipulate them, to make use of them. Instead, as Marshall McLuhan explained for a different age and technology in *Understanding Media,* they represent and actuate manipulation of each of the actors who choose to use them—and today, that's almost all of us. The actors, in turn, change the resources, even as they are again changed by them. This is especially true as usages grow, as the number of actors increases: "economies of size" always do change dynamics. At some point, something akin to a hive mind can arise, creating what amounts to an entirely new entity composed of the community of actors and the machines that bring them together. That's what the internet was long imagined to be and what it is now becoming, in fact. But that is not all it is becoming. As much as it brings intelligence together, the internet divides it and reduces it, and often in unexpected and destructive ways. We are finding that if this is not also recognized and taken into account, we will never be savvy users of the web but merely a compliant part of the environment it manipulates.

Discussion of the intelligence of systems aside, the accumulations of human intelligence and machine processing and aggregation has come to be called sociotechnical systems, which, according to Christine Borgman, start "from the premise that technology and society are deeply intertwined and mutually influencing."[1] Since the time of Gutenberg, at the very least, this has been the case for information and culture in European societies. It may, in fact, be the case for all societies in one way or another and at all times: Viking expansion and influence could never have happened had not development of the technology for ocean-going longships proved useful in war, trade, and colonization.

This latest sociotechnical system, the internet, of course, was born well into the advertising age, already a century old by the time the World Wide Web came into broad use. And it is advertising, as much as individual users, that drives internet expansion as well as a great deal of its digital creativity. In fact, the internet's principles and methodologies reflect the advertising age down to a molecular or, as we would say now, DNA level, and have only been strengthened through continuing technological development.

Journalist and cultural critic Walter Lippmann, writing in the early years of the advertising age, provided a characterization of the era that still holds true, enhancement by technology, media, and culture notwithstanding:

> Advertising, in fact, is the effort of business men to take charge of consumption as well as production. They are not content to supply a demand, as the text-books say; they educate the demand as well. In the end, advertising rests upon the fact that consumers are a fickle and superstitious mob, incapable of any real judgment as to what it wants or how it is to get what it thinks it would like. A bewildered child in a toy shop is nothing to the ultimate consumer in the world market of to-day. To say, then, that advertising is merely a way of calling attention to useful goods is a gorgeous piece of idealization. Advertising is in fact the weed that has grown up because the art of consumption is uncultivated.[2]

That weed has become a crop and the art of consumption highly cultivated. After a number of false starts in the 1990s, the internet was successfully turned into a tool for that art, with consequences that we are only now beginning to grasp.

When Lippmann's comments are applied to the internet, they illuminate three things. First, and most obvious, the internet, too, "educates the demand." Its very forms, its searches and pages, and the algorithms that lead us to them are a process of educating *us,* not the computer—doing so in a process quite separate from the explorations we are intent upon as we use the web. Second, it is not the users alone who are molding the web but the commercial interests that see our activities and utilizations as opportunities. And, third, "the art of consumption" is nowhere near as uncultivated today as it was a century ago, on the eve of World War I, when Lippmann was writing *Drift and Mastery,* which includes his commentary on commercial culture.

The progression from the start of the advertising age to our contemporary digital version of it is quite the story of technological developments and their impact on culture, refashioning what existed before, not just what is or will come to be:

> Web and Internet applications refashion the newer perceptual media of radio, television, and telephone more aggressively than they refashion print. With radio and television, the claim is not that the Internet provides a new transparency, although the quality of the audio (if not video) is already approaching the level that broadcasting or cable can provide. However, on the Internet, the listener has greater control over her listening or view experience. It is an immediacy that she achieves through the hypermediacy of the windowed interface. She now listens to Internet radio with a mouse in one hand while she looks at a web page; she reads rubrics as she listens and may chance the order of the materials by clicking on the links provided.[3]

That "hypermediacy" has its greatest impact in advertising or rather in the impact of advertising on our lives. It brings us into an illusion of a much more intimate relationship with the products advertised and the companies advertising them.

Again, though we may think that we, the public, are able manipulators of the internet, we also know that it is the internet, in most cases, that manipulates us. We may be seeking information, but what information, and how, and what we will accept as information are all being determined for us, at least to some degree. This is not necessarily a problem, but it will be, if we users do not learn to recognize and evaluate the means of our manipulation.

Given the continuities (such as advertising) it strengthens, the revolution we are in the midst of—the digital revolution—often appears less earth shattering than it really is—until we look back a bit and see how different things and attitudes were less than two decades ago. Then, people were still wondering just what the internet could be good for. In 1995, Clifford Stoll, an experienced technologist, wrote a popular book about the dawning digital age called *Silicon Snake Oil*. Not only did he argue that web commerce hadn't much of a future, but he felt that the internet would never prove to be a good source for information. For a while, especially during the dot-com bust that followed publication of his book by just a few years, it looked like he might be right; events since, of course, have proven him wrong—decisively.

Predictive abilities aside, Stoll *does* amplify at least one warning relating to information and its usage that should be heeded, though he is quite wrong there, too. In writing about libraries, he says:

One of the great promises of the online world is fast access to great quantities of information. Internet proponents talk of libraries without books, the time when essentially all publications will be available over the network. We'll be able to read and access any document from our workstations. Books will be distributed electronically.

I claim that this bookless library is a dream, a hallucination of online addicts, network neophytes, and library-automation insiders.[4]

When Stoll was writing in the mid-1990s, efforts (such as that of Project Gutenberg) at offering large numbers of books online were still in their infancy. Google didn't even exist. Books, as discrete items, were still considered the basis of knowledge. But a lack of ability to see these wasn't the only thing behind Stoll's position:

There's yet another reason why online libraries won't work. Or maybe it's a reason why they'll thrive. Thomas Mann of the Library of Congress calls it the principle of least effort. According to him, most researchers, even serious scholars, will choose easily available information sources, even when they are low-quality. Researchers are usually satisfied with whatever can be easily found rather than expending more effort to dig up better sources.

George Zipf, one of the pioneers of information science, put it a different way. Confronted with a variety of pathways to an answer, people choose the one that requires the least amount of work.

Mann writes, "If a system makes only some sources easily available—especially if those sources are very superficial or of poor quality—then it can do real damage to the quality of research, for it will encourage users simply to make do with whatever sources are readily retrievable, regardless of their quality or completeness."

In other words, people are lazy. Ease of use is more important than content. Put something online—anything—and researchers will love it, whether or not it's right.[5]

The internet, as a source of information, certainly makes life easier—at first blush (though maybe that's all that matters, these days)—for the lazy. It can provide quick backing for a stance, doing so without the necessity of real investigation or thought. Answers to questions of fact are easily established—without the bother of testing their accuracy. And the lazy mind, generally not an inquiring one, usually leaps towards the simplest conclusion in accord with its prior assumptions—something the very structure of the web search facilitates. But the lazy user will never become the savvy user, who will be able to turn the internet to real advantage, though maybe not quickly or simply. The web, as most people have learned, does not really make things easier, though it does provide the illusion of speed and accuracy to the unwary.

Stoll wasn't the only one with doubts about digital possibilities in the 1990s, of course. Keeping just to libraries, historian Douglas Greenberg, seeing a qualitative difference between digital editions and traditional printed ones, also wondered if we weren't rushing too quickly to embrace digital libraries:

> The term "digital library" may even be an oxymoron: that is, if a library is a library, it is not digital; if a library is digital, it is not a library. We have not thought as systematically as we should about the characteristics of the print library and how and whether they can, or should be, duplicated, trans-formed, or abandoned in a digital world. Digital library projects abound, but they are disparate, even contradictory, in their aims, and they are also blissfully unbothered by the unintended consequences that they presage. As the wag said: "If you don't know where you are going, any road will take you there." That is precisely our situation in the transition from the print to the digital library. Because we do not know where we are going (but want to get there very quickly), the application of digital technologies sometimes becomes an end in itself.[6]

By this logic, "digital humanities" aren't humanities. Though Green-berg's oxymoron isn't really any such thing (there's no reason a "book in a library" must take only paper form and be in a building any more than humanities must only deal with print), his point, that we have not well explored the implications of the change to digital, is as well taken today as a decade ago. It's the implication of his later comment, however, that could appear as really revolutionary (though still reflecting McLuhan's "the medium is the message" or the massage or even the mass age): it seems to be that it's not the information that's important, perhaps one should say, but the access points and the roads beyond or within. So, he's right: the application does, in some sense, become the end. On the other hand, the contemporary technological revolution could instead mean that digital technologies are abetting *real* revolutions, that the end becomes something less than "dead," but is instead the start of a new roadway—worth exploring not only for itself but for what might lie beyond.

We have accessible digital highways galore today, complete with daz-zling road signs, super-modern on- and off-ramps, and (of course) all sorts of attractive advertising. It doesn't matter that right off the highway we find just the same old information we could get to before—though by old dirt roads with streams to ford and what seemed like a lot greater chance of getting lost. Or that's how it can appear to those who never have understood the importance of the road or the way it changes the places at the end of the line—or the places beyond.

Lessening the distance between two points isn't just a matter of speed or of saved time. There's actual change in the information itself as proximity looms (as the United States and Great Britain learned, over the past 100 years, as air travel made "the pond" smaller and smaller), and serendipity's possibilities increase. So, Greenberg's criticism isn't completely deserved; the application does change the library, just as it did after Gutenberg—and that too is revolutionary in and of itself. That we don't yet have a complete map to our destination is somewhat beside the point, for any map we did have would be out of date before we arrived anywhere, anyway.

The revolution that Gutenberg sparked, like the current digital one, occurred not because of the change in technology itself (that was more a process of new application of extant possibilities and then continual refinement, more evolutionary than revolutionary) but because of the impact of the products of the technology on culture. Our image of the shift does center on Gutenberg, on a movement from what Walter Ong calls "orality" to "literacy," but Gutenberg is simply a convenient marker. It took centuries for the revolution to be completed—not surprising, given the limitations of communications prior to the 20th century—where the current, parallel revolution will probably take mere decades. Still, given the amount of time that had passed, the cultures that emerged had surprisingly little in common with what had existed before and have a focus on change that an orality culture (where the focus, intellectually, is necessarily on mastery by memorization of what is already past) cannot sustain.

The culture that emerges from this new revolution may be as radically different as that—we will see. Cultures that cannot support future changes, that do not themselves change, will wither—as did many in face of the earlier revolution. Certainly, a culture that proves unable to adapt to a form that can embrace change will not be able to compete with those that have: China, much more powerful than any European nation as late as 1800, soon collapsed in the face of the technology-embracing West. It was unable to regain its position on the world stage for two centuries, its huge population and resources notwithstanding—not until its own culture had changed enough for it to make widespread use of new technological possibilities.

The realities of the current revolution already fly in the face of the idea that all we are seeing is technological change, something that the current revolution, much as the earlier one, does allow and facilitate, but that is not itself the cause or end of the revolution. Contingent societal changes are those. The solutions to any problems along the way, then, are not simply technical, solvable by technicians. They involve culture, as well. Yet this is where discussion often centers, on technology and its wonders, not on the nontechnological implications of the use of technology. In Africa, the fast embrace of the cell phone signals a cultural shift that may allow the continent to finally start moving itself from its economic and political doldrums. This has nothing to do with the virtues of cellular technology alone; it has everything to do with cultures recognizing the possibilities for themselves in cellular technologies.

Technology, as we should all know by now, is not necessarily a good thing—not completely, not alone. As Evgeny Morozov makes abundantly clear in *The Net Delusion: The Dark Side of Internet Freedom,* technology can turn from contributory to destructive in a second—depending on the societal structures surrounding its use. He writes that "under the pressure of religious, nationalist, and cultural forces reignited by the internet, global politics is poised to become even more complex, contentious, and fragmented."[7] As a result of the web, the tools of connectivity can now be used for division: for setting one group of people off against another, for disconnection.

Morozov's view stands in sharp contrast to the "cyber-utopian" visions that often dominate discussions of the internet, lumping him with doubters such as Stoll and Andrew Keen. But Morozov's concerns are a great deal more sweeping and more troubling. He challenges the assumption "that more connections and more networks necessarily lead to more freedom and more democracy,"[8] and that more information is necessarily a good thing, doing so by taking the online world live into the real world. At one point, he quotes Radio Free Europe's Luke Allnut: "where the techo-utopians are limited in their vision is that in this great mass of internet users all capable of great things in the name of democracy, they see only a mirror image of themselves: progressive, philanthropic, cosmopolitan. They don't see the neo-Nazis, pedophiles, or genocidal maniacs who have networked, grown, and prospered on the Internet."[9]

At the end of his *Utopia,* Thomas More wrote that "there are many things in the commonwealth of Utopia that I rather wish, than hope, to see followed in our governments."[10] Humans have always wished for the best, seeing a new day around the corner, if only we (as a group) would recognize just what needs to be done and that the ways of the past need to be rejected. Even conservatives do so, though they couch their vision of the future in terms of an idyllic past. We extol our visions, much as Friedrich Nietzsche's Zarathustra exhorts:

> O my brethren, not backward shall your nobility gaze, but OUTWARD! Exiles shall ye be from all fatherlands and forefather-lands!
>
> Your CHILDREN'S LAND shall ye love: let this love be your new nobility,—the undiscovered in the remotest seas!
>
> For it do I bid your sails search and search! Unto your children shall ye MAKE AMENDS for being the children of your fathers: all the past shall ye THUS redeem![11]

Optimism is a defining feature of humanity, but it has also highlighted a naïveté just as enduring. That is not to say that the cyber-utopians are wrong in their enthusiasm, simply that they should be a little more considered and recognize that the patterns of the past developed for reasons (as we shall see later in this chapter), and they cannot be brushed away through simple desire or even by expanding digital possibilities—nor can Allnut's neo-Nazis, pedophiles, and maniacs. Lippmann, again, recognized the truth of this, and saw that balance is the essence of all good information-gathering and good decision-making. He saw that we cannot operate as though what we imagine can always be realized:

> A rational man acting in the real world may be defined as one who decides where he will strike a balance between what he desires and what can be done. It is only in imaginary worlds that we can do whatever we wish. In the real world there are always equations which have to be adjusted between the possible and the desired. Within limits, a man can make a free choice as to where he will strike the balance. If he makes his living by doing piece-work, he can choose to work harder and to spend more. He can also choose to work less and spend less. Bu he cannot spend more and work less.[12]

This remains no less true today than a century ago. Yet many of us refuse to turn away from the vision that the web can turn our lives to leisure and wealth, that the imagined online world will somehow modify our older, daily one, making the possible and the desired one and the same and erasing the crazies.

Yet it remains true: technology does change our landscapes, our roads and road maps. And it changes us and our cultures—for good *and* for bad. Borgman, focusing on the implications of technology on scholarship, writes that the "push and pull of . . . technologies for scholarship are not occurring in a vacuum. Rather, they exist in a complex environment of social, technical, economic, and political trends."[13] The same is true everywhere and of everything. As we have said, technology is never enough by itself; to mean anything, it operates within a continuum, as much the result of change as the agent of change and as vulnerable to forces of all nature as cultures are themselves. Technology in use does not presuppose democracy or a level playing field. It has no necessary cultural perspective or basis behind it but exists in synergy with culture, both good and bad.

As Morozov argues, "It may be that what we gain in the ability to network and communicate, we lose in the inevitable empowerment of angry online mobs, who are well-trained to throw 'data grenades' at their victims. This may be an acceptable consequence of promoting Internet freedom, but we'd better plan ahead and think of ways in which we can protect the victims."[14] Ultimately, those victims will include all of us, especially as we become more and more intertwined with our machines, so we had best do what Morozov suggests and prepare for negative consequences even as we hope for the positive.

At the same time, it has become evident that the online world and the world we live in have melded, becoming one and the same thing. Our devices have become integral to us, part of us, almost the image of us— maybe actually becoming how we are seen. So, our contemporary situation, down to the people who use the internet (and Morozov gives us plenty of examples of this) to target others for violence, reflects the question posed by William Butler Yeats in "Among School Children" that Paul de Man recently drew our attention to:

> O chestnut-tree, great-rooted blossomer,
> Are you the leaf, the blossom or the bole?
> O body swayed to music, O brightening glance,
> How can we know the dancer from the dance?

Are we ready to take full responsibility for the technologies that now reflect us and that we reflect? That have become us, and that we have become? Are we, as the human community, willing to see that, as technological enablers, we become at least somewhat responsible for the acts enabled, both good and bad? Furthermore, following Yeats in another direction, maybe we should be asking: how can we tell the map from our destination? From this other perspective, can we tell the technology from its uses? And, following de Man, let's go beyond, to the next step: is there really a difference between the map and what we find on the web itself? Is the information the internet, or is the web merely its visible design? How can we distinguish between the online search and the searcher?

"If you don't know where you're going, any road will take you there." Baseball great Yogi Berra famously gave directions to his home: "When you come to the fork in the road, take it." Supposedly, either way, you'd get to his house. Sometimes any road *will* take you where you want to go. This, of course, is one of the beauties of the internet: there are always multiple pathways from any one place to any other. No road is irrevocably wrong, but as Morozov makes clear, all roads are inherently dangerous. So, as Borgman's "complex environment" gets more and more so every day, we do need to continue to try to understand it, to try to map it— though today, as much as ever in the past, any map we make is flawed or worse. Yet, we need to do this, especially as the maps become more and more ourselves.

Stuart Chase discussed the problem of the relation between map, mapped, and user in relation to the spread of fascism on the eve of World War II:

> Confusions persist and increase because we have no true picture of the world outside, and so cannot talk to one another about how to stop them. Again and again I come back to the image of the map. How can we arrive at a given destination by following a grossly inaccurate map, especially when each adventurer has a map with different inaccuracies? Better language can clear away many nonexistent locations which clutter the maps we now carry. It will help us talk sensibly with one another as to where we are, why we are *here,* and what we must do to get *there*. If the characteristics of people and groups are in fact different from the characteristics our charts and theories ascribe to them, the charts are dangerous, and we run into reefs instead of sailing through open channels. If people do not in fact behave as our ideas of "fascism" expect them to behave, we are rendered helpless in dealing with the happenings which go under that label.[15]

The faith in language Chase describes, if it is just "better," seems touchingly naïve today—though it certainly does persist (or a variation of it, substituting "technology" for "language") among the cyber-utopians. The problem with this confidence in "better language" (or "better technology"), is that improvement also expands other things, creating new problems as the refinements and developments solve old ones. We may have defeated fascism, but another totalitarian system threatened soon after. Today, that system has collapsed, but the world seems even less mappable and understandable (and less controllable—a map, of course, being a symbol of control as well as understanding) than ever before. And this is more true in the world of the global positioning system (GPS) than not, for the map is no longer limited but infinitely expandable.

A further problem is that a map is not simply a representation but is the manifestation of a series of choices. What landmarks are significant enough to be represented? What makes a road? What features of the landscape should be or could be ignored? In light of such questions, a map is clearly as much a limiting factor in exploration as it is a guide—or, perhaps, that is the very nature of a guide, limitation, keeping one to a determined path. As long as we remain aware of this (and not only of the other, expansive vision of the map), it is not necessarily a problem. When we forget it, the map or guide confines our world, no matter how great the information carried. The world can become something like a limited-access highway, letting us on and off at predetermined points, the space between often effectively erased. On the internet, the very speed, the almost instantaneous movement between exits, can make us forget that there is anything out there at all beyond the growing universe of our mapped and guided destinations.

Overwhelmed by increasingly complex entities around them, people often long for an imagined map to simplicity, to knowledge they can believe in—much more passionately even than they (or others) supported, say, Barack Obama's "change we can believe in." The problem is, though, as Neil Postman describes it, that we live "in a world without spiritual or intellectual order, nothing is unbelievable; nothing is predictable, and therefore, nothing comes as a particular surprise."[16] Not even change is believable. In such an unstable situation, a map, any sort of map, can be comforting, especially if it confirms the routes we already think we want to take. It is when we take too much comfort in the map, when we rely on it completely, that the map becomes more of an impediment than a guide. Becoming prescriptive and not really descriptive, it limits the world, no matter how huge or technologically driven it becomes.

In information terms, the internet, we are finding, has at least two clear and immediate uses, depending on the mindset of the user: it can validate prior belief; or, more dangerously but usefully, it can actually do the opposite: opening the door to the unknown, to explorations off the maps. In this, it is not that different from the intellectual tools long available to us. However, if it is used primarily for the former (as is occurring quite frequently in certain parts of American culture—and especially by the lazy and the hurried), the web may become an agent of cultural calcification, helping close in cultures as certainly as China was closed in, 200 years ago. Or, if the general cultural mindset is expansive—willing to accept risk and challenge—it could lead to surprising and positive results, as may be happening today in Africa where, as we mentioned earlier, cellular technology is meeting cultural needs and opening up possibilities for societies that have felt stymied in the modern world for decades. Like the bicycle a century ago and the moped more recently, the cell phone is proving to be something that Africans can embrace and make use of on their own, perhaps breaking the grip of underdevelopment. As in China, though, and as in the United States, competing forces of cultural conservatism and cultural change will affect the speed of change and the extent of the influence of the new technology—as will manipulation of the new technologies for purposes of divisive political agendas and hatred.

Perhaps because the impact of the internet is so continually debatable, other internet skeptics followed in the footsteps of Stoll long before Morozov's more recent and more considered warnings. Not least among them is Keen who, like Stoll, had early experience with the developing digital environment. Though he was quickly dismissed by the growing chorus of web aficionados, Keen's main point—that chaos ensues when gatekeepers, maps, and rules and regulations disappear—is not as overly alarmist as it appeared to be when his book *The Cult of the Amateur* was published in 2007, a dozen years after Stoll's. Keen wrote:

> I would argue that we are easily seduced, corrupted, and led astray. In other words, we need rules and regulations to help control our behavior online, just as we need traffic laws to regulate how we drive in order to protect everyone from accidents. Sometimes it takes government regulation to protect us from our worst instincts and most self-destructive behavior.[17]

In terms of internet use within a stable, structured society, Keen may be a little more worried than need be. But his point that structure is needed cannot be denied or ignored as web tools become more readily turned to movements and networks whose intent is outside of societal norms or whose operation is within societies in upheaval. But Keen should also recognize that too often "structure" is a substitute for the status quo, that those who created structures in the past did so by building structures to keep others in check. If structure is a cell, then chaos is a friend. No matter what her purpose, legitimate or suspect, each web user brings a bias to each task, a bias that a structured environment can alleviate, too, just as traffic laws rein in the inclination of some to drive too fast. Even those who skirt the law through use of things like radar detectors are aware of the law, and they do generally keep their behavior from straying too far from it. When a country breaks down, such simple regulation is lost, and it is here where the web can prove most dangerous: not in situations of online anarchy, but where the anarchy starts far from the technology. Even so, one of the problems with attitudes like Keen's lies in the faith they show in authority. Keen may be right, as Morozov also argues (though tangentially, not centrally), that internet anarchy is not the answer, but that presupposes acceptance of general rule of law, and the law has never been anything even close to perfect.

There needs to be an exploration seeking a new understanding of the relation between structure in the world and structure online, especially as the two become more and more intertwined. The worries about misuse of the internet and about limitation of freedom can likely be met by built-in flexibility, a flexibility that can meet the needs of both sides, but it has to be based in that other part of the world, the older reality. Keen's faith in gatekeepers is as unworthy and unworkable (given that technological gates can always be circumvented) as an equally absolute internet freedom such as the one seen on the part of many cyber-utopians. As we have realized elsewhere in society, a balance of principles and flexibility is the only way of preserving both.

Cyber-enthusiasts and predictors of doom would both do well to remember what John Dewey, among others, has argued concerning the real need for both freedom and structure (something also at the heart of the U.S. Constitution, of course):

> When we say that thinking and beliefs should be experimental, not absolutistic, we have then in mind a certain logic of method, not, primarily, the carrying on of experimentation like that of laboratories. Such a logic involves the following factors: First, that those concepts, general principles, theories and dialectical developments which are indispensable to any systematic knowledge be shaped and tested as tools of inquiry. Secondly, that policies and proposals for social action be treated as working hypotheses, not as programs to be rigidly adhered to and executed.[18]

Regulation does not have to be stifling. And the experimental is not necessarily the anarchic online as elsewhere. The danger comes when structure breaks down as it has in Somalia, where digital tools now aid piracy; or in Mexico, where information from social networking sites proves a goldmine for kidnappers.

Structure needs to exist, but it must be changeable and dynamic but not static—if, that is, it is going to meet the needs to our developing digital (and offline) paradigms. And it must exist as part of a continuum that includes freedom. This, of course, has been something like the core argument behind liberal arts education, among other things, for centuries and not simply the reasoning behind the argument for instituting constitutional democracies; and it has been part of a discussion ongoing since the earliest treatises of political philosophy. That it arises in discussion of the internet, then, is not surprising—the *opposite* would be. When a new paradigm emerges, it is going to bounce between poles for quite some time before coming to rest with, one hopes, elements of both providing a certain amount of stability, until something new is injected into the system and volatility starts once again.

When the internet first began to engage the public imagination in the 1980s, it was quickly dubbed "cyberspace," by science fiction writer William Gibson, who characterized it as a "consensual hallucination"[19] in his novel *Neuromancer*. In 1990, John Perry Barlow wrote:

> Cyberspace, in its present condition, has a lot in common with the 19th Century West. It is vast, unmapped, culturally and legally ambiguous, verbally terse (unless you happen to be a court stenographer), hard to get around in, and up for grabs. Large institutions already claim to own the place, but most of the actual natives are solitary and independent, sometimes to the point of sociopathy. It is, of course, a perfect breeding ground for both outlaws and new ideas about liberty.[20]

Over the past decade, the questions of ownership were largely answered, with corporate interests taking the lead. As we have seen here, much of contemporary concern is for the mapping and the ordering and also with that other side, the outlaw possibility, with people like Morozov arguing that extolling the anarchy of the web borders on the irresponsible. When Barlow was writing, however, cyberspace seemed a place, a real new frontier, different in qualitative and quantitative ways from what we had known before or that we experienced elsewhere and removed from normal responsibility. It seemed, in addition, a place where people could don new identities, remaking themselves as creatures of something of a brave new world. It has been tamed a good deal since; even the metaphors for it have been toned down. And we have learned that it is no world reached through a rabbit hole or a wardrobe but is wholly contained by the material world even as the virtual world contains it, as in a möbius strip where the inside and the outside are one.

Over the two decades since Barlow's essay, cyberspace was either conquered or recognized as a chimera—depending on one's point of view.

In either case, it moved from the foreign—the strange, to the quotidian—the normal. Instead of being seen as a separate world we can dip into from our older one, too many see it simply as another story built onto our aging bricks-and-mortar house.

Yet there's a problem with the newer view of cyberspace as merely an extension of reality as previously known—and not simply in the changes its collective size constructs. That is, it assumes that cyberspace is constructed out of reality, reflecting it and manipulated by its citizens. It elides the impact, the reverberation that goes the other way, accepting that cyberspace is something of a tool but ignoring that old force of the tool on the user.

Oddly, on the other hand, much of what we assume today about groups on the internet appears to ignore the realities of group dynamics in physical situations, as we discussed in the previous chapter. Though there certainly can be (and is) value in the wisdom of crowds, the opposite can also be true. Mobs can turn nasty on the internet, just as elsewhere; and they do. They find ways of justifying their behavior—something perhaps a little more important down the line on the web, where everything anyone does has a permanent record. Much of the time, such justification is based on the putative rogue behavior of the other, behavior that makes the rogue a threat to the group, obviating whatever protections for the individual the group had established for those within it.

This is an old concern. The Victorian English religious philosopher James Martineau long ago described the mindset of the group in such situations, a mindset leading to a willingness to lie and to do other things otherwise considered lawbreaking themselves for the protection of the group:

> On the area of every human society, and mixed with its throngs, there are always some who are thus *in* it, but not *of* it, who are there, not to serve it, but to prey upon it, to use its order for the impunity of disorder, and wrest its rights into opportunities of wrong. Assassins, robbers, enemies with arms in their hands, madmen, are beyond the pale; and the same principle applies to those who try to turn the postulate of speech to the defeat of its own ends, and through its fidelity compel it to play the traitor. Such persons, we surely may say, can no more claim the benefit of "the common understanding," than could a spy who, by stealing the password eludes the sentry's vigilances and makes his notes of the disposition of the lines, expect to be treated as a comrade, if he is found out. The immunity and protection of the camp are not for him; he has nothing in reserve but a short shrift and a high gallows. If, then, there are persons to whom, on this principle, we are not bound to tell the truth, it is not that the intuitive rule of veracity is broken down by the admission of *exceptions*: we have not put these people into the rule, and then taken them out again: they have never been within its scope

at all; for its defined range was that of a social organism, in which indeed they may be present, but to which they do not belong.[21]

Martineau fails to explore the crucial question of who gets to decide just who is beyond the pale, who does not belong—or even why, really. The spy is too facile an example, of course, and the real spy is rarely the one targeted.

What Martineau describes is, for many of us, the great weakness of democracy. Mob rule forgets law in favor of common assumption and determination; we have now seen numerous examples, a few of them detailed in Morozov's book, of how this can also work through the web. The internet has shown symptoms of such attitudes for years, even in strictly online situations where a group can easily rile itself up against outsiders and, figuratively, ride them out of town on a rail. On the liberal blog Daily Kos, people who have attained "trusted user" status can "hide rate" the comments of others, leading to the disappearance of those comments. Though this may provide a certain amount of order, it really goes against the grain of democracy. The problem is that the troll (as the unpopular commenter is called) has not accepted the precepts of the group and is acting more like Martineau's spy. The law of the website, unfortunately (but probably necessarily, given current online possibilities), is brutal and swift—and democratic only in the most mob-oriented sense.

The political scholar Sheldon Wolin points out that for effective democracy to exist, a three-part underpinning needs to be in place: one made up of things that are not necessary conditions for participation in discussion on the web but that become extremely important when the web is seen as part of the world:

> While the principle of popular participation in decision making is fundamental to democracy. . . thoughtful participation is dependent upon certain commonplaces: first, the availability of knowledge in the form of reliable factual information and, second, a political culture that values and supports the honest effort to reach judgments aimed at promoting as far as possible the best interests of the whole society. There is a third principle, intellectual integrity. One aspect of it is the responsibility of those who, as teachers, publicists, researchers, and scientists, practice truth telling as their vocations. It is not a vocation to which many pundits, talk show hosts, for-sale journalists, and think thank residents are committed. The public vocations of truth telling cannot be consistently practiced without public and private respect for, and defense of, intellectual property.[22]

Wolin's idea of public responsibility, in its absolutes and reliance on law, contrasts sharply with what Martineau presents, for Wolin leaves no room for the outsider exception and focuses on responsibility within the group. Martineau, in describing group dynamics, exposes the dirty little secret (not so secret, really) that groups exclude. The frontier justice of the Wild West, while sometimes defended as necessary in perilous times, often takes advantage of the desire to exclude at the expense of justice and of democracy. On the web, as in the real Wild West, lack of regulation and enforcement can also lead to the strong taking advantage of the weak.

Edward O. Wilson, biologist and environmentalist, describes a different sort of view of the world than that of freedom and regulation. This other one has also become quite influential in shaping how we view the internet. It's not Wilson's own view but an exemptionalist one of the relationship between human beings and the world: "In this conception, our species exists apart from the natural world and holds dominion over it. We are exempt from the iron laws of ecology that bind other species. Few limits on human expansion exist that our special status and ingenuity cannot overcome."[23] Here again, we see something that extends to the web as well, which too many of us have seen as a playground we act upon but that doesn't, in return, act upon us; that removes us, also, from responsibility for our actions there. Though attitudes are changing, many still believe, somehow, that, if something has no immediate impact on us, it has no impact on anyone.

This is the belief that leads to views such as those of Malcolm Gladwell, that the internet lacks room for high-stakes activism: its very nature of remove from quotidian life providing a barrier between action and consequence, diffusing action in actual impact while maintaining a high-profile image. This, he sees, is a significant distinction between contemporary activism in what he sees as that fantasy, harmless internet Wild West and activism of the American past when consequences could be real, terrible, and immediate. In addition, there is a structural difference:

> The civil-rights movement was high-risk activism. It was also, crucially, strategic activism: a challenge to the establishment mounted with precision and discipline. The N.A.A.C.P. was a centralized organization, run from New York according to highly formalized operating procedures. At the Southern Christian Leadership Conference, Martin Luther King, Jr., was the unquestioned authority.
>
> This is . . . [a] crucial distinction between traditional activism and its online variant: social media are not about this kind of hierarchical organization.

Facebook and the like are tools for building *networks,* which are the opposite, in structure and character, of hierarchies. Unlike hierarchies, with their rules and procedures, networks aren't controlled by a single central authority. Decisions are made through consensus, and the ties that bind people to the group are loose.[24]

The ability to participate in high-profile, low-consequence activism through the web certainly does itself change the relationships between activists. Shared risk creates bonds that nothing on the internet can, so far, imitate effectively. That does not mean, however, that the internet is not developing its own style of effective activism or that activism there doesn't court danger.

Even so, like Morozov, Gladwell is something of a welcome antidote to cyber-utopian claims about the web, many of which present it in grandiose terms. Even such a perceptive scholar as Kembrew McLeod (though certainly a bit tongue-in-cheek and with a nod to John Perry Barlow) is willing to continue to compare the web once more to that much more dangerous and unknown environment of cowboy days:

> The Internet is a Wild West of today, sort of like hip-hop in the late 1980s before laws and bureaucracies limited its creative potential, at least as a mainstream art form. I hope the creative door won't slam shut on the Internet, though alternatives always seem to pop up, like a crazy sociological version of that Whack-a-Mole carnival game.[25]

From the mythological—and deadly earnest—to music to a carnival game! Perhaps, in this view, the web is little more than America *writ large.*

Whatever it is, conduit for positive change or also for disaster, the internet needs to be understood and not simply used. Sometimes it may appear to be organized, but it really is an extremely unsettled and unsettling place. Yet, in terms of creativity, this apparent chaos can be a good thing:

> People tend to imagine that they are getting the most out of their brains when their thoughts are well organized and focused, when they are able to clearly spell out their goals and intentions, and when the confusing world around them has been sorted out according to a distinct scheme. But actually, the mind is build around disorder on several levels, ranging from the processing of raw sensory data to the juggling of complex ideas. Our brains evolved to function in a messy world, and sometimes when we insist on thinking in neat, orderly ways, we're really holding back our minds from doing what they do best. In fact, it is when our brains seem to be efficiently putting the world around us into perfect order that they are most likely to be leading us astray.[26]

The internet is as messy and unorganized a part of our world as any any-one can imagine. This results, to some degree, from its diffuse structure, adding strength to it in a number of different ways—but also making it rife for manipulation and rationalization.

The chaos of the web also helps make it easy for the user to ignore whatever parts of the internet make one uncomfortable. Political activ-ist Eli Pariser explores the implications of this in his book *The Filter Bubble: What the Internet Is Hiding from You,* which is more accurately about how we are complicit in helping the web hide what we don't want to know from ourselves. He writes, "Democracy requires citizens to see things from one another's point of view, but instead we're more and more enclosed in our own bubbles. Democracy requires a reliance on shared facts; instead we're being offered parallel but separate universes."[27] The savvy user of the internet, for today and the future, will always have this in mind, will be aware that he or she is exploring in blinders, so he or she will move his or her head more deliberately from side to side, to catch a little of what will otherwise certainly be missed. The savvy user will fol-low the maps found and offered but will also explore the spaces between the marked exits.

One of the reasons it is so easy to miss things—aside from the tailoring to individual preferences that search engines and websites now provide—is that much of the web is repetitive. That is, very little is original to any particular site, and almost nothing is unique. Much on the web can be cop-ied exactly, with no loss either to the original or in the copy, and so it often is. Yet we tend to forget that the copy, though exact, is quite different from the original, an idea that Marcel Duchamp and Jorges Luis Borges, among many others, were able to use as an integral part of the conversations that are their art—but that we tend to overlook as we use the internet.

In "Pierre Menard Author of the *Quixote,*" Borges plays with the dis-tinction between copies to make the point that context is everything and that a copy might not even be a copy, writing that Menard:

> did not want to compose another Quixote—which is easy—but *the Quixote itself.* Needless to say, he never contemplated a mechanical transcription of the original; he did not propose to copy it. His admirable intention was to produce a few pages which would coincide—word for word and line for line—with those of Miguel de Cervantes.
>
> "My intent is no more than astonishing," he wrote me the 30th of Sep-tember, 1934, from Bayonne. "The final term in a theological or metaphysi-cal demonstration—the objective world, God, causality, the forms of the

universe—is no less previous and common than my famed novel. The only difference is that the philosophers publish the intermediary stages of their labor in pleasant volumes and I have resolved to do away with those stages." In truth, not one worksheet remains to bear witness to his years of effort.[28]

Two identical passages, Borges shows us, can have extremely different meanings, given the contexts of composition and of reception. When Cervantes writes about history as the mother of truth, to the narrator of "Menard," nothing but a rhetorical flourish has been produced. When Menard pens the same words centuries later, however, "the idea is astounding. Menard, a contemporary of William James, does not define history as an inquiry into reality but as its origin. Historical truth, for him, is not what has happened; it is what we judge to have happened."[29] Arthur Danto explains:

> Borges tells us that the *Quixote* of Menard is infinitely more subtle than that of Cervantes, while that of Cervantes is immeasurably more coarse than its counterpart even though every word contained in the Menard version can be found in Cervantes' and in the corresponding position. . . . Had Menard lived to complete his (his!) *Don Quixote*, he would have had to invent one character more than was required of Cervantes' fancy, namely the author of the (so called uniquely in Menard's case) "autobiographical Fragment." And so on. It is not just that the books are written at different times by different authors of different nationalities and literary intentions: these facts are not external ones; they serve to characterize the work(s) and of course to individuate them for all their graphic indiscernibility. That is to say, the words are in part constituted by their location in the history of literature as well as by their relationships to their authors, and as these are often dismissed by critics who urge us to pay attention to the work itself.[30]

Today, all words on the web are also constituted, in part, by their location on the internet. The digital venues (and all of the other aspects of contemporary context) have become as important as the history and the authorship. When we ignore this, we strip part of the meaning from the words.

As we see here and in other chapters of this book, the tool of language, as it existed before the advent of the internet, had different uses than it does today, if for no other reason than that language is a reflection of culture and culture works with (and reflects) the needs and possibilities (including technological possibilities) of a society. With the web, language (like everything else) is expanding and changing at an extraordinary rate. At the same time, though, the expansion stretches the tool almost to its breaking point.

As economist Stuart Chase observed more than a generation ago:

> The more complicated culture becomes, the less reliable, relatively, is ordinary language. We have seen how the printing press, the radio, advertising, propaganda, increase the havoc. At what point befuddlement becomes a dominating characteristic, and the needle swings to antisurvival, no one can say. We desperately need a language structure for the clear communication of observations, deductions, and ideas concerning the environment in which we live today.[31]

Chase was writing before World War II, but his comments are even more appropriate to the world today than they were then. With technological development comes at least the *potential* for havoc. Somehow, each of us has to learn to recognize that we are dealing with something that can be explosive when we use the internet, explosive both in a personal and in a cultural sense. When Craigslist becomes a venue for crime and Facebook a mart for those seeking victims, for our own safety we need to learn to take care as we navigate the web.

Though the internet seems to be increasing the speed of just about everything, perhaps it should become incumbent on individuals approaching it to slow it down, to take things at a more considered pace rather than complaining about danger or the lack of policing. This may be particularly important today, when discussion is often reduced to the 140 Twitter characters, one reflection of what William Scheuerman calls "a speed-obsessed society,"[32] a society that the science fiction writer Philip K. Dick envisioned in his 1979 short story "The Exit Door Leads In." "It was hell living in the twenty-first century. Information transfer had reached the velocity of light. Bibleman's older brother had once fed a ten-word plot outline into a robot fiction machine, changed his mind as to the outcome, and found that the novel was already in print. He had had to program a sequel in order to make his correction."[33] Doing anything to counter the juggernaut of the small and quick is problematic, for the slow is now perceived as the lumbering left-behind. Still, it may prove to be in reduced speed where safety on the internet lies and where real knowledge can be found.

Writing just on the eve of the explosion of internet discussion into the public sphere, Jeffrey Goldfarb argued that slowing things down could be a task taken on by public intellectuals, whose job it is, supposedly, to be more reflective than the rest of us:

> There is a deliberation deficit in contemporary societies, and intellectuals seem to be uniquely equipped to address this. They can encourage talk

about difficult problems societies face, but doing this is no easy matter. Not only do all democratic citizenries inherently distrust the elitism that is involved in the intellectual's position, but the mass media challenge the possibility of reaching the public, and the confusion of ideology with political principle, and of intellectual commitment with the demands of professionalism, make the contribution of intellectuals to democratic deliberation difficult. In order to avoid these difficulties, it is necessary to understand exactly who the democratic intellectual is, to appreciate that he or she is an autonomous agent fostering informed discussion in public. But democratic public life itself is a problem. In the twentieth century, it is in eclipse, and it is unclear whether this is because of too much democracy or not enough, or because the powers work against the public, democracy, and intellectuals, or because the public is a manifestation of power of the center against the subaltern, or because the tradition of political common sense has been broken.[34]

One result of the digital technologies developed over the past decade, though, has been the illusion, at least, that the "democratic public life" has been in anything else but eclipse. The general trend that Goldfarb writes of may continue, however, as the power of the center reasserts itself, taking back control of its own creation, the internet. Still, it won't be the public intellectuals who manage to right things. That will have to come from the public itself, which has, through the simplification and the speed resulting from new technologies, wrested control of almost all debates from those who really do know the topics. Consider the ongoing insistence that creationism be given equal standing to evolution; the birther controversy that propelled Donald Trump to a brief lead amongst potential Republican presidential primary possibilities in 2011 and that forced the White House to a high-profile response; or the controversy over whether Osama bin Laden's body should have been on public display, also in 2011. Add to this the fact that even celebrity misfortune can be monetized these days, amplifying and speeding up that entire industry of celebrity news creation, the "gossip machine,"[35] and one can only conclude that it is unlikely that that any measured approach to debate on any topic will likely emerge soon.

One of the more extraordinary aspects of the internet has proven to be the way that it works on both micro and macro levels at once, power and speed of technology allowing users to move back and forth at will. Most of what we use our search engines for takes us down to a micro level, but we can also stand back and look at information from a distance, from a dual perspective never before allowed us so easily—and can do so while also looking at the details. Psychologist William James described the distinction between these levels more than a century ago, long before this dual vision was possible through technological aids. He dwelt upon its implications for how we should imagine knowledge and our relations to it, seeing this as distinct from simply looking at data, particularly at particulars so miniscule as to hardly be worth the effort to establish. Computational power is now so great that we no longer have to take the fact of effort into consideration. But James felt at the time (given then iron-clad limitations of time, power, and memory) that it was:

> a necessity laid upon us as human beings to limit our view. In, mathematics we know how this method of ignoring and neglecting quantities lying outside of a certain range has been adopted in the differential calculus. The calculator throws out all the "infinitesimals" of the quantities he is considering. He treats them (under certain rules) as if they did not exist. In themselves they exist perfectly all the while; but they are as if they did not exist for the purposes of his calculation. Just so an astronomer, in dealing with the tidal movements of the ocean, takes no account of the waves made by the wind, or by the pressure of all the steamers which day and night are moving their thousands of tons upon its surface. Just so the marksman, in sighting his rifle, allows for the motion of the wind but not for the equally real motion of the earth and solar system. Just so a business man's punctuality may overlook an error of five minutes, while a physicist, measuring the velocity of light, must count each thousandth of a second.
>
> There are, in short, *different cycles of operation* in nature; different departments, so to speak, relatively independent of one another, so that what goes on at any moment in one may be compatible with almost any condition of things at the same time in the next. The mould on the biscuit in the storeroom of a man-of-war vegetates in absolute indifference to the nationality of the flag, the direction of the voyage, the weather, and the human dramas that may go on on board; and a mycologist may study it in complete abstraction from all these larger details. Only by so studying it, in fact, is there any chance of the mental concentration by which alone he may hope to learn something of its nature. On the other hand, the captain who in manoeuvring the vessel through a naval fight should think it necessary to bring the mouldy biscuit into his calculations would very likely lose the battle by reason of the excessive "thoroughness" of his mind.[36]

Being able to distinguish the important from the trivial situationally has always been of greatest importance; on the web, where the two are no longer distinguishable by effort, even more so, which is one of the reasons that a new educational paradigm, a new type of training that teaches one to evaluate significance on a basis other than relative effort compared to result, is going to be extremely important for the future.

This skill is somewhat different from what Gladwell identifies as thin-slicing or the ability to judge quickly and accurately on limited data:

> Thin-slicing is not an exotic gift. It is a central part of what it means to be human. We thin-slice whenever we meet a new person or have to make sense of something quickly or encounter a novel situation. We thin-slice because we have to, and we come to rely on that ability because there are lots of hidden fists out there, lots of situations where careful attention to the details of a very thin slice, even for no more than a second or two, can tell us an awful lot.[37]

Yet the two—thin-slicing and the ability to identify the particular importance of the precision of a quantity of data—are often confused through the ease and speed of internet search and information retrieval, mistaking what the computer can do for what humans do. This also leads to the mistaking of thin-slicing results for those of plodding research and consideration—at least in the realm of results. Of course, the intellectual process behind what James wrote is a great deal more laborious than the speedy evaluation that is at the heart of what Gladwell discusses in his book *Blink*. One can jump to conclusions, but verifying them can take a great deal of effort and time.

One of the reasons internet searches can seem to imitate thin-slicing is that the web consists of networked networks, the information upon it often also working as indexed indexes. This is why an understanding the distinction between data and metadata (to move James's discussion to modern terminology) becomes critical to understanding the internet. Tony Hey and Anne Trefethen explain:

> Metadata is data about data. We are all familiar with metadata in the form of catalogues, indices and directories. Librarians work with books that have a metadata "schema" containing information such as Title, Author, Publisher and Date of Publication at the minimum. On the World Wide Web, most web pages are coded in HTML. This "HyperText Mark-up Language" contains instructions as to the appearance of the page—size of headings and so on—as well as hyperlinks to other web pages. Recently the "eXtensible Mark-up Language" XML has been agreed by the W3C standards body. The mark-up language XML allows web pages and other documents to be tagged with computer-readable metadata. The XML tags give some information about the structure and type of data contained in the document rather than just instructions as to presentation. For example, XML tags could be used to give an electronic version of the book schema given above.

More generally, information consists of semantic tags applied to data. Metadata consists of semantically tagged data that are used to describe data. Metadata can be organized in a schema and implemented as attributes in a database. Information within a digital data set can be annotated using a mark-up language. The semantically tagged data can then be extracted and a collection of metadata attributes assembled, organized by a schema and stored in a database.

The quality of the metadata describing the data is important. We can construct search engines to extract meaningful information from the metadata that is annotated in documents stored in electronic form. Clearly, the quality of the search engine so constructed will only be as good as the metadata that it references.[38]

Metadata as a schema, again, reflects back to James's image of the astronomer looking at the entire ocean, not just the waves. It is also the basis of new types of research in the humanities advocated by people like Franco Moretti who focuses, as the title of his book *Graphs, Maps, Trees* suggests, on three types of metadata. He writes that "graphs, maps, and trees place the literary field literally in front of our eyes—and show us how little we know about it."[39] Moretti sees this as an expansion of the field of literary studies—and he is right, but the problem is that it is possible to concentrate so much on the metadata that data get ignored, replacing one limitation with another. This is another danger of the internet: because of our own limitations, the web can help one keep from seeing the trees for the forest, and even in arenas of study far beyond literature.

It's been interesting to see the growing reliance on the web happening without considering what we are moving aside for it; more and more often we do now look at the aggregate, forgetting the individual piece of information. What this will lead to isn't yet clear. Reliance on print reduced cultural emphasis and applause for memorization, of course, for print made much more data available without memorization than ever could be provided through it. What will web conferencing, email, chat, and so on, in replacing face-to-face discussion, also send to the junk pile? Could it be conversation itself? That really would be a loss. Even McLuhan, one of the foremost theorists of mass media and communications of his time, recognized that, in many ways, talking is at the core of invention, something Stephen Johnson, in *Where Good Ideas Come From: The Natural History of Innovation,* has been pointing out with vigor much more recently. McLuhan wrote:

the habits of the business community in demanding conference and discussion as the swift way of establishing insight into method and procedure in various specialized branches of business—these have prompted the new reliance on speech as a means of discovery. It is significant, for example, that the atomic physicists found that only by daily, face-to-face association could they get on with their tasks during the past war [WW II].[40]

The focus on the internet has taken attention away from the other, non-technological tools of invention and creation, many coming to believe that the new tools can replace the old rather than simply augmenting them, as Moretti suggests.

Theodor Adorno, a philosopher associated with the Frankfurt school of neo-Marxist social critics, was on track toward describing the encompassing (meta) nature of the internet long before it ever appeared, seeing the connectivity of media in a way that some other theorists of his time missed, making it analogous to the vision of the human mental structures imagined by (particularly Freudian) analysts:

> Probably all the various levels in mass media involve *all* the mechanisms of consciousness and unconsciousness stressed by psychoanalysis. The difference between the surface content, the overt message of televised material, and its hidden meaning is generally marked and rather clear-cut. The rigid superimposition of various layers probably is one of the features by which mass media are distinguishable from the integrated products of autonomous mass media are distinguishable from the integrated products of autonomous are, where they various layers are much more thoroughly fused. The full effect of the material on the spectator cannot be studied without consideration of the hidden meaning in conjunction with the overt one, and it is precisely this interplay of various layers which has hitherto been neglected. Whether the conscious or the unconscious message of our material is more important is hard to predict and can be evaluated only after careful analysis.[41]

The internet, so much the wide web of public imagination, also has all the depth of the deepest psyche, also something that we have yet to really adequately explore—for the most part. Certainly, as Katherine Hayles writes, the "intuitive leap made by [anthropologist Gregory] Bateson in concluding that the internal world of subjective experience is a metaphor for the external world"can help us understand the internet as well.[42] Taking the analogy with the human psyche a step further, Wilson extends it to evolution, an extremely intriguing idea in relationship to the internet, especially in light of the discussion in Chapter 1:

> In my opinion the key to the emergence of civilization is *hypertrophy,* the extreme growth of pre-existing structures. Like the teeth of the baby

elephant that lengthen into tusks, and the cranial bones of the male elk that sprout into astonishing great antlers, the basic social responses of the hunter-gatherers have metamorphosed from relatively modest environmental adaptations into unexpectedly elaborate, even monstrous forms in more advanced societies. Yet the directions this change can take and its final products are constrained by the genetically influenced behavioral predispositions that constituted the earlier, simpler adaptations of preliterate human beings.[43]

What aspect of the human being will be accented, spurred (so to speak) into change or growth by the internet? This question, of course, is the flip side of the one about what we are losing.

It remains true that, though we imagine that the internet expands our vision, helping us see much more than we ever could, we are still limited by our physical beings, by our narrow range of physical perception. Forgetting that makes the illusion of great power through the web even more dangerous than it already is. To understand just what this means, and what Wilson means, perhaps it is worth taking a look at the how the senses of another creature work, how they are also limited, and what their particular advantages are:

> The frog does not seem to see or, at any rate, is not concerned with the detail of stationary parts of the world around him. He will starve to death surrounded by food if it is not moving. His choice of food is determined only by size and movement. He will leap to capture any object the size of an insect or worm, provided it moves like one. He can be fooled easily not only by a bit of dangled meat but by any moving small object. . . . He does remember a moving thing providing it stays within his field of vision and he is not distracted.[44]

There are, of course, also limits to human senses and to the means of understanding perceptions within the brain, just as with the frog: "the eye speaks to the brain in a language already highly organized and interpreted, instead of transmitting some more or less accurate copy of the distribution of light to the receptors."[45] The frog, like the human, has evolved in response to an extremely specific environment.

One problem in understanding information arises from the vagaries and differences of conceptual frameworks. We tend, for example, to think of information as a *thing,* even though it does not act like a thing. In other words, it cannot be examined or manipulated—*used*—quite as we use things. Instead, it is a process, a dynamic that incorporates *things* as storage devices. In this way, it is more like a living being (see Chapter 1, again) than a mechanical manifestation of data. Hayles describes Humberto Maturana's view that "living systems operate within the boundaries of an organization that closes in on itself and leaves the world on the outside."[46] If so, and if the analogy holds, the same is true for information and for the internet.

With Francisco Varela, Maturana wrote on autopoiesis, or self-making. Hayles writes that, through autopoiesis, "Each living system thus constructs its environment through the 'domain of interactions' made possible by its autopoietic organization. What lies outside that domain does not exist for that system."[47] What the frog cannot see does not exist—until, of course, the hand suddenly grabs it. Its brain and senses have evolved in concert with a specific environment, one where the human hand, until very recently, did not exist. One where the human ability to problem solve and predict frog behavior was irrelevant. One so closed that a new outside observer can operate almost without consequence on the system the frog has previously maintained. Hayles quotes Maturana and Varela's claim that the "fundamental cognitive operation that an observer performs is the operation of distinction."[48] And only necessary distinction. The frog, itself an observer, can only perceive or distinguish what has developed as the frog's necessity, a composition of need and possibility, of being and environment. As Hayles explains, a "composite unity's organization is the complex web of all possible relationships that can be realized by the autopoietic processes as they interact with one another. . . [Maturana] intends *organization* to denote the relations actually instantiated by the autopoietic unity's circular processes. Structure, by contrast, is the particular instantiation that a composite unity enacts at a particular moment."[49] The coupling of an organism and its environment is therefore structural: "All living organisms must be structurally coupled to their environments to continue living; humans, for example, have to breathe air, drink water, eat food."[50]

Significantly, autopoietic systems do not develop under the eye of an observer, something that complicates any attempt to observe or explain them, for doing so imposes structures from outside, at least in description, and also changes development. Hayles writes that, in "the autopoietic account, there are no messages circulating in feedback loops, nor are there even any genetic codes. These are abstractions invented by the observer to explain what is seen."[51] She continues by quoting Maturana:

> A living system is not a goal-directed system; it is, like the nervous system, a stable state-determined and strictly deterministic system closed on

itself and modulated by interactions not specified by its conduct. These modulations, however, are apparent as modulations only for the observer who beholds the organism or the nervous system externally, from his own conceptual (*descriptive*) perspective, as lying in an environment and as elements of his domain of interations.[52]

To overcome the problem of contained systems' actual interconnectivity:

> Maturana introduces the term *allopoietic*. Whereas autopoietic unities have as their only goal the continuing production of their autopoiesis, allopoietic unities have as their goal something other than producing their organization. When I drive my car, its functioning is subordinated to the goals I set for it. Instead of the pistons using their energy to repair themselves, for example, they use their energy to turn the drive shaft so that I can get to the store. I function autopoietically, but the car functions allopoietically.[53]

Most of us would first tend to think of the internet as an allopoietic system, something applied to the goals of another (the user). However, considering it as autopoietic may perhaps prove more useful in our attempts to make us smarter in our interactions with the web. We are part of the environment making up the internet's structural coupling; we are part of what the internet needs to react to in its own evolution. Realization of this adds a new level of complexity to the broader problem here, and that lies in the choosing of what will go on online and in what order. Any choice creates a hierarchy as well as affecting the system and its future; the earlier perhaps getting more notice and more use and, then, even more notice, the system adapting as time goes on—the hierarchy established by inattention. A similar problem faces those restoring old films: Is it legitimate to restore one before another? Does the simple fact of what has been restored distort the vision of the value of each film? Does it, ultimately, change the film, making the restored version not a reflection of the original but a new entity evolved from the original?

Without consideration of questions such as this, without looking seriously at what scholars like Hayles are suggesting, we become as static (in one sense) as the restored film, changed and able to present the illusion of change through a showing, but no more an actor in our own drama than is the image of a star on celluloid. We may become like the car that Hayles is driving in the quote above, a system, yes, but one controlled by outside forces and not from within (itself, in Maturana's view, limited enough already). Our lives may no longer be our own but the environment of an evolving structure of, ironically, our own initial design. Shades of Stanley Kubrick's *2001: A Space Odyssey* and HAL.

All of this may remind us once again of Lippmann, who wrote:

> There is a indeed a dreaming quality in life: moved as it is from within by unconscious desires and habits, and from without by the brute forces of climate and soil and wind and tide. There are stretches in every day when we have no sense of ourselves at all. . .
>
> When we cultivate reflection by watching ourselves and the world outside, the thing we call science begins. We draw the hidden into the light of consciousness, record it, compare phases of it, note its history, experiment, reflect on error, and we find that our conscious life is no longer a trivial iridescence, but a professively powerful way of domesticating the brute.
>
> This is what mastery means: the substitution of conscious intention for unconscious striving. Civilization, it seems to me, is just this constant effort to introduce plan where there has been clash, and purpose into the jungles of disordered growth. But to shape the world nearer to the heart's desire requires a knowledge of the heart's desire and of the world. You cannot throw yourself blindly against unknown facts and trust to luck that the result will be satisfactory.[54]

In terms of the internet and Maturana, mastery also means recognition of one's position in an autopoietic relationship with the web, with us being not master but environment (in terms of the internet-as-being). And it means understanding human allopoietic positions as users of the web. Then, we will not be blind and mastered by our own technologies but will see and, maybe, master.

Though we might also see the internet as a great equalizer, providing power to many through the knowledge it offers, it is just as likely to be seen by those who wish to consolidate power as a tool for their efforts to upend political balance in their favor, just as it is seen by those wishing to circumvent state (or established) power and control for their own ends, as Wikipedia attempts, as do the Arab Spring and Occupy Wall Street protesters. As in the past, knowledge is power, but in a new fashion where there are differentiations in knowledge, as in metadata and data, this can lead to different types of control, of power over information in manners well beyond mere censorship. Hayles's car may be powerful, but she is more so when behind the wheel—a distinction that many who use the internet today do not understand but that politicians, more and more, do. The naïve feel that access to data is the equivalent of an understanding of metadata and operations of systems. The savvy can manipulate that understanding, though they are doing so, unfortunately, not always for the best ends.

In a democracy, as Richard Hofstadter writes, our long-term distrust of those able to manipulate information and power leads to the peculiar state where:

> we are opposed almost by instinct to the divorce of knowledge from power, but we are also opposed, out of our modern convictions, to their union. This was not always the case: the great intellectuals of pagan antiquity, the doctors of the medieval universities, the scholars of the Renaissance, the philosophers of the Enlightenment, sought for the conjunction of knowledge and power and accepted its risks without optimism or naïveté. They hoped that knowledge would in fact be broadened by a conjunction with power, just as power might be civilized by its connection with knowledge. . . Today knowledge and power are differentiated functions. When power resorts to knowledge, as it increasingly must, it looks not for intellect, considered as a freely speculative and critical function, but for expertise, for something that will serve its needs.[55]

The irony is that this expertise can only lead to limited use of power. A frog may have a powerful tongue, but its impact is limited. Perhaps a particular expertise will seem universal and complete at the moment, but soon it will be undermined by the systems that continue to evolve through and around it. Without the greater knowledge of systems, one may be a powerful frog, but one will remain a frog and nothing more, completely vulnerable to forces from outside the realm of past experience.

The expertise Hofstadter mentions is analogous to that of a film editor, one working with material created elsewhere through which one can, if skillful enough, create the illusion of new information. This, of course, is part of what has come to be called "spin," or the manipulation of the perception of information for, generally, political purposes. This is another aspect of the internet as an extension of the advertising age, back where we started this chapter. All of what we have discussed here, even if it does move away from direct discussion of advertising and the internet, does go back to that. Advertising is a system and one pumping blood through the internet, keeping it alive. It affects us just as we affect it, the symbiotic relationship as strong as any other between humans and their machines.

When we are able to understand the impact of advertising on us, how it moves us from any illusion of our position as rational consumers, we will start to comprehend just how powerful this new tool, the internet, really is. It is possible to argue that given knowledge of the position and purpose of the writer or editor or producer, one can discount the "spin" in a story or the manipulation in an advertisement and judge it on what does lie behind, on the reality being manipulated. Henry Jenkins writes:

> Spin is in some ways a product of television culture. In the old days, it oc-curred without much fanfare, and much of the public didn't know that every interviewee was pushing a predesigned agenda. In more recent elections, the news media has focused enormous attention on the spin process—even as campaigns have more systematically coordinated their talking points. The public has been educated about the ways spin works. The process of crafting and spinning messages has become a central part of the drama on shows such as *The West Wing* (1999) or *Spin City* (1996). As spin is publicly acknowledged, the two campaigns dismiss each other's spin for what it is—an attempt to shape the meanings of events to their partisan advantages.[56]

That may well seem to be, but Jenkins does not take his discussion to the next level here, considering the impact of education about spin on those doing the spinning, not just on their audience. If things are being spun, and people know this, then they can be spun around the knowledge of the spin-ning. An evolution commences, and where it will end is anyone's guess.

It would be much easier to predict the future of the web were we, each of us, not also responsible for our own personal spin. Unfortunately, though, as George Orwell wrote:

> we are all capable of believing things which we *know* to be untrue, and then, when we are finally proved wrong, impudently twisting the facts so as to show that we were right. Intellectually, it is possible to carry on this process for an indefinite time: the only check on it is that sooner or later a false be-lief bumps up against solid reality, usually on a battlefield.[57]

But even the battlefield rarely does slow spin more than temporarily.

Yeats liked to see history as a gyre, another type of spin, returning to the same spot but widened. With all change comes, Yeats seems to have believed, a good dollop of "the same." So, no matter how much of an in-telligence may develop out of our machines, no matter if they do attain a level of self-awareness, no matter if they influence us as much as we do them, there remains—and will remain for a long time—functional truth in what the father of cybernetics, Norbert Weiner, had written:

> The machine will still be literal-minded on its highest level, and will do what we have told it to do rather than what we want it to do and what we imagine we have told it to do. Here we dig into the moral problems which earlier generations have faced on the level of magic. W. W. Jacob's story

The Monkey's Paw, Goethe's poem *The Magician's Apprentice*, and the Arabian Nights legend of the fisherman and the genie call this matter to our attention. The Monkey's Paw gets its owner a small fortune at the cost of the mangling of his son in the machinery of the factory in which he works. The Magician's Apprentice has learned the words by which the broomstick was made to tech water but has not yet learned the words to stop it. The genie in the bottle, once it has been released by the fisherman, has a will of its own which is bent on his destruction. These tales of imagination cease to be tales of imagination once we have actually made working agencies which go beyond the complete comprehension of those who have constructed them. There is nothing which will automatically make the automatic factory work for human good, unless we have determined this human good in advance and have so-constructed the factory as to contribute to it. If our sole orders to the factory are for an increase in production, without regard to the possible aspects of this new and vast productivity and without regard to the problems of unemployment and of the redistribution of human labor, there is no self-working principle of *laissez-faire* which will make those orders redound to our benefit and even prevent them from contribution to our own destruction.[58]

Anyone who forgets this does so at his own peril. Machines may take on lives of their own, but they are also still machines. The internet operates, yes, within a much wider framework than merely its machines and connections, within a network that not even Facebook can rival—or ever will, for that matter. Still, though what we have today isn't an effective or real artificial intelligence (as the previous chapter also suggests), it certainly is quite a bit different from what Weiner envisioned as the literal-minded machine. In some respects, as we have seen in previous chapters, the internet may now represent a symbiosis between human and artificial intelligences. But it is still, at its core, mechanical, though we should no longer think of it as simply so, for it is also becoming something else. We cannot forget this any more than we can forget the machine base, not if we are going to approach our technological milieu with savvy.

SIX

The Fault of Epimetheus

In October of 2008, during the peak of the U.S. financial crisis, an opinion piece by Richard Dooling, author of *Rapture for the Geeks: When AI Outsmarts IQ,* appeared in the *New York Times.* Dooling's article drew attention not to the complex financial instruments that Wall Street traders and hedge fund managers used to fuel the real estate bubble, but to the process by which those instruments had been developed. When the discussion involves words and phrases such as "mortgage-backed securities" and "derivatives," that language often appears in close proximity to "Wall Street talent" and "greed," not "computer-generated," "Darwin," or "evolutionary algorithms." While the nation was cackling over the Fed, the bailout, and Main Street, here was an article asking us to shift our attention from the trust the American people put in the financial industry to the trust the financial industry puts in the intelligence of computers.

Dooling explains that the people he lovingly calls "The Wall Street Geeks" when he is being cute or "quantitative analysts" (aka "quants") at other times, used computer algorithms (aka "algo trading")—not their own creativity—to make vast networks of wealth through bundling derivatives of mortgage-backed securities insured by credit default swaps, none of which we now know were safe investments but were packaged for no other reason than the attempt to create more wealth for the wealthy without anyone taking the risk.[1]

Wealth, it turns out, is not really solely a function of accumulating more money. It is actually quite like information. As historian of technology George Dyson explains, wealth is a function "of the velocity with which money is moved around," a condition that has had the effect of leading people to realize "that money, like information but unlike material objects, can be made to exist in more than one place at a single time."[2]

Dooling explained that traders don't really know themselves how the derivatives of the bundled securities actually worked but left that up to the computers. Making a bold claim, he wrote: "No one understands default obligations and derivatives, except perhaps Mr. Buffett and the computer who created them."[3] Don't get confused concerning the role of Warren Buffett; Dooling is being cagey here. What Dooling means is not that Buffett created derivatives, but that he understood them—as a negative force to the economy, calling them "weapons of financial mass destruction." The only ones who understood the true nature and specifics of the investments and cause for the crises were the machines themselves, and yet, even here there is an interesting wrinkle—the machines didn't understand them at all. How could they? Since the machines are not conscious or reflective (not yet, anyway), they know not what they do. If they did, then maybe we would have a chance for them to communicate that information to us. What the machines *do* know is how to execute algorithms, and it is by these algorithms that the U.S. economy swam—and sank.

Dooling writes:

> Somehow the genius quants—the best and brightest geeks Wall Street firms could buy—fed $1 trillion in subprime mortgage debt into their supercomputers, added some derivatives, massaged the arrangements with computer algorithms and—poof!—created $62 trillion in imaginary wealth. It's not much of a stretch to imagine that all of that imaginary wealth is locked up somewhere inside the computers.[4]

The key to all of this may be contained in an interesting statement made by Dyson: "The problem starts, as the current crises demonstrated, when unregulated replication is applied to money itself. Highly complex computer-generated financial instruments (known as derivatives) are being produced, not from natural factors of production or other goods, but purely from other financial instruments."[5]

Like all complex adaptive systems, the financial sector is highly decentralized. Because the wealthy have successfully lobbied, bought, bribed, and corrupted almost anyone or any agency that they have come into contact with since Carter left office with the promise of making more money, the U.S. economic system is also highly deregulated. Because of increased technologization and resulting globalization, corporations are able to hire labor of all kinds, from unskilled workers to neuroscientists across the globe at cheaper salaries than would be possible in the United States. Because cultures are healthier and a sense of community fabric is more tightly woven, education is stronger in other parts of the world. America, the world gossips, is soft. Haven't you heard?

However, while America is no longer a powerhouse producer, it is still able to compete because of economic globalization. Those few American-owned companies that actually make products are those able to bring their product to market at extremely competitive price points. Because of low labor costs, goods and services are able to be bought and sold in the United States at extremely competitive rates, while the people at the top of those corporations make more money than ever before. Americans are expected to purchase the goods that are made in other countries, but they are considered too expensive to be the ones hired to make those goods. Unemployment rises, and insanely wealthy corporations continue to get richer because, in addition, they are considerably alleviated from paying taxes. Americans are still, unfortunately, gullible enough to buy the propaganda put forward by the wealthy stating that companies should not be taxed because they are the ones who create jobs—that by taxing them, Americans would lose work. The fact of the matter is that American manufacturers don't employ Americans. If it can be done cheaper elsewhere, then it will be. In an age of globalization, international companies will exploit those in China and India and sell their goods in America. This is a backward and unsustainable system, one where already rich people get richer and richer in the short term.

It's all part of a massive machine of decentralized and unregulated desire to create wealth, but American businessman and (the few) women working for large financial firms, while they reap all the benefits, have neither the savvy to pull it off continually, as the meltdown indicates, nor the knowledge to understand even what they were attempting to do in the first place and certainly not the talent to make it happen. They left the calculations to these so-called evolutionary algorithms, allowing evo-math, Wall Street's version of the Lower East Side's emo-punk, to fly as though algos were nothing more consequential than a new wave band. But these kids weren't Warren Buffet. Most of them weren't past the age of 30. It didn't seem to matter: so long as the computer created massive amounts of wealth by making 10 cents leverage like 100 dollars, evo-algos were making everyone rich. The Fed. Bernanke. Paulson. Obama. Directly or indirectly. All that glitters was gold. Evo-kids, their algorithms, BlackBerrys, and Macs were buying a stairway to heaven. It made you wonder.

Until 2008.

Much is to be made from the point that the financial industry has given over too much information to the machines. Dooling writes:

> we are still fearful, superstitious and all-too-human creatures. At times, we forget the magnitude of the havoc we can wreak by off-loading our minds onto super-intelligent machines, that is, until they run away from us, like mad sorcerers' apprentices, and drag us up to the precipice for a look into the abyss. As the financial experts all over the world use machines to un-wind Gordian knots of financial arrangements so complex that only machines can make—"derive"—and trade them, we have to wonder: Are we living in a bad sci-fi movie? Is the Matrix made of credit default swaps?[6]

Powerful stuff. The key point, of course, is not even that traders used mathematical algorithms to create bad investments. The issue is that the computer-generated financial instruments had been (and were being) generated by other computer-generated financial instruments. Dooling, for his part, gets quite alarmed by the situation, declaring that we have entered an age where the intelligence of machines have taken over human intelligence to the point where we allow machines to govern our financial lives. This is quite an ironic statement but also quite scary. It is not as though we have allowed computers to control our philosophy so they could determine the morality and ethics of our lives, but we have allowed machines to control our financial lives: the very portion of life that ideally creates enough surplus to make philosophy, art, and other noble pursuits possible. For Dooling, the idea that computer-generated financial instruments are the architects of the derivatives and trading practices that sent the U.S. economy spiraling is proof enough that we have left the most important decisions to machines. While some may want to focus more on the traders, Fed, policy, or greed, the trust given to financial algorithms whose sole purpose is to "make magic happen," by making money appear in more than one place at a given time, should give us serious pause.

When Dooling launches into high-flying alarmist concern, it would serve us well to recognize that Kevin Kelly may have missed this one, that the machines (innocent as they may still be) may have a desire, a want, a *zoe* different from our own.

This chapter considers three perspectives concerning the telematics of the internet as they relate to participatory culture. We look at three writers and some of their influences: Malcolm Gladwell, Clay Shirky and, to a lesser extent, Jaron Lanier. While the second two are often grouped with the so-called social media gurus, Malcolm Gladwell, in light of his well-known *New Yorker* article "Small Change: Why the Revolution Will Not be Tweeted," is considered an opponent.

The purpose of this chapter is not to argue along the lines of any of these writers. We are not interested here in who is most convincing or who wins the war or even who wins the battle. Are the telematics of the internet good or bad? Do we have better ways of organizing information? Is the culture of sharing and exposing creating problems that we are not prepared for? These are all important questions, and we will consider them as they come up in due course through this chapter. But the fact of the matter is that the ecology of network culture is a self-generating, self-perpetuating force that will continue to unfold according to its own logics.

The only way for possibly changing course is to appeal to the engineers and designers of internet technologies, to convince them to create designs and new technologies that embody and encourage a particular ethic that will help bring out the best in the human being. Ultimately, however, even though the writers we discuss here all have significantly different points of views and projects, we want to point out a particular commonplace in their orientations of how to think about social media and participatory culture.

An underlying assumption guiding all three writers is the way they see the relationship between the human and the technology. That is, they see technologies primarily as tools and, since they do, they posit the human in a position of master over technology. We want to draw your attention to this positioning for one essential reason: as long as writers as influential and wide read as Gladwell, Lanier, and Shirky continue to propagate a view of technology that fails to see that the human has a parasitic and symbiotic relationship to technology in a way that is, and has always been, fundamental to the ontological condition of the human (that is, the very nature of being human), then we will continue to live in a way where the technologies that are created by engineers and designers will determine our behaviors and our situation while we tell ourselves untruths. People using the internet will simply continue to think that they are the ones in control of the technologies. As we go on to explain, every technology embodies an ethic, a tendency. Each technology implies a value. These values, in turn, give shape and meaning to who we are as human beings because they give shape and meaning to what we do and how we behave.

If it will soon be possible to get the internet through contact lenses, then there is a value that is implied by that device. This value is a natural extension of the developmental progress of the internet, one that increases the mediation between us and our exposure to the world around us. But what about the technologies that imply values other than virtualization? What technologies exist that bring us closer into touch with the world around us?

We will also look at the underpinnings of collective intelligence in this chapter. If, in a previous chapter we studied the difference between collective intelligence as it belongs to the hive mind and looked at how collective intelligence applies differently to humans, we now look a little further at how these so-called knowledge communities function to create another kind of intelligence. We will come to see that in quite a contrast to Kevin Kelly and the swarm logic that dominates a considerable portion of the social media utopians, such logic, as the above example shows, buckles under its own weight on the internet. We will argue that to have a more productive relationship with technology, then a reorientation to the way we conceive of the human's relationship to technology must occur in the mainstream intellectual climate. We must begin to see that in contradistinction to Lanier's *You are Not a Gadget,* that we, in fact, are our gadgets and that we always have been—whether those gadgets are our iPods, our nail guns, or the word itself. Each technology, like every word, can be seen to have a denotation (its definition or its function) as well as a connotation (its value or its implication). Too long have we operated on the assumption that tools are singular units, apart from humans, that we pick up and put down at will. Tools are also part of a culture and ecology. As such, each tool influences its environment and extends itself outward towards those things it touches. We use the tool, but we too are transformed by that tool. In order to have a productive relationship with the technologies we use, these values and their implications need to be accounted for in technological designs.

This is the biggest hope that we might have toward steering our technological culture in a beneficial way.

Are computers supposed to be having such a negative effect that they can send an economy spiraling out of control? Was it supposed to be like this? Weren't the machines supposed to make things *better*?

Evolutionary algorithms are computational programs that belong to the domain known as evolutionary computation, itself an area of the computational intelligence aspect of artificial intelligence. Computer scientists working in computational intelligence pursue the ability for computers to mimic the evolutionary processes that are part of complex adaptive systems. These algorithms simulate reproduction and evolution in order to solve problems that humans are not capable of solving.

According to scientist and futurist Ray Kurzweil:

The list of ways computers can now exceed human capabilities is rapidly growing. Moreover, the once narrow applications of computer intelligence are gradually broadening in one type of activity after another. For example, computers are diagnosing electrocardiograms and medical images, flying and landing airplanes, controlling the tactical decisions of automated weapons, making credit and financial decisions, and being given responsibility for many other tasks that used to require human intelligence.[7]

Dooling's outrage is fueled by this very procedure, specifically of the use by evolutionary algorithms to create wealth in an unstable economy. They use models of replication, reproduction, and fitness found in nature to solve problems that have specific answers. If the problem we want to solve is how to generate more money trading derivatives and hedging risk, then the computational algorithm will seek to solve that problem. It will not take into consideration the stability of the underlying commodity or the sustainability of the financial instrument in comparison to the long-term health of the market. Given this, according to Dooling, the financial crisis is evidence that evolutionary computation may spell disaster. For Kurzweil, on the other hand, the day the machines completely surpass humanity (the so-called singularity) will be a happy day—mankind will finally free himself of his debilitated trapped condition of living inside a human body unfit for extended life and a brain unable to tap its potential because of the slowness of its computational ability. Which will prove out?

In presenting the differences between collective intelligence and human collective intelligence, the question being pursued in Chapter 3 was to ask whether participatory culture should be considered collective intelligence. We looked at the differences between intelligent systems as they apply to human collective intelligence and as they applied to natural systems. We saw that the conditions for intelligence are substantially different. The above example of the financial crises is a case in point in how the computational algorithms of artificially created complex systems can have devastating effects. The year 2008 was an interesting one not only because of the financial crisis but also because this was the breakout year for social media; this was the year YouTube had 10 percent of all internet traffic[8]; the year Facebook surpassed MySpace in terms of unique monthly worldwide visitors to become the largest social media site[9]; the year that Twitter exploded with a 752 percent growth[10]; and, of course, the year that social media helped put Barack Obama, the first African American president, into office.

In looking at the financial situation and the explosion of social media in 2008, one can clearly see two different kinds of intelligences at work. As our earlier analysis showed in comparing the wisdom of human crowds versus the wisdom of nonhuman ones, the emergent intelligence of complex systems would appear to work with greater chances of success than human group intelligence because humans would be eliminated from the situation. But humans were not eliminated from the financial crisis; they just weren't part of the system. The algorithms were supposed to work to create wealth that humans could benefit from, but the human element was not accounted for in the whole of the algorithm. What happened was the condition necessary for making complex systems work—allelo-mimesis. Copy your neighbors. If there is enough diversity in the situation, then more will be different, but that does not mean (as social media theorists contend) that more is *always* different. As we showed in Chapter 3, when insufficient diversity is present, copying your neighbors leads to a cascade—just like ants in a circular mill, walking until they drop dead just because that's what the ant in front of them is doing. If one jumps off a bridge, they all jump off a bridge. Financial bubbles are built from the elements of complex adaptive systems going wrong. Part of the reason for wanting to determine the difference between intelligence at work in natural systems and intelligence at work in human systems is for just the reason that when nonhuman intelligent organizations are applied to human situations, the chances are high that they will fail miserably—just as the financial meltdown indicates.

In the past 10 to 20 years, quite a number of advocates have heralded the liberations that come with the internet. The systems of communications during the pre-internet days certainly had their problems; and the underground, almost hacker-like qualities of some of the discussion boards of the early internet painted a much different picture than the spirit of conformity prevalent today. As Barlow pointed out in the first installment of this trilogy, the establishing mythology of the early internet concentrated on taking power from broadcast media and putting it into the hands of citizens. Speaking of the rise of blogs, Barlow wrote, "the news media in America is in peril. Technology has shown that it can be replaced. The news profession will have to do something to prove its worth, or citizen journalists and another will, one day, take over its place."[11]

While this threat has not disappeared, a new set of problems has been revealed. Part of the work of political strategists of the past was uncovering aspects of private life that belonged to political opponents, in order to create a scandal; but with the rise of social media, a considerable portion of the bottom feeders' job seems to take care of itself. Today, the news media have become quite adept at picking up on the inherent dangers associated with life in the network. If journalist bloggers used to threaten news organizations with a rigorous attention to reporting, political leaders now sabotage themselves by posting lascivious photos on social networking sites, and all big media need to do is report it.

We should ask what kind of collective intelligence is embedded in social media and participatory culture? Is it similar to the intelligence of complex adaptive systems where the emergent phenomena is greater than any one of its single parts? Is it a kind of diversified, independent, and aggregated intelligence of the kind that is able to solve a problem of locating a lost submarine? Perhaps this kind of intelligence—if it can even be called that—does not necessarily *do* anything, but it does bring people together in a sometimes disorganized and haphazard way. Is social media of the likes of YouTube, Facebook, and Twitter (to name the big three) more than just a way of connecting with friends and family to share photos of the senior prom; reading Sarah Palin's most recent humdinger; or where Anthony Weiner posts pictures of his, uh, wiener? No doubt, a remarkable achievement has occurred in terms of personal convenience for millions of people since sites such as Facebook have made it possible to share information, but what does it mean when political leaders consistently post inaccurate information to Twitter feeds? What does it mean that 13-year-old children "sext" each other naked pictures of their classmates? What does it mean when college kids "out" their gay roommate by streaming a tryst over the Net? What is all of this noise, and what are we supposed to do with it?

In "Why the Revolution Will Not Be Tweeted," one of his best essays, Gladwell argues that the major difference between the so-called social media revolution and true activism, the likes of which Gladwell epitomizes in the 1960s grassroots civil rights movements, is the difference essentially between making a connection and making a commitment, or what he calls "strong ties" and "weak ties." A person who is committed to a cause will do whatever is necessary in order to effect a change in the status quo. The other kind of connection is expressed by your average "friends" on Facebook where each one might make a small commitment, so long as it's convenient and painless.

Drawing from Jennifer Acker and Andy Smith's book *The Dragonfly Effect,* a book that describes how social media can effect social change, Gladwell recounts the story of Sameer Bhatia, a young entrepreneur of South-Asian descent working in the computer industry who was diagnosed with acute myelogenous leukemia. Bhatia needed a bone marrow transplant, but no matches were found in the national registry. His colleague sent out approximately 400 emails to friends and other colleagues, asking them to forward the word to help save Sameer. Social media kicked off. Facebook, Twitter, and YouTube all became active in getting the word out. As a result, 25,000 people registered their bone marrow, and Bhatia was eventually able to find a donor.

Acker and Smith use this anecdote to show that social media helps to increase *motivation,* but Gladwell disagrees. For Gladwell, social media helps increase *participation* specifically by *decreasing* the motivation that participation typically requires. Gladwell explains that the level of commitment required to get your name on the national registry is minor: it requires merely swabbing the inside of your cheek and sending in the sample. If you happen to be the unlikely match, then donating your bone marrow requires an afternoon in the hospital for the procedure. While Gladwell admits that donating bone marrow is not a trivial matter, he is sure to make his point of the difference between doing something like donating bone marrow and staging a civil rights movement: "It doesn't involve financial or personal risk; it doesn't mean spending a summer being chased by armed men in pick-up trucks. It doesn't require that you confront socially entrenched norms and practices. In fact, it's the kind of commitment that will bring only social acknowledgment and praise."[12] Social media does not increase motivation. Rather, it is good at increasing *participation* because is decreases the motivation that you would otherwise need to participate.

Gladwell calls Shirky's *Here Comes Everybody!* the "social media bible" and goes on to recount the story with which Shirky opens his book. This is a story about a young woman who, having lost her phone in a New York City taxi, later called her number and asked the person who recovered the phone to return it; she was denied and through a series of internet-based appeals, was able to draw from the intelligence of the community in a way that eventually led to the recovery of her phone. Shirky doesn't tell the story so that the reader can see how the world can be changed by the internet; the recovery of a phone does not equal a government's overthrow. Rather, Shirky tells the story to show the potential inherent with the organizing power of people when they are asked to do things simply out of the goodness of their hearts. Those who helped the young woman recover her phone were able to do so because they were following the story from their connected online rumor mill; saw the opportunity to chip in by making a phone call or offering advice based on professional expertise (one respondent was familiar with New York police procedures); and collectively, either by offering emotional support or more specific guidance, the members of the group were each able to make minimal effort; but, because the numbers were many, they were able to make a change that Shirky claims, and Gladwell agrees, would not have been possible in pre-internet days.

But Gladwell points out that in all the hype about the power of connection on the internet, social media utopians miss out on the nature of the connection. Just like a face-to-face connection has more strength than a phone call, a phone call has more strength than an email, and so on. For Gladwell, the nature of the connection is more important than the connection itself; and, for this reason, Gladwell invests very heavily in his insight into the difference between weak ties and strong ties, claiming finally that the internet is good at solving problems that require little to no effort from those in the group: simple or low stakes problems such as the loss of someone's phone, but because the internet thrives on the weak-tie connection, it will not be able to make any significant changes on its own.

While Gladwell's argument raised a few eyebrows and stirred up healthy debate concerning the role of social media, nobody predicted that in the spring of 2011, after the humiliation and self-immolation and martyrdom of street vendor Mohamed Bouazizi, Tunisia and Egypt would overthrow their governments; Libya would break out in civil war; major unrest would stir the governments in Syria, Yemen, and Bahrain; and significant protests would take place in Algeria, Morocco, and Oman. While there is considerable debate concerning the extent to which social media served to help spread Middle East uprisings, no one denies that it played some role: protest events were announced on Facebook pages, the news of the revolt in Tunisia spread like wildfire across Middle Eastern blogs, and the Egyptian government ordered the internet shut down during the protests. Mohammed Jamjoom at CNN said that "In the case of Egypt it really played a critical factor in getting out the word on how to organize." "There was one group in Egypt that was one of the key groups in getting people out on the street. . . . Last week in a matter of days they went from 20,000 fans to 80,000 fans. . . . We can see that these sites were used in order to get the word out about how to bypass checkpoints, how to get across bridges, how to get to places where people wanted to demonstrate. So it was a critical tool in getting people out into the streets."[13] In light of these events, commentary partly in reply to Gladwell's article started to pop up across the internet as writers discussed what they were seeing and experiencing. "Gladwell was not the only deep thinker rendered ridiculous by the remarkable events of early 2011," wrote Matt Welch in *Reason* magazine.[14]

What Gladwell's article does do very well, however, is speak to the issue of convenience. No one denies that information can spread like wildfire over the networks, and the ease with which people can participate has made all the difference. If we—or Gladwell for that matter—were going to organize a rally, it would not make any sense to use pre-internet era techniques. Today's rallies, organizations, and protests require the internet, texting, phones, Facebook, Twitter, YouTube, and more. Gladwell is smart to point out that when you increase convenience, you decrease the amount of energy (motivation) that needs to be spent in order to move from doing nothing to doing something. But he makes the mistake of assuming that while social media only *requires* small levels of commitment, that it will be used only when people have little to no commitment.

This isn't splitting hairs. It's a fairly large difference. If you were going to throw a party of over 200 people, you wouldn't visit each one to invite them. Sending out invitations or calling them on the phone would require less effort than paying each one a personal visit, but choosing the more efficient option would not mean that you were not committed.

The major flaw is that the article is overly simplistic by setting up what amounts to a false dualism. On the one hand, Gladwell suggests, are people and their strong connections. Civil rights protests were possible because people risked life and limb and yet—because they were committed—organized 70,000 students across multiple Southern states "without email, texting, Facebook, or Twitter."[15] These organizations were made up of people, and they required truly committed individuals who believed in the cause for equality for Americans of African descent.

On the other hand are technologies and their weak connections. Those who type out their names on web petitions to "Save the Whales," click "Like" on a Darfur Facebook page, or hit "Send" on prewritten emails to their lawmakers don't exhibit any significant commitment. Such actions are generated by the technology that makes it so easy for people to become involved that they would never have become involved were it not for the convenience. Because their involvement lacks personal sacrifice, it means little to nothing at all.

But the problem with Gladwell's divisions is that like many false dualisms, the divisions cannot be qualified or quantified. Furthermore, in this case, we are seeing that; they simply do not hold up.

Gladwell's argument implies a causal connection between technology and commitment, suggesting that if you use social media, you do so because it is convenient, and so you exhibit a lack of commitment. But using social media does not mean *necessarily* that a weak connection is present, though it may be. People have strong connections to their family members, and they use social media with them more than with anyone else. You have a strong connection to the people coming to your party, but you order invitations rather than paying each one a visit.

To say that one uses social media is not sufficient to also say that one's ties are weak. What's new about social media is that it creates a level between no commitment and a strong commitment, and so it allows first for the possibility of weak ties and second for the proliferation of them. To be a senator and to receive 5,000 emails from constituents that all say the same thing is something quite different from receiving 15 letters from constituents that all say something different. Not only does social media allow for the proliferation of weak ties, but it supports and reinforces strong connections; and it can, under some circumstances, *generate* strong connections and even bona fide real friends. Gladwell doesn't explore these issues, and neither does he address the most obvious function of social media—the way that it seems to have primarily been used in the Middle East protests—as a means for delivering information. You might just make a Facebook page announcing your party. In fact, although everyday use of Facebook, Twitter, texting, and YouTube may very well proliferate and feed the narcissism and churlishness that haunts America when little is at stake, in actual times of crisis, few tools may be as important.

Underlying Gladwell's point is a deeper assumption, one that plays off of the technology/human split. Unlike the dualism that Gladwell sets up, the divide between technology and the human is a much stronger dualism with quite a bit at stake. There are various ways the relationship between the human and the technological can be approached—and there are even some discourses in a generalized area of research called the *posthuman* where that split can be resolved, both theoretically and practically. A considerable number of people currently live a posthuman life, for instance, and cybernetic professor Kevin Warwick has had chips implanted into his body on numerous occasions that have allowed him to experiment being part machine by allowing him to transmit signals with his brain. Amputees are quickly becoming the modern cyborgs, using very high-tech machines such as myoelectric arms that as Amanda Booher, an English professor specializing in the area of biotechnology, explains, allows them to "communicate directly with nerve impulses in the body."[16]

As we have already mentioned, Ray Kurzweil sees the hybridization between human and machine to be the literal and actual course that future that homo sapiens will take. Reading Kurzweil is a blast from the future, but it is less fiction than it is hypothesis about what is *likely* to happen based on what is *actually* happening now. Quite a number of other thinkers come to mind: Donna Haraway, Katherine Hayles, Manual De Landa, and Bernard Stiegler, among others. There are networks of discourses concerning the posthuman in the sciences and the humanities, but Gladwell is not interested in exploring the way the human is changed by the interactions with machines. Gladwell is more interested in establishing how humans are and have been able to function without computers.

When Gladwell published his piece in the *New Yorker* he was being timely, responding to the current intellectual climate by offering a welcome point of view outside that of the so-called social media utopians. Advocates for social media, people such as Shirky, Chris Anderson, Henry Jenkins, and Howard Rheingold were beginning to dominate the mainstream intellectual discourse on social media. However, Gladwell and his publishers could not have foreseen the role social media would come to play in the Arab Spring. In retrospect, while Gladwell's article contains a few strong points, Gladwell and his supporters such as Evgeny Morozov, author of *The Net Delusion,* have been placed in the unfortunate position of having to defend even its weaknesses.

As a number of people have argued, there has been a considerable amount of hype surrounding the contribution that social media played in the Middle East uprisings; and so, if Gladwell were to have written that article today, it would likely gain considerable strength by incorporating, measuring, and comparing the hype and the actual impact social media played in the protests. Being able to investigate the role that social media played would have helped Gladwell build an essay that might have contributed substantially to the discourses on the impact that social media is having on cultural life rather than offering a point of view that dismisses internet communication as practically irrelevant for anything of social importance.

For decades, science fiction writers and philosophers of technology have speculated and feared the increasing mediation and virtualization of our connections to the earth and to each other, so Gladwell's unstated apprehension is most understandable. Gladwell wants people to connect with people and not to be overmediated. He believes that the technology is getting in the way, and he correctly recognizes that when people see the convenience of communicating via Twitter and other similar platforms, communications that are largely *asynchronous,* then the strong connections that people have to each other will be substituted by weak connections, a condition that leads rapidly to increasing mediation and virtualization, substituting virtual life and virtual relationships for "real" relationships and connections.

Among the plethora of prescient stories and worlds painted for us since the dawn of the industrial age, it looks like we've begun to live in an early version of the world that E. M. Forster wrote about in "The Machine Stops." Consider the following:

> She knew several thousand people, in certain directions human intercourse had advanced enormously. But when she listened into the receiver, her white face wrinkled into smiles, and she said:. . . . "Be quick, Kuno; here I am in the dark wasting my time." But it was fully fifteen seconds before the round plate that she held in her hands began to glow. . . .and she could see the image of her son, who lived on the other side of the earth, and he could see her. "I want you to come and see me." . . . . "But I can see you! she exclaimed. . . . "I see something like you. . . but I do not see you. I hear something like you. . . but I do not hear you. . . I want to see you not through the Machine," said Kuno.[17]

Pondering the relationship between the internet and the world created by Forster at the beginning of the internet but after the publication of Kevin Kelly's *Out of Control,* internet critic Mark Slouka wrote:

> Today, the technologists use that very metaphor to describe the interlinked hive nature of the Net. (The cover of Kevin Kelly's book *Out of Control,* for example, features drones flying from an apartment building in which each window/cell is a computer screen.) Seventy years ago, Forster wrote: "Under the seas, beneath the roots of mountains, ran the wires through which they saw and heard." Today, the prophecy has been fulfilled. Our "wired planet," Kevin Kelly notes, is rapidly becoming "a torrent of bits circulating in a clear shell of glass fiberes, databases, and input devices." . . . .Forster's fiction describes an incremental apocalypse; increasingly enervated, impatient, and irritable, humanity entrusts everything to the machine. And the machine stops. In our lifetimes, it's just getting started.[18]

That was in 1996. Thirteen years later, in 2009, with the internet well into the 2.0 era, professor of philosophy Hubert Dreyfus recognized in his interpretation of Forster's short story what Marshall McLuhan said decades ago: that "artists are the antenna of the human race." Dreyfus wrote:

> Artists see far ahead of their time. Thus, just after the turn of the last century, E. M. Forster envisioned and deplored an age in which people would be able to sit in their rooms all their lives, keeping in touch with the world electronically. Now we have almost arrived at this stage of our culture. We can keep up with the latest events in the universe, shop, do research,

communicate with our family, friends, and colleagues, meet new people, play games, and control remote robots all without leaving our rooms. When we are engaged in such activities, our bodies seem irrelevant and our minds seem to be present wherever our interest takes us.[19]

Quite a number of others, including Jaron Lanier, inventor of virtual reality in the 1980s, could be quoted in order to illustrate how prescient Forster's story was. There is no shortage of those who fear the oncoming moment where we will live in small compartments, increase our Facebook friends into the tens of thousands, doing everything from the comfort of our little home universes. There is a value implied in such a life, and it is easy to see that increasing virtualization and physical isolation begins with relationships. Humans are social animals as much as they are technological animals, and when our technological inventions substitute the connections we make with other members of our species, it is easy to see how concern might set in and how arguments might be made to suggest that these technologies, no matter how ubiquitous, addictive, and seductive they are, have little consequence on our daily lives—or don't have to have consequences—if we don't want them to. Thus, Gladwell's argument that social media tools really don't matter after all. In comparison to human-to-human connections, the weak connections made by social media cannot compare, so nothing of consequence is likely to result from them. From this point of view, Twitter and Facebook are much to click about nothing.

"Social media utopian" has become a recent buzz phrase. Clay Shirky, author of *Here Comes Everybody!* and his more recent *Cognitive Surplus,* has argued that there is an intelligence at work in social media that is unprecedented and more powerful than anything that has been witnessed before. You can't become as popular as Shirky without receiving your fair share of critics. In a ribbing that Shirky was glad to get, Gladwell called Shirky's first book "the social media bible."[20] There couldn't be two people on further sides of the participatory culture divide, and yet they still both hold the same basic assumptions about the human's relationship with technology to be true.

For Shirky, Web 2.0 technologies encourage participatory culture primarily by giving us the opportunity to share things that could not have been shared in the past. Shirky offers the example of the Mermaid Parade that takes place in Coney Island each summer in June. The parade is a celebration of eclectic weirdness where people paint and dress themselves, their cars, their dogs, and each other in scantily-clad costumes honoring creatures from the sea. Shirky's point is that before the popular photo-sharing site known as Flickr, there was no way to see the photos that people took of the parade. In addition to being able to upload and post them on the internet for all to see, the ability to "tag" your photos opened the possibility that photos carrying the same tag but uploaded by very different people would connect and categorize tens or hundreds of photos coming from very different sources under the same heading. The same reasoning has led to the use of the "hashtag" (#identifier) on Twitter. As a result, before Flickr, many people took photos of the Mermaid Parade, to be sure, but they remained private or, in the 1.0 days of the web, they might have been uploaded to a server and then hand coded in someone's personalized web page.

If someone had the idea of bringing together a large number of photos from different photographers, this would have created a whole set of logistical requirements. Such an event would have to be organized; professional photographers would have to be hired, paid, and sent to the event. Their photos would have to be processed, published, and aggregated—all of this requiring many hours of labor and significant amounts of overhead. With Flickr, the photographs simply appeared, organized under the same headings and publicly available. Spontaneous events, such as the tornadoes that hit Joplin, Missouri, and swept through Alabama in the spring of 2011; the London train bombing in 2005; or the Japan earthquake-tsunami also in 2011, would have gone uncovered and unreported until crews could be assembled and reporters dispatched. Reporters and photographers would eventually cover the stories in the aftermath, but no significant information would be made available until a significant amount of time had passed. Shirky suggests that no matter how seasoned, even the best journalist can't take the place of an amateur videographer looking straight into the vortex of a tornado.

This narrative, however, should not be accepted too readily. Just as in the case where using social media to communicate planned events for social and political uprising puts tools into the hands of those who need them, so too are cameras in the hands of amateurs crucial to helping the necessary agencies and organizations bring help and/or relief to situations when it is needed. But one should not confuse times where social media is an essential tool with times when it is not. Being able to upload photos to Flickr or use YouTube in similar ways—at times when spreading that information is essential—is not enough to make a determination that the technology is beneficial. Not only does the mainstream literature on telematics, from Shirky to Gladwell to Lanier and on and on, fail to make the distinction that differing technologies imply different values, it also fails to make the distinction that different values are often appropriate to, and thereby contingent upon, different situations.

Shirky and others fail to make the simple distinction that certain tools are best for certain situations, believing that participatory culture services like Flickr and YouTube can be a positive cultural force, as a rule and without question. These services allow us to connect easily with each other and to share. The crucial issue here, however, lies in the need or the desire that these technologies help us to realize. For Gladwell, humans have basic social desires for strong connections. Simply because social media thrive on weak ties and are overly convenient does not mean they are meeting a basic human need. Likewise, for Shirky, humans have basic social desires for *sharing*. As a species, apparently, humans like to share—photos, music, stories, information, videos, and, as too many male politicians and athletes have let us know, other things as well. For Shirky, social media sites, then, help us realize human potential. Shirky explains:

> The essential advantage created by new social tools has been labeled "ridiculously easy group-forming" by the social scientist Seb Paquet. Our recent communications networks—the internet and mobile phones—are a platform for group forming, and many of the tools build for those networks, from mailing lists to camera-phones, take that fact for granted and extend it in various way. Ridiculously easy group-forming matters because the desire to be part of a group that shares, cooperates, or acts in concert is a basic human instinct that has always been constrained by transaction costs. Now that group-forming has gone from hard to ridiculously easy, we are seeing an explosion of experiments with new groups and new kinds of groups.[21]

Again, we return to the motif that we saw with Gladwell. Both he and Shirky agree that humans share certain desires and instincts; what they disagree about is the role technology should play in helping people meet those desires. In both cases, then, we see another instrumentalist view of technology. We are here. We have our instincts and our desires. The technology is there, outside of us. Does it help us to meet our desires? Either it does, as Shirky says; or it does not, as Gladwell says. In both cases, what's central is whether the human need is being met by the technology itself. From such a perspective, desire flows in a single direction, out from the human and into the technology: a technology that is neutral, just simply waiting to be used. A tool.

In Chapter 1, we discussed the desire of *zoe*: of a nonhuman, nonorganic desire, a self-perpetuating force that expresses itself differently according to different modes or situations. In this view, desire exhibits a tendency because it has a value, one that is part of its design. Shirky claims that Flickr allows us to tap into our need for sharing that has always been a basic human instinct. That is certainly an uncomplicated, positive way of looking at it. Consider, however, Jean Twenge and Keith Campbell's investigation in *The Narcissism Epidemic* concerning how social media affects the young:

> Web 2.0 and cultural narcissism work as a feedback loop, with narcissistic people seeking out ways to promote themselves on the Web and those same websites encouraging narcissism even among the more humble. The name "MySpace" is no coincidence. The slogan of YouTube is "Broadcast Yourself." The name "Facebook" is just right, with its nuance of seeing and being seen, preferably looking as attractive as possible. In December 2006, *Time* magazine officially made *you*—yes *you*—their Person of the Year for promoting Web 2.0. So: the founders of Google, LonelyGirl15, the nutty guys with the Mentos and Diet Coke, and *you* are responsible for the success of the internet. The cover came complete with a mirror, allowing you to gaze at yourself and think about how important you were for blogging about your lousy day at work and buying a vintage T-shirt on eBay. . . . In her eye-opening book *Generation MySpace,* high school teacher Candice Kelsey lists four messages young people absorb from social networking sites like MySpace and Facebook:
>
> 1. I Must Be Entertained All the Time
> 2. If You've Got it, Flaunt It
> 3. Success Means Being a Consumer
> 4. Happiness is a Glamorous Adult (with adulthood defined primarily in terms of sexuality)

Twenge and Campbell go on to quote a university student:

> "Sure, our generation seems more into ourselves than ever before, but that is from an older (and outsider) perspective," wrote a University of Michigan student in 2008. Previous generations weren't given the same tools as us. We can't be blamed for growing upon a time when outlets (MySpace, Facebook, blogging . . .) were created specifically for us to talk about ourselves."[22]

Shirky, of course, isn't one of these young people. Being from an older generation, he might just miss the idea that sharing is oftentimes really just about telling others to "look at me." Using the search function in Google

Books, a search for the word *narcissistic* and its variants in Shirky's *Here Comes Everybody!* yields just one result. In this single hit, Shirky actually accused "old media" newspapers of suffering from narcissism, explaining that the profession exhibited a "sort of narcissistic bias."[23] A search for the word *share* and its variants, however, yields 89 results. Twenge and Campbell help us to realize what everyone pretty much already knows and already accepts: what goes by sharing is oftentimes just showing off.

The problem is not that Web 2.0 technologies such as Flickr, YouTube, Twitter, and others allow photos, videos, and other information to be easily aggregated and shared; the problem is with the claim that these technologies express a positive value *all the time.* In certain situations, during political unrest, natural disasters, and other kinds of trouble, these technologies shine as beacons. But, because all media now converge on the computer, there has become a fine line between working, goofing off, disseminating crucial information, creating art, and showing off how cool you are by posting a picture of your new shoes that generates 75 comments.

Of course, it's true that people are not required to act narcissistically, yet they do. They could be sharing things that matter, and the tools will allow them to do so. It's not necessary to contribute to a narcissistic culture, yet many do. Shirky would say that doing so is a basic human instinct. But do such social media utopians delude themselves by saying that acting narcissistically is actually sharing, and that doing so is a positive cultural force? In a recent speech, Shirky made the point that a person who does what one might call "wasting their time," on the internet actually has positive cultural value. His reasoning was that a person who does nothing better or more creative than making pictures of lolcats and posting them up on the web, an activity he says can be seen as "the stupidest possible creative act," is still "doing a creative act." He goes on to explain that doing something is better than doing nothing. A person who does nothing by making a lolcat has already made the transition from doing nothing to doing something, that there is a range of quality in a so-called creative act, where making something entertaining like a lolcat is on the one end of the spectrum and writing a brilliant treatise or finding a cure for cancer is on the other end. A person, Shirky reasons, can create something within this entire spectrum, that creative acts don't have to be good, but what is of the highest value is that they do *something* rather than nothing because the difference between doing poorly and doing something well is smaller than the difference between doing nothing and doing something.[24]

That's it. That's Shirky's argument for his second book, *Cognitive Surplus.* To be sure, there is more in the book than that, but that's the heart of the argument. Such a proposition doesn't require much of a response. In fact, words in the spirit of Jon Stewart will do. As a response, one might say, "Hmm. It sounds like Mr. Shirky is appealing to our common sense, that he is using an argument that most of us would agree to—that is, until you think about it for about five seconds!" What's a creative act? One could easily appeal to the underbelly of what might be called a creative act by referring to the negative acts that have occurred through the internet. Of course there are the many sensationalist sex scandals involving pictures and videos of politicians, athletes, and celebrities. But then there are the more solemn examples involving children or suicide.

According to The Cisco Visual Networking Index, more than 91 percent of the web's global consumer traffic will be video by 2014. Aside from the so-called creative acts of lolcats, what are the implications of this transition that will be taking place concerning participatory video? Recent phenomena involve numerous incidents of tragic consequences; each one of them that could fit into Shirky's discussion of creativity. Of particular importance is the phenomenon of exposure, a phenomenon easily grasped by considering the story of Tyler Clementi, a Rutgers student who committed suicide in September 2010 after his roommate broadcasted a video of him engaged in a homosexual act.

Technologists Langdon Winner, Sven Birkerts, and others have argued that the ubiquity of technology collapses the usual distinctions between public and private life. Video culture speeds this collapse, and more needs to be done than to question how lolcats could show "signs of human progress." Rather, our best technology thinkers, Clay Shirky and people like him, should interrogate issues such as what are the ethical implications that result when people's lives are exposed to a video culture that can often be mean spirited and ruthlessly public. Our culture has not yet begun to grasp how or why these acts of exposure lead to generalized acts of cruelty to one's self and others.

Much of the existing work on participatory culture lauds its ability to create civic change for the positive, but the picture is more complex. Consider the following four examples:

First is a project that YouTube critic Sarah Arroyo is working on, the case of Alexandra Wallace, a UCLA college student who uploaded an anti-Asian rant on YouTube called "Asians in the Library." This video reveals not only the risks of digital delivery but also how participatory culture can often fire back with a troubling and provocative fervor of its own. Wallace's video served as a catalyst for hurtling racist views into an online culture that was ready to respond, remix, and provoke, as evident in parodies like comedian Jimmy Wong's wildly popular song "Ching Chong." The embarrassment Wallace suffered: endless responses; parodies; and name calling, including a video that the president of the university made and published to the online community where he apologized for Wallace's actions while disassociating himself and the rest of the UCLA community from her, led Wallace to eventually leave school and go into hiding.

Second, another example currently being explored by Robert Leston, one of the authors of this book, is the case of Tyler Clementi, a promising Rutgers University college student who, in 2010, jumped off the George Washington Bridge because his roommate showed a video of him having a sexual encounter with another man. Or consider another case, also being explored by Leston, that of Abraham Biggs. Biggs, a 19-year old man, committed suicide live on camera while 1,500 people watched. Drawing from work on "being exposed" forwarded by rhetorician Diane Davis, Leston argues that these acts of violence need to be addressed in our mainstream literature of participatory culture, not lolcats. It is crucial that in this new age, we come up with methods of helping each other deal with the consequences of being publicly exposed.

Third, consider another project that social media critic Sherrin Francis is working on, a project she titles "My Name is Evan Emory. My Classroom Video Turned into a Felony Sex Charge." This project examines public servants who deliberately expose parts of their private lives through YouTube. In these instances, the exposure opens a gateway into uncomfortable territories that are ignored by most social media critics. Evan Emory is a Michigan youth who was charged with manufacturing child pornography for splicing together a children's performance with sexually explicit lyrics. Such a case raises serious questions about the relationship between YouTube culture and legal consequences as well as the limits of parody.

Lastly, consider Geof Carter's project where teacher Donald Wood suffered viral infamy when his outburst in front of his high school class was posted to YouTube, a standout among "angry teacher" posts. In addition to raising questions about classroom surveillance, Wood's rage connects to the public taste for tantrums as exemplified in the 2009 documentary, *Winnebago Man*. This portrait of Jack Rebney, a victim of a viral VHS tape that surfaced during some commercials he shot during the late '80s shows not only the long-term consequences of video, it also paradoxically suggests that sometimes, through overexposure, something good can emerge.

At the time of this writing, these projects are currently being pursued for an upcoming conference presentation and being developed into an essay that could eventually turn into a full-length book. Unlike much work in participatory culture, they expose the "underbelly" of social media and show just how large the stakes can be when the bells and whistles stop and the internet is considered in a rigorous, critical way.

THE FAULT OF EPIMETHEUS

In a paper at the College Composition and Communication national conference in Atlanta in 2011, Jason Helms, a professor of rhetoric and communications, reminded his audience that the human has the same origin as the technological. In presenting his lecture, Helms drew from Bernard Stiegler's *Technics and Time: The Myth of Epimetheus.* Most of us are familiar with the story of Prometheus, who stole fire from Apollo's sun chariot and gave it to humans. But it was Epimetheus, the brother of Prometheus, who set this development into motion. Whereas Pro-metheus means forethought, Epi-metheus means afterthought. The two titans have often been seen to act as representatives for the lower creatures, and they were both given the responsibility of giving a positive trait to each animal, including humans. But by the time Epimetheus was to give humans their special quality, he had already given out all the traits, and there was nothing left to give. In order to compensate for his brother's mistake, Prometheus gave humans the gift of fire, the gift of technology.

But the ironic part, as should be clear, is that this gift of technology was not incorporated into the being of the human. Where the snake had venom or camouflage, the predator both tooth and claw, the human is weak and slow footed and unable to defend itself at birth. For Martin Heidegger, the word that is used in *Being and Time* and throughout his career to designate the human who is concerned with his being: that is, the ontological condition of what it is and what it means to be, is *Dasein. Dasein* is the human undertaking the investigation into being. When we are concerned with ontology, then we are *Dasein.* The word *exist* has an interesting origin. *Ex,* to be outside of. *Sist* comes from the Latin *sistare,* which means to stand. To exist means to stand outside. To be is to be external to, outside of, to stand outside of ourselves. Our being is defined by our externality to ourselves. Drawing from Stiegler, Helms explains:

> This is our curse: we are always already in need of prostheses, tools with which to enable ourselves. "Man invents, discovers, finds, imagines, and

realizes what he imagines: prosthesis, expedients. A pros-thesis is what is placed in front, that is, what is outside, outside what is placed in front of. However, if what is outside constitutes the very being of what it lies outside of, then this being is *outside itself.* In order to make up for the fault of Epimetheus, Prometheus gives humans the present of putting them outside of themselves." At a certain point in prehistory, evolution moved out, from the biological to the technological. Since then humans have been defined as external to themselves. Dasein ek-sists.

We are in turn propped up by these false limbs, in fact defined by them. Humankind's dependence upon prostheses, its inherent externality, results not just from our beginnings but from our modes of living. To be is to be outside oneself: to "ek-sist." As a result that which makes us human, *technology*, is forgotten. Forgetting becomes part of our humanity. Forgetting how we define technology creates a situation in which technology defines us.[25]

Step 1: To be is to be defined by our tools. Our tools exist outside of ourselves; but at the same time, they are our being, defining who we are and our very *ability* to live. Step 2: We forget that we are defined by our tools. In *The Parmenides,* Heidegger explains that the Greek word for truth is *alethia.* It is a rather interesting word, particularly because the root of the word, *lethe,* means to forget. The prefix *a,* what is known in linguistics as the privative-*a,* is added to adjectives and nouns to designate negation. The force of the word *alethia* that is translated positively as truth has, as its root, to forget. Truth literally means unforgetting. While we might quickly replace this word with remembering, doing so loses the quality of the positive force of the word. The positive force is to forget, to conceal. What this suggests is that the normal course of things is a propensity and a tendency to forget. Truth is a matter of grabbing onto what is forgotten and wresting it back from oblivion. Heidegger writes, "Therefore it could be that an invisible cloud of forgetting itself, the oblivion of Being, hangs over the whole sphere of the earth. . . a cloud which is forgotten not this or that being but Being itself."[26] This oblivion conceals not because of the cognitive failure to remember but by a concealment that perpetually withdraws.

On the one hand we have Dasein, who is defined by *ex-sistare,* to stand outside of oneself. We are outside of ourselves because we are defined by technology that is outside of ourselves. On the second hand, our being also moves in the pattern of perpetual concealment. To remember is to pull events back from their natural course. We forget that we are defined by our technology, and as Helms writes, "forgetting how we define technology creates a situation in which technology defines us."

DO ARTIFACTS HAVE A POLITICS?

The tendency to forget how technology defines who we are makes all the difference in the world. Why we forget, since it is the normal course, is understandable; but once we are made aware that we should remember our relationship with technology, then it becomes a responsibility to ourselves and to each other. As long as we continue to forget, an instrumentalist orientation to technology will dominate. Over 30 years ago, Langdon Winner famously brought up this issue. Oh my, how we continue to forget!

> To our accustomed way of thinking, technologies are seen as neutral tools that can be used well or poorly, for good, evil, or something in between. But we usually do not stop to inquire whether a given device might have been designed and built in such a way that it produces a set of consequences logically and temporally *prior* to any of its professed uses. Robert Moses's bridges, after all, were used to carry automobiles from one point to another; McCormick's machines were used to make metal castings; both technologies, however, encompassed purposes far beyond their immediate use. If our moral and political language for evaluating technology includes only categories having to do with tools and uses, if it does not include attention to the meaning of the designs and arrangements of our artifacts, then we will be blinded to much that is intellectually and practically crucial.[27]

We suffer—our discourses and our intellectual progress suffers—by the failure to make the appropriate distinctions between whether a technology is beneficial or harmful. Different moments in time require different responses, and technologies are the media that give shape to the response; but they also give shape to who we are and who we might hope to become. Technologies have values, and these values are expressed in their designs. And the value of a technology, though we often don't think of it in this way, is expressed in us. More important than the denotation of the word is the connotative function of the word. We have long recognized that words can do damage, but we have not generally recognized the connotative functions of technologies. That's what Winner is talking about.

Shirky has a point that participatory culture encourages sharing, but Shirky, we are afraid, keeps the instrumentalist perspective toward the technology alive. It's a tool to be used. It can be used positively and negatively. This is the most common way of thinking. But how might this tool be used, what kind of use does the design of this tool encourage? A bridge may be a way to move cars from one place to another, but it is also a target to drop a bomb. Today's participatory culture technologies have incredible potential, but not only is that potential wasted by promoting narcissism, it actually can do significant damage, even to the point where people kill themselves as a result. On the other hand, oftentimes there are great goods that can come from it. Many possibilities are open, but technologies can be designed that promote a healthier, better culture. But it is up to the designers, and so it is also up to us to write books where we encourage designers to create better designs and to become designers ourselves, such as Douglas Rushkoff discusses in his revealing book *Program or be Programmed*. We could ask what would happen if the 500 million people on Facebook used their energy to solve the world's problems? But a better question would be what if Facebook had been *designed* so they would?

SEVEN

Education Amid the Digital Revolution

"This is one of the disadvantages of wine: it makes a man mistake words for thought." Samuel Johnson's epigram could be transformed, today, to "This is one of the disadvantages of the Internet: it makes people mistake words for thought." Words without thought? That shouldn't be possible—any more than, say, information without education. Each pair is completely intertwined. Words derive from thought, and thought requires words. Information is educating; education is informing, the strengths and weaknesses of each notwithstanding. We've all seen drunks babbling, word and thought disconnected. Just so, as cultural critic Neil Postman said 20 years ago, "we have directed all of our energies and intelligence to inventing machinery that does nothing but increase the supply of information. As a consequence, our defenses against information glut have broken down; our information immune system is inoperable. We don't know how to filter it out; we don't know how to reduce it; we don't know to use it."[1] Why? Because we haven't educated ourselves to it. As a result, we babble like Johnson's drunk.

When we try to talk about the place of information in society—about how society's relation to information is changing—we are also talking about the place of education in society, about how society's relation to education is changing. If not, we are discussing only a part of the picture, skewing our conclusions and sounding inebriated. Unfortunately, this is almost always the case.

Information is simply inert material until it has an intelligence (even a mechanical intelligence) interpreting it, reading it. This intelligence necessarily brings some sort of education (or programming) to the task and continues this education through the process of interaction with the information and with the interface between it and the user. But there is a problem with this: there is, of course, bad education just as there is bad information. As philosopher and mathematician Bertrand Russell has written, "We may say, generally, that what commonly passes as knowledge is not all equally certain, and that, when analysis into premisses has been effected, the degree of certainty of any consequence of the premisses will depend upon that of the most doubtful premiss employed in proving this consequence."[2]

In the 1990s, at about the same time as the internet was beginning to make its influence felt in the broader culture, American schools were renewing emphasis on standardized testing as a means of evaluating education, culminating (in the next decade) in the No Child Left Behind push of the Bush administration and, after that, Obama's Race to the Top. Both of these initiatives presuppose the idea of education as quantifiable, static, and transferable. That is, they rank success in education by measurable results based on established standards that should be attainable in all situations (that should be transferable and replicable). They reduce education to information.

Historian of education Diane Ravitch, once a supporter of the Bush education policy, has become an outspoken critic of attempts to reduce decisions on education to reliance on the quantifiable. At the same time, she, and the chorus of others who have been criticizing the way testing numbers are being used against teachers and unions and in favor of things like charter schools (as is done, for example, in Davis Guggenheim's 2010 documentary *Waiting for Superman*), have perhaps missed (or ignored, maybe seeing it as outside the current debate) another critical point: the mindset established through an emphasis on testing is antithetical to effective use of the internet and other digital tools. Not only is it an inadequate way of judging educators and institutions, but it leads to a type of education that is serving students poorly as they prepare for life in the digital age. Yes, the problems of education may arise from things far from the web, but the needs of education to change to meet a digital future become more pressing each day as the internet becomes a stronger and stronger presence in all of our lives.

One person who does understand the need for substantial and fundamental change is British education specialist Sir Kenneth Robinson. In a talk sponsored by the Royal Society for the Encouragement of Arts,

Manufactures, and Commerce for his acceptance of the Benjamin Franklin Award in 2008, he asked:

> How do we educate our children to take their place in the economies of the 21st century? How do we, given that we can't anticipate what the economy will look like at the end of next week? . . . The problem is, they [educators] are trying to meet the future by doing what they did in the past. . . . The current system of education was designed and conceived and structured for a different age. It was conceived in the intellectual culture of the Enlightenment and in the economic circumstances of the Industrial Revolution. . . . There's . . . built into it a whole series of assumptions about social structure and capacity. . . . This model has caused chaos.[3]

And it continues to cause chaos, focusing debate over education on exactly the wrong things: on standards and on teachers (among other things) and not on the needs of the students and on learning. And not at all on the digital future, whatever that may prove to be. All of these standards, teachers, needs, and learning should be redefined in light of the present and the forming future before real revamping of education can even be considered. Otherwise, as Robinson says, we will continue focusing on what was and not on what should be or could be.

Indeed, though they certainly have a function, measurable standards are regressive. Speculation cannot be utilized for measurement, for it is inherently variable and, therefore, nonstandard. The same is true of personal judgment. Standards, with their false sense of stability, present the image of a rigid, unchanging world: one of absolutes, of truth, of certainty. A world unlike the one we experience or the one that we find (and create and superimpose) on the web.

One of the consequences of the contemporary quest for standards in education has been an increasing reliance on standardized tests, most of which take the form of multiple-choice exams. Unfortunately, the outward form of a search engine, its "skin," looks a lot like a multiple-choice test: a question and an array of possible answers. Though the user is the one who concocts the question (or search parameters) and not a distant test designer, the form retains this familiar aspect, perhaps leading users to assume that a correct answer exists among the "hits," much as the test taker assumes that one of the choices presented must be correct. This assumption is fraught with danger and is one of the many things that needs to be addressed (but is not) through our contemporary educational structures. It is not answers that one finds on the web but information—information that needs to be constantly evaluated, within itself and its contexts, if it is to prove useful. By assuming "correct" is but something to find, we bypass that evaluation completely.

In the future, our web browsers will likely be less dependent on the written word than they are today and will become something more like the computers of the television show *Star Trek* where one needed only preface a question with "computer" to activate the machine. Here, the answer returned can be even more dangerous, for it comes back without a menu of choices—and without any indication of the provenance of the information. It is just assumed, by Captain Kirk and Mr. Spock, that the computer is accurate—a situation potentially more fraught with danger or error than is reliance on our current search engines.

Not only do our multiple-choice tests actually hurt effective utilization of the internet, they don't work for education in general. The reasons for the failure of reliance on testing in the digital world were apparent *even before* the internet came into being. The cultural critic Jacques Barzun easily put his finger on them 50 years ago:

> Taking an objective test is simply pointing. It calls for the least effort of mind above that of keeping awake: recognition. And it is recognition without a shock, for to a veteran of twelve years old, the traditional four choices of each question fall into a soothing rhythm. No tumult of surprise followed by a rallying generalship and concentration, as in facing an essay question; no fresh unfolding of the subject under unexpected demand, but the routine sorting out of the absurd from the trivial, or the completing of dull sentences by word- or thought-clichés. No other single practice explains as fully the intellectual defects of our student up to and through graduate school than their ingrained association of knowledge and thought with the scratching down of check marks on dotted lines.[4]

The sort of dumbing down that Barzun describes has made itself felt today in the way people approach the information available to them on the internet—and with disquieting results. The debate over evolution, which has actually grown over the past several decades as a more vocal and growing percentage of Americans come to reject it, is enabled in part by the fact that a theory cannot be presented as an absolute answer but as something that itself evolves as our knowledge grows. Having become used to simple truths packaged for recognition, many people turn away from a subtle argument almost before it is proposed.

The mindset fostered by multiple-choice testing has had unexpected side effects, particularly in relation to the internet and its search engines.

That is, students have been trained to answer questions from a limited array of choices, generally four, of which one is correct. Rarely is the choice "none of the above" presented. Students work to determine the right choice through a number of strategies—if they don't already know the answer. Even with a math problem, they will eliminate answers that cannot be the one they want, leaving only those within the realm of possibility. They work backward, scratching out wrong answers rather than solving for the right one—unless they absolutely have to—using a process that only works with answers already known by the test creators and then offered. In other instances, students will decide which answer fits best with the ideas of the world that have been taught to them (original thought and ideas, of course, rarely leading to correct choices in such situations). And sometimes they will guess, especially if they have been able to eliminate an answer or two.

The tendency today is to use the strategies one has learned for determining answers on multiple-choice tests in order to choose which hit provides the answer to the question posed through keywords on a search engine. This isn't a conscious choice, of course—simply the result of habit, but it still limits the possibility for developing real knowledge through the web. Tara Brabazon argues in her screed *The University of Google* that "the popularity of Google is facilitating laziness, poor scholarship and compliant thinking,"[5] compounding the problems spawned by overreliance on multiple-choice testing. This should not be surprising, for the "cultural orientation of the search engine was engineering and mathematics, not education, library, internet or media studies,"[6] where greater use is now found. Though the first search engines were developed at universities, they were not considered as aids in education; their searches were not even thought of as research any more than flipping through a card catalog would be.

Because it can look like research and appears to help in the gaining of knowledge, the popular conception has been that the search engine is already a valuable tool for education. It may be, but it is also a dangerous tool:

> Google, and its naturalized mode of searching, encourages bad behaviour. When confronted by an open search engine, most of us will enact the ultimate of vain acts: inserting our own name into the blinking cursor. This process now has a name: googling. This is a self-absorbed action, rather than outward and reflexive process. It is not a search of the World Wide Web, but the construction of an Individual Narrow Portal.[7]

Beyond that, the very design of most contemporary search engines causes them to make choices for the user that she might not even be aware of:

Google ranks their search results via the popularity and number of links and hits to that site. . . . The links with less hits, but perhaps more critical information, are far lower on the rankings. . . . Ponder the more serious consequences when students click onto highly ideological sites that are assessed by popularity, not qualitative importance or significance. There are many other ways that this ranking could be assembled, particularly with intervention by librarians and information managers. The assumption of Google is that the popularity of sites is a validation of quality. Google is the internet equivalent of reality television: derivative, fast and shallow. In an era of the supposedly "long tail" of niche markets and plural interests, Google's top return receives 42.1 per cent of click throughs, with the second listed link gaining 11.2 per cent.[8]

As a tool for education without careful oversight of its use, Google leaves a lot to be desired. In fact, it can lead to actual harm. Former *Playboy* centerfold Jenny McCarthy, advocate for not vaccinating children because of fear of autism (based on the apparently fraudulent work of Andrew Wakefield), says she "did a lot of digging on my own, the 'University of Google' "[9] The idea that vaccinations can lead to autism, never widely accepted in scientific circles, has now been completely discredited but, in part because of McCarthy's crusade, untold numbers of children in the United States and Britain have not been vaccinated against diseases that do pose real threats. Writing in the *New York Times,* historian Michael Willrich, author of *Pox: An American History,* agrees that "thanks to the internet, a bottomless archive of misinformation, including Dr. Wakefield's debunked work, is just a few keystrokes away."[10] McCarthy alone can't be blamed for this newest vaccination hysteria.

Multiple-choice tests reflect received knowledge of some sort, within defined parameters. They fit very well with attitudes of trust in truth, in knowledge that can be established as absolute and immutable—in the fixed aspects of American foundationalism. Test results allow no room for shades of gray or for disagreement. They also place responsibility for knowledge outside of the individual, not in the results of debate and the trappings of discussion, but in authority. They change the very nature of the way we view argument and the location of truth. They replace argument with identification, what pragmatist philosopher Richard Rorty calls "rational certainty" with the confidence of belief. Rorty describes what is lost:

If. . . we think of "rational certainty" as a matter of victory in argument rather than of relation to an object known, we shall look toward our interlocutors rather than to our faculties for the explanation of the phenomenon. . . .

Our certainty will be a matter of conversation between persons, rather than a matter of interaction with nonhuman reality. So we shall not see a difference in kind between "necessary" and "contingent" truths. At most, we shall see differences in degree of ease in objecting to our beliefs. We shall, in short, . . . be looking for an airtight case rather than an unshakable foundation.[11]

We will, in other words, be looking around rather than looking for. On the other hand, when people search the web, they most often search from an unshakable foundation, seeking only confirmation for what they believe instead of development of an airtight case. The latter course, however, is dangerous: one might prove oneself wrong.

In his talk, Postman said that "School teachers. . . . will, in the long run, probably be made obsolete by television, as blacksmiths were made obsolete by the automobile."[12] This is a view still common, probably more so, as the mechanistic view of teaching has, if anything, grown. And it is being put into practice: "over 7,000 students in Miami-Dade County Public Schools [are] enrolled in a program in which core subjects are taken using computers in a classroom with no teacher. A 'facilitator' is in the room to make sure students progress. That person also deals with any technical problems."[13] This belief that teachers can be superseded by technology is one of the reasons many find it so easy to attack teachers today, and their unions—they see no danger in it, for they see no place for teachers in the world of the future. But it is teachers, and not machines, who are best able to help make digital information, for those attempting research on the web, pliable and useful.

Working together without direct intervention from a teacher, as Barzun pointed out more than a generation ago, we continue to believe that a group of people can do as well as they could under direction of an expert, a teacher, that "pooled ignorance"[14] sometimes can provide answers. For many students in Barzun's time, such attitudes came "usually, out of the parents' dim recollections, aided by a search through the *Britannica*. This collaboration is expected, though it rather contradicts the boasted invention of 'independent research.' "[15] Today, still expected, it comes from the internet. Though group work has proven an effective part of education, it cannot succeed without plan and trained oversight.

Since well before the web appeared, we were making judgments without the background necessary for making our conclusions meaningful, something that hasn't changed. Just look to today's deniers of climate change: their own arguments come more from that pooled ignorance than from knowledge.

202 Beyond the Blogosphere

"An influential 2006 congressional report that raised questions about the validity of global warming research was partly based on material copied from textbooks, Wikipedia and the writings of one of the scientists criticized in the report, plagiarism experts say."[16] Unfortunately, this is the kind of research we continue to train our students to conduct and accept—compounding the failure of our test-oriented educational system.

In his book *The Global Achievement Gap,* Tom Wagner lists seven "survival skills" that he sees as meeting the needs of employers (and citizens) in contemporary society, in this digital age. Not surprisingly, none of these include the ability to memorize and pick answers on multiple-choice tests. Not surprisingly, none of them is particularly new but have been goals of American education for generations. They are:

1. Critical thinking and problem solving;
2. Collaboration across networks and leading by influence;
3. Agility and adaptability;
4. Initiative and entrepreneurialism;
5. Effective oral and written communication;
6. Assessing and analyzing information;
7. Curiosity and imagination.[17]

Even the teaching of proprietary software tools (or of Computer Management Systems, or CMS), especially the use of such, does little to help students meet the real needs of potential employers as Wagner sees them—though such teaching is highly touted today as providing digital literacy while ignoring the more basic code levels where real digital literacy begins. This simply teaches them to be consumers of technology and not creators of it or even adapters. It teaches students to be little more than data-entry drones, but they are often fooled into thinking they are content strategists working with CMS when they have been given no understanding of the construction underlying the systems themselves and, consequently, have developed no ability to do anything but work within defined constraints. All they are doing is becoming adept with interfaces, forgetting the need to grapple intelligently with the information accessed or the meaning of access.

Though there are problems with our schools, we do know how to solve them. Wagner's list is but one of many laying out sensible goals: all useful, and all backed with methodologies that have been shown to be successful in meeting such goals. Yet we find ourselves in a peculiar position, where powerful forces in society, like Barkan's venture philanthropies, have hijacked the debate, turning it down a road that won't likely make for better education. As education blogger Adam Bessie writes, "the corporate reformers, such as Bill Gates and Michele Rhee [former Chancellor of the Washington, DC public schools]—present the public with a false choice: that there is, on the one hand, the 'status quo,' one that doesn't work, and, on the other, their 'reform' movement, which is the only pathway out of our morass of mediocrity. Unfortunately, the mainstream media has unquestioningly bought into this limited conception of educational reform."[18] As Ravitch explains it, these forces see education quite narrowly and view its failures as systemic:

> The problem is not money. Public schools already spend too much. Test scores are low because there are so many bad teachers, whose jobs are protected by powerful unions. Students drop out because the schools fail them, but they could accomplish practically anything if they were saved from bad teachers. They would get higher test scores if schools could fire more bad teachers and pay more to good ones. The only hope for the future of our society . . . is escape from public schools, especially to charter schools, which are mostly funded by the government but controlled by private organizations, many of them operating to make a profit.[19]

Instead of utilizing the skills we possess in our public school systems today—skills that could be turned toward developing a coherent and useful program for dealing with education in a digital age—they are attempting to establish a new model for education, to turn schools into profit centers with fewer of those problem causers, teachers. Unfortunately, this won't change the success rates of our schools, for it does not address the problems faced by student learners. It is not the systems or the teachers that are the problem but the expectations of the institutions from beyond.

The work necessary to teach students Wagner's skills cannot be completed by an administrative emphasis on testing or on teacher evaluation. Because of the nature of the skills themselves, the focus has to be on the student and on student (not teacher) activity. In relation to his sixth skill, assessing and analyzing information, students can't be told or shown how to do this but must be guided in learning to do it themselves. Otherwise, they are going to repeat the sloppy process used in the 2006 climate change report mentioned earlier or will find themselves in the position that author Joy Masoff was in when, on October 20, 2010, the *Washington*

Post reported that a textbook she wrote for use in Virginia claimed, in the face of the opinions of most scholars, that black soldiers fought for the Confederacy in the Civil War. "Masoff, who is not a trained historian but has written several books, said she found the information about black Confederate soldiers primarily through internet research, which turned up work by members of the Sons of Confederate Veterans."[20] Astonishingly, Masoff refused to back down when questioned about what she had written: "As controversial as it is, I stand by what I write," she said. "I am a fairly respected writer." Yet what her publisher sent the *Post* as her research links only "referred to work by Sons of the Confederate Veterans or others who contend that the fight over slavery was not the main cause of the Civil War." Masoff may be a respected writer, but she clearly lacks the credibility to give value to her standing by research based on inept use of digital resources, research that seems not far removed from looking something up in an almanac or encyclopedia and then drawing unwarranted conclusions from careless reading of even that. "Masoff said one of her sources was Ervin Jordan, a University of Virginia historian who said he has documented evidence—in the form of 19th-century newspapers and personal letters—of some African Americans fighting for the Confederacy. But in an interview, Jordan said the account in the fourth-grade textbook went far beyond what his research can support."[21]

The dangers of reliance on the web for research on blacks serving in the Confederate Army in the Civil War, in particular, are shown through a presentation given in 2005 by Jerome Handler and Michael Tuite called "Retouching History: The Modern Falsification of a Civil War Photograph."[22] The authors show that some unknown person took a photograph of Northern black troops and altered it so that they appear to be Confederate soldiers. Copies of the altered photograph were offered for sale on the web; an unwary researcher could easily mistake them for proof of something for which there is no proof at all.

Reflecting an approach to the internet where research through it is only used to verify what one already believes, Masoff clearly did not understand the weakness in her methodology. Fast and simplistic, Masoff's research must have been—and it was not that different from what students in high schools and colleges today are passing off as research for their papers, or from what many people do, when using the internet, to validate what they already believe. If our schools don't start leading students to an understanding of the weakness of such research, we will be producing graduates of little value to any future research projects, in academia or in business.

There's another underlying danger in the type of research and writing that Masoff has participated in and presented; and that is the emphasis on speed, often at the expense of accuracy. Though we have no idea what the pressures on Masoff might have been, the possibilities for quick turn-arounds presented by digital technology can make it difficult for anyone to spend the time necessary on any project for careful research and vetting. This, too, is part of a trend that started long ago, as technology began to make for less and less time between completion of the work of the re-searcher and author and actual publication. Students will have to learn to take their time on their projects, not to rush through them—as timed tests now encourage them to do.

This trend toward speed has led us to focus more on the "now" than ever before. The past becomes merely a source of justification for contempo-rary views, as may be the case in the Masoff incident, where conforming to certain current ideas about the world may have been more important than any presentation of historical accuracy. This is certainly the case in Texas where, in 2010, a Christian-Conservative dominated Board of Edu-cation accused textbook producers of whitewashing Islam, holding it to a different standard than Christianity. They claim to have found patterns "pejoratives toward Christians and superlatives toward Muslims, calling Crusaders aggressors, 'violent attackers,' or 'invaders' while euphemizing Muslim conquest of Christian lands as 'migrations' by empire builders."[23] One side or the other has taken the study of the past and replaced it with attempted justification for contemporary attitudes.

This concentration on "today" is merely an acceleration of something that has been happening for generations, now, exacerbated by digital pos-sibilities, but it continues to weaken education as a whole, just as it did when Barzun was writing *The House of Intellect* 50 years ago:

> Woe to the teacher or textbook that refuses to be up to date, either by hold-ing lessons for today or by leading up authoritatively to the events of last week. The truth is that dealing with the contemporary prepares the mind poorly for a thoughtful life, shortening judgment and distorting perspective. The contemporary, moreover, is extremely difficult to assess and teach, though dealing with it makes the teacher popular. His references to the liv-ing satisfy in students the illusion of being at last in the know.[24]

Graduate students are sometimes told not to bother with anything written more than a decade ago: if the earlier is important, it will be encapsulated in the contemporary; the contemporary, to what John Palfrey and Urs Gas-ser call the "digital native," becomes the explicit standard by which all else is judged. This is now no longer simply the fault of the teacher who ignores the past—for the teacher has no choice but to concentrate on standardized tests and measurable results—but of a society that is unable to recognize the importance of intellectual skills, which include knowledge of the past, to all who attempt to use the internet—the very skills Wagner advocates, and that we need to recognize as the necessary underpinnings of future success.

As Harvard Law School professors, Palfrey and Gasser have the opportunity to observe some of the best young students in America. They notice the processes developed by digital natives in their use of the internet:

> Digital Natives gather information through a multistep process that involves grazing, a "deep dive," and a feedback loop. They are perfecting the art of grazing through the huge amount of information that comes their way on a daily basis. Imagine an eighteen-year-old college freshman. . . . When she opens her browser, Google is her home page. It features headlines from sources that she has preselected, on topics of her choosing. She might even have plugged keywords into Google or Technorati . . . so that those services could send her alerts when relevant stories appear. She grazes all day through the news feeds that she sees on her Facebook profile.[25]

When these "grazers" want to delve more deeply, according to Palfrey and Gasser, they go to established news sites or others that also provide selected perspectives—which have gatekeepers or other interference between the grazer and any sort of raw data. This "deep dive" relies on a process "where news organizations, especially powerful and wealthy institutions—those able to afford bureaus and the like—can add the most value."[26] The "feedback loop," which consists of active response and further distribution of what the seeker has found, offering it to friends, family, and interested parties on the web (through social networking sites, through blogs, through comments, etc.). The deepest these grazers go, unfortunately, is not very deep at all:

> While grazing, the Digital Native will absorb a headline or a bit more— perhaps a paragraph—about any given story. The most important features of information in this context are speed, accessibility, and how well it has been sorted. The information is valuable insofar as it is timely, relevant, and easy to process. The fact that it can be accessed from anywhere—that Facebook news feed is channeled through a cell phone that is constantly attached to a Digital Native's body—is equally important. And the interface through which the Digital Native gets this information is more useful and attractive

the more it can enable her to sort through the vast rivers of information flowing around her all the time.[27]

Interestingly, the focus is on the process and the sources of information and not really on the digital native, who becomes something of a cipher, a taster but with no particular taste. This description of the wonders of the new information possibilities also begs questions of value and related utility. If information value is based on speed and timeliness, accessibility and relevance, and sorting and processing, then its value is removed almost totally from the information itself (only relevance and, to some degree, timeliness, relate to the information and not to its position) and, almost paradoxically, even from the grazer. This is a situation where a bit of guided learning could significantly change the digital native's relationship to the information used so cavalierly.

Unlike Masoff or the grazing digital native, any person who is comfortable with and conversant in the new digital environment will understand the weaknesses of any simple web search or of grazing—from choices of search phrases to the dangers of incomplete examination of lists of results to the limitations of the various interfaces and beyond. Such an educated person will also be aware that an answer is not somehow "out there," that the universe of the web is not complete in the way that of a multiple-choice test is assumed to be (that is, containing answers).

Web pages do not provide anything similar to the choices one marks on a Scantron form, certainly not in terms of reward or as choice. Most people do know this, but, on an emotional level, they are so used to operating within the closed systems of testing (especially within the context of education) that they carry their learned attitudes over into the wider spaces of the internet. Most people, also—like Masoff—are easily satisfied when they find, say, three websites (that, on first appearance at least, seem distinct and independent) agreeing with what the seeker was expecting to find. Most of us are, on many levels, lazy—unless forced by our own training into rigor—and we are willing to trust in the certainties we have already imagined.

Our inclination to accept what we find on the web, like our tendency to grant truth to what we read in books or newspapers, makes us vulnerable to error in judging texts. This is understandable. After all, as Walter Ong writes, "There is no way directly to refute a text. After absolutely total and devastating refutation, it says exactly the same thing as before. This is one reason why 'the book says' is popularly tantamount to 'it is true.' "[28] In a way, this is the essence of foundationalism. This is also part of the emotions behind the reading of the United States Constitution in the House of Representatives in January 2011. Putting the words into the record somehow makes them more real than otherwise (though, ironically, it was a redacted version that was read). The Constitution has also become something of an impenetrable wall for the Tea Party movement and much of the Republican party, something through which no argument can pass: "All active mass movements strive . . . to interpose a fact-proof screen between the faithful and the realities of the world. They do this by claiming that the ultimate and absolute truth is already embodied in their doctrine and that there is no truth nor certitude outside it."[29] In this, the American right has become somewhat akin to the mass movements Eric Hoffer was writing about in *The True Believer,* 60 years before the Tea Party movement emerged. "In the beginning was the Word" (John 1:1) remains extremely difficult to argue against.

The economist and sometime writer on words Stuart Chase (perhaps most famous today for being mentioned at the end of George Orwell's "Politics and the English Language") explored the problems of certitude and faith in words in his *The Tyranny of Words,* explaining at one point that "The lesson of this study is to beware of eternal certainties. There are none which the fingers of experience can verify. There is no perfect 'truth,' 'happiness,' 'Heaven,' 'peace.' To rely upon them is to feel hopeful before being betrayed. Look to the context. Find the referent. What is true about this? What is useful about that? What possibilities of survival and happiness may be found here?"[30] Orwell saw Chase as coming "near to claiming that all abstract words are meaningless,"[31] but Chase's questions remain relevant. These, unfortunately, are *not* questions raised in many classrooms or that many web users ask themselves today. Users of the internet have no patience for the betrayal that inevitably follows hope (for a time, at least) in any real research project. Trained to believe in answers, our experience with tests assures us that we can find them if we look—that they are most certainly there and only await identification. When not immediately satisfied, we often make ourselves satisfied by doing no more than reconfiguring our own words.

The truth is that the mountains of information in front of us have become so vast that not even our wandering eyes can encompass but a small part of the whole—and, in the whole of it, the answers we want might not exist. As Alexander Pope suggests in *An Essay on Criticism,* each intellectual hill topped simply reveals more beyond—higher and broader and with no end in sight: "But those attain'd, we tremble to survey / The growing Labours of the lengthen' Way." We have developed aids in negotiating

these hills, maps—our search engines—but these are now proving problematic, the way just as long as ever. The algorithms we have learned
to depend on work in ways unknown to most of us as their users—they
are maps constructed not by past human use but for and by machines.
Instead of presenting the placement of roads and landmarks from experience, these operate, one might say, through surmise—assuming pathways
and, if finding them blocked, positing alternatives. They do not serve as
maps for people and not necessarily for answers. We are, then, relying on
supposition and possibility rather than on the tried and true.

The writings of another pre-internet thinker, semiotician Charles Morris, can also help us recognize the problem we face when addressing this
aspect of the internet, the problem of making it into a viable tool whose
workings (whose maps) we can read and understand—and the dangers this
tool presents when used without careful thought and preparation—without
education in, among other things, the nature of signs (critical to understanding maps):

> Even at the level of animal behavior organisms tend to follow the lead of
> more reliable signs. This follows from the basic laws of learning, accord-
> ing to which habits are strengthened or weakened depending upon whether
> connections of stimuli are or are not accompanied by a reinforcing state of
> affairs which reduces the need of the animal. At the human level, where
> signs are themselves signified, great effort is spent to find out what signs
> are true and what reliability signs have, and the resulting knowledge about
> signs becomes an additional factor determining which signs are to be fol-
> lowed in behavior. Such knowledge is gained not only about the denotation
> of signs, but also about the adequacy with which certain signs fulfill certain
> purposes. And this knowledge, as well as knowledge about the truth and
> reliability of signs, tends to influence the adequacy of signs. For if an indi-
> vidual knows that a given sign is unreliable this knowledge will affect the
> extent to which he is subject to influence by a second individual who uses
> the sign to exert such influence.[32]

Great effort? Unfortunately it is not often there, not when people rely on
the internet. We have abandoned, for the sake of speed and ease, any of
our once-growing understanding of the unreliability of signs—or of the
idea that the web is, itself, simply signs, simply linkages with no more
strength than that classic weakest link. Perhaps partially because of our
test-taking mindset, we have come to treat all information equally, regardless of provenance. We don't want to face the task of rating it, of evaluating it in terms of other information, of studying it.

One of the offshoots of the rise of reliance on algorithmic patterns (without really taking the time to understand the particulars or the philosophies behind them) has been acceleration toward the demise on the web, of the gatekeeper and the teacher: in journalism, education, and elsewhere—a demise that is, perhaps, the cause of the problems of the bumbling internet user or researcher. Compounded by that attitude of the test taker (All I need is a quick prep course), this has also resulted from a sense of egalitarianism in approaches to the web that denies the need for education regarding it. The users, or so the advocates of the new leveling believe, can learn by doing. Information, anyway, can be sorted and explored through mechanical pathways (mistakenly believed to be nonbiased), so who needs human help there? This attitude is exacerbated by developments during the 20th century that led to something of an enforced passivity (in education and in entertainment, among other areas) on the part of many in the broader population in America, certainly, but also in the rest of the developed and, now, the developing world. A somewhat mythic passivity that the internet, certainly, has shown to be false.

The discomfort of this restive passivity did not become apparent, really, until the World Wide Web and those algorithms of its search engines (along with the lack of vertical controls) released people from the constraints of knowledge presented in books of (apparent) finality and authority and of predominately one-way electronic media. This has expanded possibilities for learning through avenues that were rarely contemplated before. But schools still stick with their reliance on limited-choice testing, on hierarchical and teacher-focused classrooms, and on the static world, though more and more students and their parents—and educators, too—are discovering that there are choices beyond those offered on the exams and are beginning to awaken to the need for a new educational paradigm.

What can be done to improve preparation for internet usage and to improve our systems of education so that they train students adequately for the digital age? The question is more difficult than it sounds for, as we have said, we have come to view the web as the ultimate level playing field, needing only personal ambition and talent brought to it for success. This view doesn't only reflect Ayn Rand but can be found in works such as Thomas Friedman's *The Earth Is Flat*. Responsibility for education, from this perspective, devolves upon the individual—for the resources are all available, as is mechanical assistance in sorting it and organizing it. Over the past decade, this attitude, this belief in a simplified version of self-reliance, though it runs back at least to Benjamin Franklin, and has become the driving force behind many uses of the internet. Coupled with a growing dissatisfaction in America with teachers and the educational system (witness the growing popularity of home schooling), many people have become emboldened enough to reject the idea that they need education at all. They can find what they need on the web themselves, they believe; all one needs is basic ability to read and to perform a Google search.

Education, in this vision, need not come from schools at all or from teachers but best arises from the individual. In a situation where so much information is so readily available, all one needs is the desire, and one can learn. The autodidact is king. Of course, it is not so simple. In fact, rather than offering a chance for real education unaided and effortless, the web often seems to be providing the opposite.

As many critics of the internet, like Clifford Stoll and Andrew Keen, have claimed, without constructing new models that reflect recognition of the problems the internet can pose, the web becomes as much of a danger as an asset—certainly in informational terms, as Americans saw quite quickly after the election of Barack Obama. The so-called birther movement of those who refused to believe that Obama is a natural-born American relied for its strength on web statements that linked one to another, giving a sense of validation to each, and on interviews and documents presented on the web that *seemed* to show proof of Kenyan origins or Hawaiian skullduggery. Little more than a diversion and an amusement in this particular case, widespread reliance on faulty information from the internet will prove increasingly hazardous unless users become more judicious and expert in their searches—something that will not happen without work and care, and without direction from outside of the individual.

Today, there is plenty of room on the internet for new types of intellectual fraud (not to mention the financial frauds that have been a web mainstay since the early 1990s—the best known being advance-fee scams where people send money in hopes of getting more). People are taking advantage not only of naïveté and lack of experience but of expectations developed through years of education as an activity based on choice (as in choice between answers on a test), not on real investigation or learning. Though there are plenty of actual frauds (in legal terms) on the web, there are many more legal intellectual frauds perpetrated on the internet. People set up websites that look legitimate, that seem to present coherent arguments, but that prove to be nothing more than attempts to promote specific agendas by skewing information (sometimes intentionally, sometimes by belief). Websites that will come up as parts of search results, buried among legitimate sites, can be used to fool the unwary—and they are.

One such is Wallbuilders.com, a panoply of information (in the form of books, videos, and the website itself) purporting to show that the United States was founded on explicitly Christian principles—that is, as a Christian nation. The site presents a document signed by Thomas Jefferson that contains "explicitly Christian language that President Thomas Jefferson chose to use in official public presidential documents."[33] While seeming to stick to the tenets of historical research by presenting an image of the document that seems to be the basis for this claim, the statement contains clear deceit—of a sort a historian would notice but that an average reader, especially one uneducated in research or already inclined to accept the conclusions the site presents, could easily miss. And that is use of the word *chose*. There is no indication, in the document or elsewhere, that Jefferson chose the wording of this document, most of which is clearly a printed form, and an international one, at that (it is dual-language: English and Dutch).

Even a president of the United States does not always choose the wording of documents signed. Someone has deliberately made the site look scholarly and professional but provides only that look, not the reality. The site ignores information that runs counter to its a priori assumptions. There is no real substance behind it—something easy enough to miss when one surfs the web without education.

Do a Google search on "Joseph Wesley Newman." On the very first page of over 600,000 hits, you have to look to the bottom before finding any link to something that doubts the claims of his energy machine—and that's to the Wikipedia article about it (itself not considered the most reliable source). The first site listed is josephnewman.com, which tells you his invention is one whose time has come (though he first came to attention for it over 20 years ago) and asks you to buy DVDs and follow links to proof (as if the efficiency of a machine could be proven on the web). A little ways down is a link to a Facebook page: "Joseph W. Newman Energy Machine—U.S. Patent Protection Petition."[34] The links on Facebook take one back to josephnewman.com. Nothing on the page immediately lets one know that a patent application for the machine was denied long ago.

In his book *Voodoo Science,* Robert Park describes how Newman's machine came to be known, through a naïve and uncritical fluff piece shown on the *CBS Evening News* on January 11, 1984. It was "the sort of story Americans love. A backwoods wizard who never finished high school makes a revolutionary scientific discovery. He is denied the fruits of his genius by a pompous scientific establishment and a patent examiner who rejects his application for a patent on 'an unlimited source of energy' without examining it, on the grounds that all alleged inventions of perpetual motion machines are refused."[35] Park, a professor of physics at the University of Maryland, goes on to say that most scientists "simply ignored Joe Newman. The prospect of someone with little education and no record of scientific accomplishment overturning the most basic laws of physics, laws that have withstood every challenge, seemed much too unlikely to bother with."[36] Finally, "God's plan, according to Newman, is to completely decentralize the production of energy. Every home, business, and far would have its own Newman Energy, producing unlimited, pollution-free energy."[37] Yet, more than a quarter of a century since its invention, the Newman device has produced nothing—nothing, that is, except a web presence and, one would assume, enough believers to keep Newman in funds.

It may be rare for anyone to really believe in something as unlikely as perpetual motion, but the internet can be used to substantiate all sorts of discredited but popular theories or conspiracies. Some of these, like doubts about who wrote Shakespeare's plays, and belief in the "truth" of the putative origins of "The Protocols of the Elders of Zion," have been around for many decades (Mark Twain having been one of the Shakespeare doubters). Because the Shakespeare question has attracted more attention by Shakespeare scholars than Newman's machine did among physicists, there's much more on the web defending Shakespeare's name than there is regarding Newman's claims: A Google search on "Who wrote Shakespeare's plays?" comes up with more websites defending the bard than questioning him—on the first page, at least (there are more than a million hits). The first of almost 150,000 hits on the Protocols conspiracy leads to a Wikipedia debunking. The second, however, brings one to the document itself—through a site called biblebelievers.org.

Attitudes toward education as conducted via the web, through both the new for-profit and more traditional educational institutions, have reinforced the idea of the teacher as, at most, a facilitator, as "the guide on the side" instead of the "sage on the stage." That the dichotomy is a false one doesn't negate its impact. The implication is that the guide works with doers, while the sage speaks to passive audiences. One problem with this is that it completely avoids questions of motivation, moving it outside the realm of teaching. It also sidesteps the question of expertise. It's not content that the guide is responsible for, simply the map providing directions to it—the interface and not the information.

A guide doesn't motivate but merely shows the way. A sage (a word choice made by advocates of facilitation, one meant to demean the traditional lecture class rather than showing it fully as flawed, yes, but playing a valuable role when not the only part of an education) only offers wisdom. A teacher, any successful teacher, both guides and offers wisdom—but also leads and motivates, something the dichotomy elides. In each case, however, one assumption does remain: that help is needed by the student—something we are losing sight of in the digital environment, where programs people use, even in education, are not seen as help but as tools, another concept completely, especially in an environment where few believe it takes training to use these tools.

If the web has opened up possibilities for communication and access to information, schools need to do so, too. They need to learn from the examples the internet sets, both good and bad: of the dangers of creating an environment where misinformation can triumph, of providing new venues that can be used for deceit as well as illumination, of allowing reduction of the level of discussion too often instead of enhancing it. They need to learn that opening access to information does not itself lead to knowledge. The egalitarianism promoted by our new online environments is all well and good, but it is not always sufficient.

There is still a need for teachers, for leaders, for exemplars. And, if their space is not filled by people who are themselves well trained and prepared, their roles will be taken on by demagogues and opportunists. David Barton, who founded WallBuilders, for example, bills himself as one whose "exhaustive research has rendered him an expert in historical and constitutional issues."[38] He claims his books are on "subjects being drawn largely from his massive library of tens of thousands of original writings from the Founding Era."[39] However, he shows no training at all in research or in effective utilization of a library. . . itself not a barrier to effective scholarship or writing, but something that should lead one to take a closer look at his methodology and purpose.

For reasons both good and bad, this sort of look at a researcher's background has become suspicious over the last few years, with many feeling leery of exclusionary, elitist results. Though Barton is untrained, one cannot conclude that he is unskilled or that his conclusions are incorrect. This very fact, however, creates a conundrum: If training can lead to establishment of hierarchy through its resulting bona fides, then training itself might be part of the problem that the internet is, in some minds, rectifying. But, without training, the likelihood is that misinformation will too often trump information, leading to chaos rather than knowledge.

An important concern for educators today, then, lies in how to train and certify without making the training and certification exclusive or exclusionary. It also lies in how to lead people to learn effective uses of the new tools without seeing them simply as tools for ratifying prior belief. The question, in a time when a huge proportion of the people who use the web come to it from a foundationalist mindset (or for some other reason come looking to the internet for confirmation of what they already know), is how does one lead people to a better mindset and methodology—and how does one justify the arrogance in claiming to know better? Because the internet exists outside of established hierarchical or educational structures, it would be extremely difficult to impose order on it from outside. Users want (and should have, quite frankly) the freedom to approach and use the web as they see fit.

How, then, do we solve the problem of the lack of gatekeepers on the internet? How do we stop abuses while still promoting freedom?

By doing what has always been necessary for successful democracy. By providing early and universal education designed to meet the needs of a people faced with an uncertain technological future. Once people have the knowledge and experience necessary for making considered and accurate judgments on what they find on the web, they will be a lot less vulnerable to fraud, self-deception (seeing only those sites we want to see), and error. Though much else may have changed in the digital age, the need and reason for education has not.

There are many ways education for the digital age could be built, but most are going to include as a basis something like the concepts Wagner lists as his survival skills. All of them, if they are going to be effective, will concentrate on the student as doer—but doer in situations created, observed, and led by an expert teacher. All of them will focus on collaboration skills and on communication. All of them will stress flexibility and will be so in their design and in the variety of their approaches. None of them will expect one teaching tool or method to be sufficient but will use curricula designed around a variety of activities with plenty of room for invention and spur-of-the-moment change.

One strategy for teaching effective utilization of the web relies on divergent thinking, which moves students from attempting to see the process of learning, researching, and writing as something more than a treasure hunt. According to Robinson, " 'Divergent Thinking' isn't the same thing as creativity. I define creativity as the process of having original ideas that have value. Divergent Thinking isn't a synonym, but it's an essential capacity for creativity. It's the ability to see lots of possible answers to a question, lots of possible ways of interpreting a question."[40] Consisting of techniques used by generations of teachers, what's important about divergent thinking for learning and for successful web use is that it, if not creative, is expansive rather than reductive or restraining. It works *from* the individual rather than *toward* a predetermined answer, relying on questions, on opening possibilities rather than eliminating them.

By its nature, divergent thinking provides no pathway, no formula; its second step is a panoply of activities, any one of which might lead to further exploration. Before that, the divergent thinker conducts a bit of self-evaluation, arraying what she or he knows and believes—and enjoys—before setting out on any research project. This both makes one aware of the constraints personality and the biases we all carry place on how we view material we find and encourages one to pursue lines of personal concern, for we all do better—and communicate better—when interested in the project. It also balances the work, keeping the focus from being too heavily on that sought by keeping an eye on the seeker, also.

Divergent thinking dovetails well with principles of investigation associated with the scientific method and with what Russell called philosophic analysis:

> We start from a body of common knowledge, which constitutes our data. On examination, the data are found to be complex, rather vague, and largely interdependent logically. By analysis we reduce them to propositions which are as nearly as possible simple and precise, and we arrange them in deductive chains, in which a certain number of initial propositions for a logical guarantee for all the rest. These initial propositions are *premisses* for the body of knowledge in question. Premisses are thus quite different from data—they are simpler, more precise, and less infected with logical redundancy.[41]

Both this and the scientific method, like divergent thinking, rely on process for learning and progress, not on command of established information.

Through a number of related activities, which could involve a personal journal, brainstorming, small group work, free writing, and mapping, the student begins to ask questions about the subject of inquiry, starting each with the student herself or himself: What do I know about the subject? How do I feel about the subject? The point of divergent-thinking techniques is that this student-focused approach to learning leads to internalization of thinking skills. The next step moves the student beyond herself or himself, leading to a process of real investigation much like Russell describes and that all good scientists know so well.

The divergent thinking concept could work efficiently for schools trying to develop Wagner's skills in its students. These skills cannot be attained through traditional classroom methods, for many of these are antithetical to the mindset necessary for successful utilization of the skills. This should not be surprising, for American education was designed for providing something completely different from that required in the digital age. According to *21st Century Skills, Education and Competitiveness: A Resource and Policy Guide*:

> beginning in the 1970s, labor input of routine cognitive and manual tasks in the U.S. economy declined and labor input of non-routine analytic and interactive tasks rose. This finding was particularly pronounced for rapidly computerizing industries. As firms take up technology, computers *substitute* for workers who perform routine tasks—but they *complement* workers who perform non-routine problem solving. . . . Hence, computerization of the workplace has raised demand for problem solving and communications tasks, such as responding to discrepancies, improving production processes, and coordinating and managing the activities of others.[42]

Here again, it's clearly not simply the ability to operate systems that should be the focus of education but how to deal with situations the systems do not encompass. The *Guide* goes on:

> All Americans, not just an elite few, need 21st century skills that will increase their marketability, employability and readiness for citizenship, such as:

- Thinking critically and making judgments about the barrage of information that comes their way every day.

- Solving complex, multidisciplinary, open-ended problems that all workers, in every kind of workplace, encounter routinely. The challenges workers face don't come in a multiple-choice format and typically don't have a single right answer.

- Creativity and entrepreneurial thinking. . . . Many of the fastest-growing jobs and emerging industries rely on workers' creative capacity—the ability to think unconventionally, question the herd, imagine new scenarios.

- Communicating and collaborating with teams of people across cultural, geographic and language boundaries.

- Making innovative use of knowledge, information and opportunities to create new services, processes and products.

- Taking charge of financial, health and civic responsibilities.[43]

None of this is new, of course, especially the last. But there are also dangers in it all, dangers Barzun pointed out rather sarcastically 50 years ago and dangers whose avoidance requires a guiding presence, a teacher:

> The best activities are of course those than bring into one "project" the entire group, for then noise and agitation can reach their educative peak. The intention, one may suppose, is to inure the young to the ways of collective journalism, though it would be supposing too much to assume that all children are destined for it. Another purpose is to make the children self-governing. They decide what to do, how to do it, and who does which part. This looks like good practice for young democrats, but all it seems to develop is a taste for committees as a substitute for work, while teaching the identity of committee meetings with undirected thought and small achievement. No pupil, for instance, is shown how to lead a committee to discover its own best opinion—a difficult feat which the teacher herself does not demonstrate.[44]

Training for democracy and training for the internet are not that different—and both require teachers' vision and a sense of order in education. Both require all of the skills that Wagner and the Partnership for 21st Century Skills advocate. And both require skills that no test-centered classroom can give and skills that need continual renewal. Both require directed learning, advice, and guidance from outside, showing what the particular individual, through his or her narrow perspective, may otherwise miss. We cannot rely on ourselves alone to learn, certainly not on what we might believe right now. As Orwell wrote even earlier than Barzun:

> To see what is in front of one's nose needs a constant struggle. One thing that helps toward it is to keep a diary, or, at any rate, to keep some kind of record of one's opinions about important events. Otherwise, when some particularly absurd belief is exploded by events, one may simply forget that one ever held it. Political predictions are usually wrong. But even when one makes a correct one, to discover *why* one was right can be very illuminating. In general, one is only right when either wish or fear coincides with reality. If one recognizes this, one cannot, of course, get rid of one's subjective feelings, but one can to some extent insulate them from one's thinking and make predictions cold-bloodedly, by the book of arithmetic.[45]

This last point is critical: Learning to separate feelings and thinking—and past belief—must be a part of any process of education, and it is not something one can figure out for oneself, for it takes an ability to face cognitive dissonances that, without necessity, we tend to elide or ignore.

Brendan Nyhan and Jason Reifler, in a study of misperceptions in politics, write that "We find that responses to corrections in mock news articles differ significantly according to subjects' ideological views. As a result, the corrections fail to reduce misperceptions for the most committed participants. Even worse, they actually strengthen misperceptions among ideological subgroups in several cases."[46] In other words, if people are not trained to recognize their own misperceptions, most won't, not even if confronted with them directly. The researchers also discovered that the "backfire effects that we found seem to provide further support for the growing literature showing that citizens engage in 'motivated reasoning.' While our experiments focused on assessing the effectiveness of corrections, the results show that direct factual contradictions can actually strengthen ideologically grounded factual beliefs."[47] The only remedy for this is effective prior education focusing on skills such as those Wagner lists, not on performance on standardized tests, which ignore (by their own structure) situations such as those Nyhan and Reifler explore.

What might a viable educational system for the digital age look like? Certainly, it would not be built on teacher-centered classrooms and evaluated solely by standardized (or other sorts of multiple-choice) tests. To meet the needs for skills such as Wagner lists, it could not pass students on simply through time or test but would need to assess progress through actual demonstration of skill acquisition.

Using a system like Benjamin Bloom's mastery technique, where students demonstrate command of discrete units before moving on to the next, each student progressing at her or his own pace, the problems of standardization and comparison can be broken up by the very fact of individual learning speed:

> Bloom . . . recognized that what was important in education was not that students should be compared, but that they should be helped to achieve the goals of the curriculum they were studying. Goal attainment rather than student comparison was what was important. The process of teaching needed to be geared towards the design of tasks that would progressively and ineluctably lead to the realization of the objectives that defined the goals of the curriculum. Mastery learning is an encomium to such a conception. The variable that needed to be addressed, as Bloom saw it, was time. It made no pedagogical sense to expect all students to take the same amount of time to achieve the same objectives. There were individual differences among students, and the important thing was to accommodate those differences in order to promote learning rather than to hold time constant and to expect some students to fail. Education was not a race. In addition, students were

allowed, indeed encouraged, to help one other. Feedback and correction were immediate.[48]

Mastery, within the context of something like the Fred Keller's Personalized System of Instruction (PSI), which combines mastery-like techniques with a panoply of other activities, including lectures and group projects, could provide a strong basis for an educational model that meets the needs of the digital age. Both of these emphasize student participation in the learning process as tutors rather than simply as learners, adding an element that the standard teacher-centered classroom generally lacks. The basic parts of PSI are:

1. Self-pacing, allowing students to move at their own rate in keeping with their abilities and other time demands;
2. Advance to the next unit only on demonstration of complete mastery of the current one;
3. Motivation through demonstrations and lectures (instead of reliance on them as information sources);
4. Utilization of written communication for teacher-student interaction;
5. Utilization of proctors, allowing for quick scoring and repeated testing, incessant tutoring, and a focus on the social aspect of learning.[49]

What's notable about PSI is its flexibility, its desire to make student learning possible in ways varied enough to meet the needs of many different types of learners:

> A student beginning a Keller course finds that the course work is divided into topics or units. In a simple case, the content of the units may correspond to chapters of the course text. At the start of a course, the student receives a printed study guide to direct his work on the first unit. Although study guides vary, a typical one introduces the unit, states objectives, suggests study procedures, and lists study questions. The student may work anywhere—including the classroom—to achieve the objectives outlined in the study guide.
>
> Before moving on to the second unit in the sequence, the student must demonstrate his mastery of the first by perfect or near-perfect performance on a short examination. He is examined on the unit only when he feels adequately prepared, and he is not penalized for failure to pass a first, second, or later examination. When the student demonstrates mastery of the first unit, he is given the study guide for the next unit.[50]

The student has a great deal of flexibility in how to approach the course. The problem with PSI, the reason it slowly disappeared after the 1970s, was that it requires a great deal of work on the part of the teacher, and it's work that is not always in the traditional place at the front of the classroom. Worse, those who did use it found that it worked best with small units and frequent tests, adding to the burden on the teacher in terms of preparation and paperwork.

What may lead to a resurgence of PSI is the increase in digital possibilities that can assist the teacher and the student in a PSI situation. Where much of the grading and test preparation once had to be done by hand, most of the work can now be automated and managed with a small percentage of the effort once required, leaving the teacher more time for the motivational and leadership duties that probably drew her or him to teaching in the first place. A strong digital component to PSI helps in other ways, too, decreasing the amount of oversight needed of student tutors and proctors and increasing development of digital skills (if the courses are well designed) on the part of the students.

Neither PSI nor the Mastery concept it encompasses are the only way effective education can be structured, but they do move learning from pattern to patterning, keeping the student the focus and allowing him a great deal of control in how the education will take shape and place—but without losing the teacher and his or her role in leadership, design, and shepherding.

As Trebor Scolz writes, "Many educators continue to resist the use of digital media in the classroom and still subscribe to what the Brazilian theorist and educator Paolo Freire called the banking model of education, which is based on teacher isolationism, top-down modes of learning, and extensive memorization. Contemporary learners are at odds with this approach and the consequences are pernicious."[51] Keller began developing his PSI in Brazil, Freire's home country, and there are certain affinities between them, though Freire is better known for describing what's wrong with educational systems while Keller tries to put something better in place. The fact that both Keller and Freire were actively developing their viewpoints in the 1960s is a telling indication that it is not just contemporary learners who have problems with the banking-model approach. The problem is an old one.

Writing in 1971, the French philosopher Roland Barthes asked his readers to:

> Imagine that I am a teacher: I speak, endlessly, in front of and for someone who remains silent. I am the person who says *I*. . . . I am the person who,

under cover of *setting out* a body of knowledge, *puts out* a discourse, *never knowing how that discourse is being received* and thus for ever forbidden the reassurance of a definitive image—even if offensive—which would *constitute me.*[52]

Though he is exploring the teacher, and not the learning, Barthes makes a point of the one-sidedness of much of what is set forward as teaching, providing one of the reasons that educators have fallen into such low repute—they cannot see how silly they sometimes look for they have become oblivious to response through a system where no response is needed or wanted, except in specific testing situations.

Though most famous for pointing out the limitations of that banking model of education and for motivating a generation of teachers to move away (perhaps too far away) from traditional models of teaching, Freire's purpose was much greater and his proposal much more extensive than simply moving the teacher from a position of continuous centrality. He wanted teachers to move away from any oppressive "imposition of their own truth."[53] To Freire, the heart of education lies in dialogue—and in a specific type of dialogue that doesn't presuppose that one previously specified truth can be found:

> Finally, true dialogue cannot exist unless the dialoguers engage in critical thinking—thinking which discerns an indivisible solidarity between the world and men and admits of no dichotomy between them—thinking which perceives reality as process, as transformation, rather than as a static entities—thinking which does not separate itself from action, but constantly immerses itself in temporality without fear of the risk involved.[54]

Real education occurs through development of active minds, not merely through receipt of information.

Real education, for the development of active minds, needs to encompass student creativity, providing room and encouragement for their own writing and exploration (necessary components of dialogue). All programs, then, need to be constructed on a flexible enough platform to allow student work to have a real impact not only on the discussion but on the very structure of their education (working through the guidance of educators, however, and not simply on their own).

In keeping with a flexible program, a flexible environment would also need to be created, replacing the rows of classrooms that our schools and colleges consist of today. Just as college dorms in the 1970s began to be remodeled from rows of rooms into suites, so could our schools be. Each suite could house a number of courses, creating learning communities each with a particular (but nonexclusive) accent. The suite for a college could contain (though it wouldn't have to) a traditional classroom space; a small, comfortable auditorium (for lectures and other performances); spaces for small-group work; a small reference library; wired carrels for individual study; writing and tutoring; offices for the teachers providing space for private discussion but at least visually open to the rest of the suite; laboratory space that can be formed and reformed for differing needs; a gallery for display of student work; and lounge areas for informal discussion. None of the suites would be dedicated to a particular department or field of study but would be determinedly cross-disciplinary in environments suited to each particular aspect of the task.

Neither students nor teachers would need to be constrained by inclusion in a particular suite but would be encouraged to move around at specified points. Students, when they have completed work in one sequence; teachers, when breaks built into the structure of the school year occur. The goal would be to structure the whole in such a way as to allow students to be able to pursue their studies in directed, though customized, fashion.

This structure would also work well with what is sometimes called the hybrid course or blended learning, courses with both an online and a face-to-face component:

> "There is no doubt that blended learning can be as effective and often more effective than a classroom," said Mr. [Michael] Moore [Pennsylvania State University education professor], who is also editor of T*he American Journal of Distance Education*. He said, however, that research and his experiences had shown that proper design and teacher instruction within the classroom were necessary. A facilitator who only monitors student progress and technical issues within virtual labs would not be categorized as part of a blended-learning model, he said. Other variables include "the maturity and sophistication of the student," he said.[55]

In fact, almost all education, today should contain the possibility for such blending but with, as Moore implies, teaching and not just facilitation (which demands too much reliance on the mechanical online aspect of learning). *Every* classroom (or educational suite) should have access to digital possibilities, and students should also be able to access class material online from home. The terms *hybrid* and *blended learning* should disappear from use, for all classes should contain them.

Because students, to succeed in their future careers, will need to be trained to meet something akin to Wagner's goals, they have to be involved in the design of their own educational program. This can be a problem, for students (naturally) don't have the skills or knowledge necessary for such design. They can, however, be eased into this responsibility through steps monitored by their teachers.

The role of the teacher would change dramatically in this new environment. No longer would any one teacher control that little kingdom—the classroom—that has for so long been the center of American education. No longer could the teacher isolate himself or herself behind office walls. Instead, the teacher would operate within a number of different physical situations, interacting with students rather than simply directing them. One day, he or she might provide a lecture, introducing students to new aspects of a field of study and providing motivation for following up with real study in that area. At another time, the teacher would be meeting with a group of more advanced students involved in tutoring: those having more difficulty in the particular subject. At another, the teacher might be reading and responding to student writing or participating in discussions with students. The teacher would be continually revising the sequence of lessons the students must master for completion of the course and would be reviewing student work; shepherding small groups; and organizing other activities, including some completely outside of the classroom and campus:

> The instructor will have as his principal responsibilities: (a) the selection of all study material used in the course; (b) the organization and the mode of presenting this material; (c) the construction of tests and examinations; and (d) the final evaluation of each student's progress. It will be his duty, also, to provide lectures, demonstrations, and discussion opportunities for all students who have earned the privilege; to act as a clearing-house for requests and complaints; and to arbitrate in any case of disagreement between students and proctors or assistants.[56]

The classroom suite should be structured for a number of teaching styles and philosophies, allowing for real diversity in approaches to learning and participation by students in choosing what works best for each of them. Assessment, also, should be able to encompass a variety of styles. Any universal methodology provides a straitjacket that will limit students in their eventual ability to operate within a digital world. As students would also be involved in instruction (another part of the learning that would prove beneficial in addressing the new digital environment), the physical space would have to be able to accommodate the needs of tutors and proctors, ensuring an atmosphere "of 'mutual reinforcement' for student, proctor, assistant, and instructor."[57]

Within these suites, students would study a variety of subjects but always with the purpose of using them as conduits for thought and expression. A chemistry student wouldn't simply learn symbols and formulae, but the meanings behind their usage, and would write about what she or he had learned under supervision of a composition instructor. This would be a significant step toward remedying the current situation where, as Richard Arum and Josipa Roksa note, students "are also not learning much, even when they persist through higher education. In general, . . . undergraduates are barely improving their . . . skills in critical thinking, complex reasoning, and writing during their first two years of college. Even more disturbingly, almost half are demonstrating no appreciable gain in these skills between the beginning of their freshman year and the end of their sophomore year."[58]

Whatever it may be (and it could have a number of different configurations), a system of education preparing students for the digital age should:

1. Develop a level playing field by bringing parents more directly into the educational process, from the time children are born, providing parents with the training and tools needed to meet their children's needs. Parents need to be able to work with their children from their earliest years and need to understand what they are learning. Ralph Tyler, writing 40 years ago, pointed out that "The day-by-day environment of young people in the home and in the community generally proves a considerable part of the educational development of the student. It is unnecessary for the school to duplicate educational experiences already adequately provided outside the school."[59] At the same time, it is necessary for the school to provide the experiences not provided outside the school—or to help parents and community meet their responsibilities to the children. Information isn't confined to schools but is part of life, emphatically so in the digital age.

2. Develop systems based on exploration and discussion, not on discovery or answers. When students aren't looking for "planted" answers or asking "What are you looking for?" they gain confidence in their own ability to search and to examine. Divergent thinking becomes the basis for creativity and for problem solving outside of artificial situations and for, as Robinson says, original thinking. Here, writing, both as skill and as a means of exploration, becomes extremely important, for it provides the basis and record for dialogue—one of the most important factors in any system of education or learning. Here, also, emphasis would lie on the mechanics behind writing in a digital situation, on

programming and code as they dovetail into how writing (and other creative endeavors utilizing digital tools) is accomplished today.

3. Develop a system of real research instead of promoting the cobbling together of bits and pieces in its stead. Very little of the putative research that students participate in does anything but cover old ground. Teachers can easily set up research questions where they don't know the answers and where answers are not easily obtainable. The trick is for the teacher to broach research possibilities that he or she doesn't know the answers to, guiding students in particular directions but not to particular answers. The trick, also, is to get students to understand that the means of research are not the research itself: the real research comes in what the student herself or himself does with the information found. Use of the scientific method of gathering data, developing a hypothesis and means of testing, the test itself, analyzing results, and ensuring replicability would be at the heart of this. Here, too, writing and other creative expressions become extremely important parts of the education—communicating one's results is as important as achieving them.

4. Develop a system based on trust in the methods of individual teachers but that does not focus exclusively on the teacher. Different teachers have different strengths. If we move away from classroom-based instruction, we can encourage individual teachers to gravitate toward roles reflecting their strength. One might provide lectures, another supervise tutors, another work with students to develop group projects. Instead of trying to meld teachers into identical and quantifiable pieces of a seamless whole, work with their differences to meet the needs of students—whose personalities and needs are as distinct as those of their teachers.

5. Provide space for motivation within the educational structures. Students need to have a reason to learn. Telling them education will get them good jobs isn't going to be enough, nor is saying they have a responsibility to do well in school. The teacher needs to learn enough about individual students to help develop particular methods of motivation. Schools should be able to work with students within the contexts of their cultures but without the generalizations that often come with racial, ethnic, and class identification. There should also be attention paid to the attitude of the students in the classroom. They don't need to be having fun, but if they are not engaged, corrective steps need to be taken.

6. Start where the students are. Because they come from such different homes, ethnicities, and classes, students have differing needs at the start of their educations, needs that continue to differ throughout their schooling. The educational process needs to be able to accommodate differences in speed of learning, in interest, and in outside support. As Tyler wrote, "Learning takes place through the active behavior of the student; it is what he does that he learns, not what the teacher does. It is possible for two students to be in the same class and for them to be having two different experiences."[60]

7. Teach the ability to work slowly and with continual self-evaluation. We now put too much emphasis on speed, and leave work behind without any but the most cursory glance back. The "stretch" system of allowing students, if need be, to complete the work of a course over two semesters instead of one, is an attempt to ease the time pressures that education currently puts too heavily on students, but others can be developed—including abandonment of lock-step progression through grades (at the K–12 level) and semesters (in college).

Essentially, what we need to do if our educational system is to provide graduates that are able to successfully negotiate a digitally informed world, is to redesign our schools, doing away with the traditional classroom and broadening the teacher's role, making it more collaborative and ensuring there is room for tailoring it to the strengths of the individual teacher and the needs of individual students.

If we are ever going to get beyond the blogosphere, making the digital environment into something really useful to and integral to human endeavors, we are going to have to address more concretely the internet's place in modern cultures—and how we prepare "information's children" to deal with this massive new presence in society. The web doesn't work in a hierarchical, formulaic structure of the sort our schools are still fond of, a model relating more to industrial structures of the 19th and 20th centuries than to the needs of 21st-century workers.

The barriers between words and thought, information and education need to be removed. Our digitally informed world requires self-reflection at the same time that it becomes more outer directed and more able to take over from the individual many of the routines of research and exploration. Only an educational system taking this into account will be effective for the new world of the 21st century.

EIGHT

The Excess of the Internet and the Waste of Information

As a rule, internet users consume more than they produce. This imbalance is not necessarily a problem: the cost of copying on the web is nil, and consumption of the copies does not reduce stock. Because the act of consumption is higher than the act of production, the ability for knowledge to organize on the internet is best illustrated by showing how human potential is wasted. Knowledge communities illustrate this through the potential they harbor, the waste of that potential, and a suggestion that continued study of the internet requires an investigation into the relationship between waste and information.

Henry Jenkins, in *Convergence Culture,* works from one of the themes that has been a consistent mainstay of *Beyond the Blogosphere,* one that should prove to be crucial to any nuanced study of the internet—the notion of collective intelligence. Jenkins explores fan communities of television programs to illustrate how they assemble to create a form of collective intelligence that works differently from the complex adaptive systems and human group intelligences investigated in Chapter 3. Acknowledging an intellectual debt to Pierre Levy's influential *Collective Intelligence: Mankind's Emerging World in Cyberspace,* Jenkins suggests that his knowledge communities serve as future indicators to collective intelligence by showing how human intelligences spontaneously organize on the internet, create emergent knowledges that are beyond the strengths of the smartest members of the group, yet still maintain group member distinctiveness and individuality.

Jenkins does not use the term *convergence* the same way that we have used the term in previous chapters. Previously, we have indicated that the internet is a place where media converge—where sound, image, video, and text come together to be delivered through a single medium; here, the network is more of an uber-medium, platform, and fabric where other media are its content. Following McLuhan, different mediums in the past implied different messages, but those media now converge, making it so that now different aspects of life (work and play, public and private) not only *converge* but, as so many social media scandals frequently indicate, also find ways to *implode* (Anthony Weiner, Brett Favre, and so on). Jenkins has a less medial and more cultural orientation to convergence, however. For Jenkins, convergence is the notion that old media and inter-net communities converge in the sense that people use the internet to talk about television, and it is in this sense that the internet is a space for both new and old media.

Compared to the broad canvases of others working in the field, what Jenkins undertakes may seem trivial to some because his investigation involves reality TV shows such as *Survivor* and *American Idol*. But that triviality soon gives way to a notion of apprenticeship. The idea for Jenkins is that studying these kinds of pop-culture phenomena reveals how internet communities learn to produce collective intelligence in nonexpert, low-risk environments. Jenkins explains: "convergence culture represents a shift in the ways we think about our relations to media, that we are making that shift first through our relations with popular culture, but that the skills we acquire through play may have implications for how we learn, work, participate in the political process, and connect with other people around the world."[1] Fan communities don't necessarily solve any important problems, but they are not supposed to. They exist as play and serve as an apprenticeship for humans learning to use forums and online communities in more serious pursuits.

A fansite devoted to *Survivor* shows collective intelligence at work through "spoiling." Spoiling is what it sounds like, when one reveals the end of a show; but in spoiling *Survivor,* people try to figure out before airing who will be eliminated and at what stage. Spoiling arises from the fact that the season is shot and edited before it is broadcast and that the network keeps all information concerning the show top secret. The fan community investigates whatever clues it can get its hands on to figure out as much about the show as possible; it researches locations, the individual players, the food, weather patterns—anything it can learn from in order to create a composite picture. Then it begins working toward figuring out the nuances to the show, who will be booted off, when, why, and who the leaders will be.

Jenkins introduces his readers to one duo—Wezzie and Dan—who work together to find out as much as they can about the location of each season before it airs. Wezzie explains some of the research involved: " 'We look at latitude, climate, political stability, population density, road system, ports, accommodations, attractions, culture, predominant religion, and proximity to past Survivor locations.' " Dan explains how he uses that information to discover locations: " 'In Africa I overlaid demographic maps of population, agricultural areas, national reserves, tourism destinations and even city lights seen from satellites at night. Sometimes knowing where Survivor can't be is important. That's how I found Shaba Reserve.' "[2] The group engages in a process of elimination based on clues that they are able to find.

The conditions that Jenkins establishes meet the requirements discussed in Chapter 3, when we asked what the difference was between collective intelligence as it applies to complex adaptive systems and collective intelligence as it applies to humans. We made the point that human forms of collective intelligence require four key principles: independence; diversity; decentralization; and, finally, the ability to aggregate that information.

In complex adaptive systems, the key trait is allelo-mimesis, copying what others do. But, for the most part in human organizations, allelo-mimesis leads to groupthink and cascade, canceling out independence and diversity. If everyone just follows what the group says, there is a good chance that the chosen course will not be effective. On the other hand, in a sufficiently diverse crowd, each person putting in his or her best guess of an answer—this done along with a way of aggregating those results— chances are good that a solution will be found.

While Jenkins's discussion of fan communities is an enlightening account of the potential for collective internet intelligence, a number of difficulties remain, however. These difficulties are not with how intelligence functions in the fan communities; Jenkins has articulated those operations well; rather, the difficulty is with the composition of the communities themselves and their unrealized potential, a condition that pushes our final query toward the notion of waste.

Though Jenkins's fan communities do exhibit the rules of diversity, independence, decentralization, and aggregation, it is difficult to ascertain how broad of a group participates in online communities. Most people are "lurkers," posting infrequently, if at all. This internet phenomenon of the participation of the few is easily expressed by a graph known in internet studies as a "power law distribution" and was made most famous by ex-*Wired* editor Chris Anderson in his book *The Long Tail* (2004). A look at the graph illustrates the long tail. The majority of internet users are those who produce little to nothing on the internet, comprising the long train of a typical power law distribution. They are unactualized human potential (see Figure 8.1).

While it has a few different applications, when the long tail is applied to participatory culture, it is simple to grasp: most social media systems function through just a few active users. Of all the people who read blogs, only a few keep blogs. Of all the blogs on the internet, a very small number generate the vast majority of traffic. Of all the people who use Wikipedia, only a few ever contribute to an article. Of the 500 million plus users on Facebook, most only check their accounts once a week. In the case of Jenkins's knowledge communities, of all the people following the community of spoilers, only a few do the work and thereby only a few of them create knowledge. Online participation is primarily driven by few producers while most are consumers, even though it may appear, at first glance, that many do the work.

From an infrastructural perspective, the long tail is necessary: imagine the amount of information that the internet would be flooded by if everyone started to participate at the same time. Indeed, the internet functions fairly well because there are billions of global internet connections; any

Figure 8.1   Power law distribution: Few generate most online production; a small to medium number generates some, and most generate little to none.

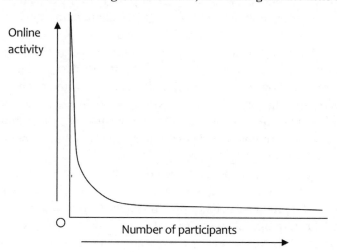

time one server fails, other servers continue to function.[3] But servers for individual companies and organizations crash or get hacked as a matter of doing business.

When Amazon decided to release Lady Gaga's *Born This Way* album in May 2011 as part of its campaign to bring more users to its cloud service, it did so by offering downloads of the album for a release-day special of 99 cents. Amazon didn't count on the popularity its offer would generate, and the site went down for the day. Twitter has experienced similar problems during its phenomenal growth, unable to handle the 2010 World Cup or the tweets discussing being generated during the Tunisian and Egyptian uprisings in 2011.[4] During Justin Bieber's peak of popularity, Twitter dedicated 3 percent of its servers just to handle the traffic related to him.[5] If everyone on the internet produced as much as they consumed, we would be living in a different internet, a world where the prosumer (producer + consumer) neologism would ring more true.

To move closer to the excess of technology and information waste, we need to keep the so-called long tail of the power law ready to hand. For Anderson, the long tail of the power law distribution reveals the unrealized potential of the internet. We should be very clear about who makes up this long tail, about all these people floating along on the internet, clicking Groupon and LivingSocial deals, reading Yahoo! News, following the tides and flows of wherever the browsing experience takes them, acting as the more basic type of flâneur described in Chapter 2. We could say that the people on the long tail don't exist; and from the perspective of a knowledge community, they don't. That is, those who are on the long tail of the culture of participation, those who use the internet primarily as a tool of consumption only exist as potential: the potential to *do* something productive that, in the end, could possibly help in the bottomless barrel of important struggles. They have the potential of becoming the second type of flâneur, but it is unrealized.

But they *do* exist, don't they? And we are they, at least some of the time, aren't we? They/we exist as consumers and to places such as Facebook, Google, Netflix, Amazon, and every other company trying to sell you something; what they/we do, in the sense of what links we/they click, what pages we/they like, what articles we/they read, and what purchases we/they make is the very stuff that drives the growth of the internet.

In 2011, most online consumers realized or intuited that the majority of the ads they receive are algorithmically produced based on the preferences they have exhibited while visiting various sites. Eli Pariser, author of *The Filter Bubble,* shows how Google filters news information based on these preferences. At first, this kind of technology may seem innocuous. If you are a Mets fan, Google bots read that you have clicked on Mets-related articles recently. So, more articles on the Mets start showing up in your news queue. Along with the new articles, you may start seeing baseball-related ads. In general, most people accept this situation as simply a part of navigating the internet. But Pariser takes a closer look, asking two of his friends, with similar political views and profiles, to do a Google search for "Egypt" during the week of January 25, 2011, the week of the Egyptian Revolution. One of his friends loves to travel, and the other one is more focused on politics. The one interested in politics received that day's news concerning the revolution. The other one, however, received articles concerning travel to Egypt, important news of the day appearing at the bottom of the page, almost hidden from view. If this second friend only had internet access to media for that day, it's possible that nothing significant would have been learned. News delivery—a staple of the internet—was replaced by travel information through taste profiling. Pariser argues that internet users should be exposed to more than just the things they prefer.[6]

Pariser's point is important, but, as we have said throughout this book, technology exhibits desires that are different from our own. We may want to have a wide variety of news, but we'll get what the technology thinks what we want, much of it designed to help advertisers cash in.

The phenomenon described above is typically referred to as a user's "taste" or "preference" profile, but there's much more to it. The next move of the semantic web is to combine preference profiles with a more powerful "persuasion profile." Of interest to rhetoricians (and to politicians), a persuasion profile is what the computer thinks will be most effective in getting a user to purchase a product. Until recently, the logic at work in the semantic web has been *associational,* following the formula—if you like X, then you might also like Y. Now, the logic of the network is growing in sophistication, making other types of association that appeal to an individual's sense of reason, emotion, and authority.

Pariser describes an experimental bookstore set up by a group of Stanford University doctoral students. They asked participants in their study to browse the bookstore as though they were going to purchase some titles. As the experimental customers browsed, they were presented with appeals to authority (Malcolm Gladwell recommends this book), appeals to social groups (Facebook friends are reading this book), appeals to simplicity (this one is a page turner). The researchers were able to track which arguments worked best for each person and, by honing those appeals, were able to increase the efficacy of the recommendation 30 to 40 percent.[7] The consequences may be significant. Pariser explains:

> Consider what could happen if they knew that certain customers buy things compulsively when they're stressed or feeling bad about themselves. ("Our analysis of your Facebook photos says you're overweight and ugly. Buy our makeup.") If persuasion profiling makes it possible for a coaching device to shout "You can do it" to people who like positive reinforcement, in theory it could also enable politicians to make personalized appeals based on each voter's particular fears. If your persuasion profile shows that you're a sucker for social pressure, Joe Candidate could target you with ads saying that your friends will be told whether or not you voted. Persuasion profiling potentially offers quick, easily transferable, targeted access to your personal psychological weak spots.[8]

Pariser suggests that there are ways to avoid being so insidiously and persuasively profiled, but, without sounding defeatist, if persuasion profiling does indeed become as ubiquitous as taste profiling, internet users will likely just accept it. Like so many that we've discussed in this book, Pariser believes that humans have the ability to control the technology that gives shape to their behaviors *after* the design is implemented; until more books get written in the mainstream that begin to change what we can actually influence—the attitudes people have toward technology—then technology will continue to express a desire that oftentimes runs counter to the well-being of the human. If people will have an influence on technology, that influence must be made *before* the designs are implemented.

Perhaps the biggest problems the long tail exposes is the waste of human potential, but this waste is nothing new; just think of those who are undereducated, underemployed, below poverty, underfed. The study of fan communities by Jenkins reveals that most of the intelligence created in these knowledge communities is done by the very few, not the many, resulting in considerable waste that Jenkins does not account for. Take another example, this time the well-known article "The Rise of Crowdsourcing" that Jeff Howe wrote for *Wired* magazine and went viral in 2006: In this article, Howe gives four examples about how the crowds of the internet can fix problems that would not have been previously possible: a woman who needed photos for interactive kiosks, a producer of the VH1 show "Web Junk 20" looking for viral videos, the founder of InnoCentive website, and Amazon.com's Mechanical Turk website. The Mechanical Turk website, for instance, a site designed to connect businesses with people willing to pick up contractual jobs, is outright laughable. A visit to the site reveals mind-numbing jobs that ask human workers to complete tasks such as "please copy text from this business card into the text fields below"; typical of the jobs on the site, this ad offers to pay 2 cents for 10 minutes of work; 12 cents an hour. $9.60 for the day. $38.40 for the week. $1,996 for a 40-hour work week for the year. Is this what crowdsourcing thinks human beings are worth? None of the examples Howe offers solve or point to solving any significant problems, yet the influence of his article was overwhelming; again, because companies are looking to cash in on cheap labor.[9]

In an ideally anthropocentric and unrealistic world, such "cognitive surplus" (to borrow Shirky's term) would be utilized. Humans have always seen that energy should be used to suit some human purpose or good. For many (and we share certain sympathies with this idea too), the idea that the wasted human potential that exists on the internet should be used to heal the wounds of a civilization is a given—especially when the internet reveals the potential to embark on a course of unrealized human collective potential. Many wish that human potential of the internet *should* be realized, but the actual truth of the situation reveals that human potential is wasted, that the long tail is excess.

But what is the nature of this excess, and why does it comprise such a large portion of what happens on the internet? What is the relationship between all of this excess energy and its use value? How do we think about the internet as part of a sustainable and post-sustainable network culture? When most humans spend considerable time on the internet using technologies that have the potential to collectively organize and do important cultural work, why do these possibilities remain unrealized? How does all of this waste fit into the broader cultural economy and longevity of the internet? Can we continue to see technology as being in the service of the human? Can all of this energy be used?

While we do not pretend to know the answers to these questions, we do believe that further internet studies will need to undergo a cultural investigation into the relationships among tools, energy, excess, and capital. When a collective force as ubiquitous as the internet continues to grow at alarming speeds and when most of its energy is wasted, some sketches of understanding need to be made so that we can begin to better understand this growing, pulsing, emerging organism called internet.

Notes

PREFACE

1. James Gleick, *The Information,* 403.
2. *2010 Digital Universe Study: A Digital Universe Decade—Are You Ready?,* April 26, 2010, 1, http://www.ifap.ru/pr/2010/n100507a.pdf.
3. Alfred Bester, "Fondly Fahrenheit," 489.

ONE

1. Kevin Kelly, *Out of Control,* 8.
2. Ibid., 10.
3. Craig Reynolds, "Boids (Flocks, Herds, and Schools: a Distributed Behavioral Model)," http://www.red3d.com/cwr/boids/.
4. Kevin Kelly, *Out of Control,* 28.
5. Ibid.
6. Kevin Kelly, *What Technology Wants,* 16–17.
7. Kevin Kelly, "TEDxSF—Kevin Kelly—What Technology Wants." YouTube. Accessed May 22, 2011. http://www.youtube.com/watch?v=nF-5CMozGWY.
8. Reidar Due, *Deleuze,* 8
9. Ibid.
10. Michael Hardt, *Gilles Deleuze,* 64.
11. For a full account, see Lewis Feuer, *Spinoza and the Rise of Liberalism* (1987).
12. Christian Kerslake, "Desire and the Dialectics of Love: Deleuze, Canguilhem, and the Philosophy of Desire," 78.
13. Rosi Braidotti, *Transpositions,* 37.

14. Ibid.

15. Marshall McLuhan, *Understanding Media: the Extensions of Man,* 88.

16. Ibid.

17. Tim Wu, *The Master Switch,* 5.

18. Ibid., 5–6.

19. See also Siva Vaidhyanathan, *The Googlization of Everything.*

20. Kevin Kelly, "Web 3.0," http://www.youtube.com/watch?v=J132shgIiuY.

21. "U.S. & World Population Clock," Census Bureau Home Page, http://www.census.gov/main/www/popclock.html.

22. "Statistics Facebook," Facebook, http://www.facebook.com/press/info.php?statistics.

23. Paul Virilio, *Open Sky,* 24.

24. Babak Parviz, "Augmented Reality in a Contact Lens," IEEE Spectrum.

25. Matt Richtel, "Growing Up Digital, Wired for Distraction," *New York Times,* November 21, 2010, A1, http://www.nytimes.com/2010/11/21/technology/21brain.html?_r=2&ref=technology&pagewanted=1.

26. Ben Sisario, "In Lady Gaga's Album, Evidence of a New Order," *New York Times,* http://www.nytimes.com/2011/06/02/arts.

27. Donald Norman, *The Invisible Computer,* 6.

28. Friedrich A. Kittler, *Gramophone, Film, Typewriter,* xxxix.

29. Jan Li Harris and Paul Taylor, *Digital Matters,* 67–68.

30. In Nicholas Carr, *The Shallows,* 29.

31. Ibid.

32. Ibid.

33. Jan L. Harris and Paul A. Taylor, *Digital Matters: Theory and Culture of the Matrix,* 68.

34. "Friedrich Kittler—Professor of Media Philosophy—Biography," The European Graduate School—Media and Communication—Graduate & Postgraduate Studies Program, http://www.egs.edu/faculty/friedrich-kittler/biography/.

35. See Chapter 6 in *What Technology Wants.*

36. Kevin Kelly, *Out of Control,* 192–193.

37. Kevin Kelly, *What Technology Wants,* 270.

TWO

1. Jonathan Klein, quoted in "Special Report With Brit Hume," September 14, 2004, partially transcribed and posted September 17, 2004, on *FoxNews.com,* http://www.foxnews.com/story/0,2933,132494,00.html.

2. Sarah Palin, quoted in Linda Bergthold, "Palin Calls Bloggers 'Kids in Pajamas,'" *The Huffington Post,* November 10, 2008, http://www.huffingtonpost.com/linda-bergthold/palin-calls-bloggers-kids_b_142872.html.

3. Philip K. Dick, *Confessions of a Crap Artist,* 169–170.

4. Philip K. Dick, in a letter dated January 19, 1975, quoted in Paul Williams's "Introduction" to Dick's novel *Confessions of a Crap Artist,* x.

5. Ibid.

6. Philip K. Dick, *Confessions of a Crap Artist,* 1.

7. Ibid., 169–170.

8. Andrew Marr at the Cheltenham Literature Festival, quoted in "Andrew Marr Attacks 'Inadequate, Pimpled and Single' Bloggers," *The Telegraph,* October 10, 2010, http://www.telegraph.co.uk/technology/internet/8053717/Andrew-Marr-attacks-inadequate-pimpled-and-single-bloggers.html.

9. Jay Rosen, "Bloggers vs. Journalists Is Over," *PressThink,* January 21, 2005, http://archive.pressthink.org/2005/01/21/berk_essy.html.

10. Adam Gopnik, "The Information," *The New Yorker,* February 14, 2011, http://www.newyorker.com/arts/critics/atlarge/2011/02/14/110214crat_atlarge_gopnik?currentPage=1.

11. Charles Baudelaire, *The Painter of Modern Life and Other Essays,* 9–10.

12. Eric Larrabee, and Rolf Meyersohn, "Introduction" to *Mass Leisure,* x.

13. Mercedes Paulini and Marc Aurel Schnabel, "Surfing the City," 385.

14. Robert Luke, "The Phoneur," 187.

15. Andy Clark, "Out of Our Brains," *New York Times,* December 12, 2010, http://opinionator.blogs.nytimes.com/2010/12/12/out-of-our-brains/?ref=opinion.

16. Charles Baudelaire, *The Painter of Modern Life and Other Essays,* 3.

17. John Le Carre, *The Night Manager,* 300.

18. Ibid., 321.

19. Simon Lindgren, "From Flâneur to Web Surfer," November 2007, http://www.transformationsjournal.org/journal/issue_15/article_10.shtml.

20. Bertrand Russell, "In Praise of Idleness," 8.

21. Clive Bell, "How to Make a Civilization," 32–33.

22. Lev Manovich, *The Language of New Media,* 273.

23. Charles Baudelaire, *The Painter of Modern Life and Other Essays,* 12.

24. Wayne Franklin, *Discoverers, Explorers, Settlers.*

25. Chia Chi Wu, "A Space Beyond," http://chiachiwu.com/a_space_beyond/index.html.

26. Simon Lindgren, "From Flâneur to Web Surfer," http://www.transformationsjournal.org/journal/issue_15/article_10.shtml.

27. Walter Benjamin, *The Arcades Project,* 417.

28. Malcolm Gladwell, "Does Egypt Need Twitter?" *The New Yorker,* February 2, 2011, http://www.newyorker.com/online/blogs/newsdesk/2011/02/does-egypt-need-twitter.html.

29. Stephen Ramsay, "Who's In and Who's Out," *literature mundana,* January 8, 2011, http://lenz.unl.edu/wordpress/?p=325.

30. Stephen Ramsay, "On Building," *literature mundana,* January 11, 2011, http://lenz.unl.edu/wordpress/?p=340.

31. Matthew Kirschenbaum, "What Is Digital Humanities and What's It Doing in English Departments," *ADE Bulletin,* Number 150, 2010, 6.

32. David Berry, "Digital Humanities: First, Second, and Third Waves," *Stunlaw: A Critical Review of Politics, Art and Technology,* http://stunlaw.blogspot.com/2011/01/digital-humanities-first-second-and.html.

33. Fran Berman, Geoffrey Fox, and Anthony Hey, *Grid Computing Making the Global Infrastructure a Reality,* 819.

34. Tony Hey and Anne Trefethen, "The Data Deluge: An e-Science Perspective," 13.

35. Bertrand Russell, "In Praise of Idleness," 14.

36. Charles Baudelaire, *The Painter of Modern Life and Other Essays,* 12.

37. Jorge Luis Borges, "The Book of Sand," 118–119.

38. Jorge Luis Borges, "The Book of Sand," 121–122.

39. Marcel Duchamp, quoted in Michel de Certeau, *The Practice of Everyday Life,* 177.

40. Lawrence Lessig, *The Future of Ideas,* 41.

41. Johann Wolfgang von Goethe, "The Sorcerer's Apprentice," trans. Edwin Zeydel, http://www.fln.vcu.edu/goethe/zauber_e3.html.

42. Howard Eiland and Kevin McLaughlin, "Translators' Foreword," x.

43. Ibid., xi.

44. Ibid.

45. Walter Benjamin, *The Arcades Project,* 460.

46. Sergei Eisenstein, "The Dramaturgy of Film Form," 95.

47. Ester Leslie, "Walter Benjamin's *Arcades Project,*" http://www.militantesthetix.co.uk/waltbenj/yarcades.html.

48. Franz Kafka, "In the Penal Colony," trans. Ian Johnstone, http://records.viu.ca/~johnstoi/kafka/inthepenalcolony.htm.

49. Ibid.

50. Ibid.

THREE

1. Henry Mitchell, *The Intellectual Commons,* 25.

2. Marcus Boon, *In Praise of Copying,* 43–44.

3. Sherman Frederick, "Copyright Theft: We're Not Taking It Anymore," *The Las Vegas Review-Journal,* May 28, 2010, http://www.lvrj.com/blogs/sherm/Copyright_theft_Were_not_taking_it_anymore.html?ref=164.

4. Richard Posner, "Misappropriation: A Dirge" (revised), originally presented at the 2003 IPIL/Houston Santa Fe Conference, sponsored by the University of Houston Law Center's Institute for Intellectual Property and Information Law, June 6, 2003, http://www.houstonlawreview.org/archive/downloads/40–3_pdf/Posnerg2r.pdf.

5. Ibid.

6. James Boyle, *The Public Domain,* 63.

7. Marcus Boon, *In Praise of Copying,* 43–44.

8. Kembrew McLeod, *Freedom of Expression,* 169.

9. Henry Mitchell, *The Intellectual Commons,* 25.

10. Mary Bono, speaking on the floor of the House, October 7, 1998, *The Congressional Record,* Volume 144, page H9952, http://thomas.loc.gov/cgi-bin/query/F?r105:1:./temp/~r105dNTzrX:e46923:.

11. Paul Farhi, "Now on DVD: The Sanitizer's Cut," *Washington Post,* April 18, 2005, p. A01.

12. Richard Posner, "Misappropriation: A Dirge" (revised).

13. Senior District Judge Richard P. Matsch of the United States District Court for the District of Colorado, "Huntsman v. Steven Soderbergh," July 6, 2006, http://www.eff.org/files/filenode/Huntsman_v_Soderbergh/CleanFlicksDistCt Opinion.pdf.

14. Copyright Law of the United States of America, http://www.copyright.gov/title17/92chap1.html.

15. Steve Green, "Righthaven Extends copyright Lawsuit Campaign to Individual Web Posters," January 12, 2011, http://www.lasvegassun.com/news/2011/jan/12/righthaven-extends-copyright-lawsuit-campaign-indi/.

16. Corynne McSherry, "A Field Guide to Copyright Trolls," Electronic Frontier Foundation, https://www.eff.org/deeplinks/2010/09/field-guide-copyright-trolls.

17. David Kravetz, "Newspaper Chain's New Business Plan: Copyright Suits," *Wired,* July 22, 2010, http://www.wired.com/threatlevel/2010/07/copyright-trolling-for-dollars/.

18. Anandashankar Mazumdar, "Righthaven's Litigation Tactics Raise Concerns for Online Publishers" Bureau of National Affairs' Professional Information Center: Intellectual Property, http://ipcenter.bna.com/pic2/ip.nsf/id/BNAP-8A9MUL?OpenDocument.

19. David Kravetz, "Newspaper Chain's New Business Plan: Copyright Suits," *Wired,* July 22, 2010, http://www.wired.com/threatlevel/2010/07/copyright-trolling-for-dollars/.

20. Wendy Davis, "Publisher Sued For Reposting Article Based On His Own Research," *The Daily Online Examiner,* June 28, 2010, http://www.mediapost.com/publications/?fa=Articles.showArticle&art_aid=131043.

21. Maureen O'Connor, "*Men's Health* Editor Plagiarizes His Own Writers," *Gawker,* January 26, 2011, http://gawker.com/5738017/mens-health-editor-plagiarizes-his-own-writers.

22. Quoted in Maureen O'Connor, "Plagiarizing Editor's Boss: Byline Doesn't Take Credit for the Work," *Gawker,* January 26, 2011, http://gawker.com/5744178/plagiarizing-editors-boss-byline-doesnt-take-credit-for-the-work.

23. Kurt Opsahl, "Democratic Underground Responds to Righthaven Copyright Troll Lawsuit," Electronic Frontier Foundation, http://www.eff.org/deeplinks/2010/12/democratic-underground-responds-righthaven.

24. "Motion for Summary Judgment," *Righthaven v. Democratic Underground,* United States District Court for the District of Nevada, 1, December 7, 2010, http://www.eff.org/files/filenode/righthaven_v_dem/PlfMSJ.pdf.

25. Ibid., 2.

26. Ibid., 7.

27. Kembrew McLeod, 165.

28. James Boyle, *The Public Domain,* 9.

29. Henry Mitchell, *The Intellectual Commons,* xi–xii.

30. Ibid., 13.

31. Marjorie Heins, *"The Progress of Science and Useful Arts": Why Copyright Today Threatens Intellectual Freedom,* 8–9, http://www.fepproject.org/policyreports/copyright2d.pdf.

32. "Motion for Summary Judgment," 12/7/10, *Righthaven v. Democratic Underground,* United States District Court for the District of Nevada, 10, http://www.eff.org/files/filenode/righthaven_v_dem/PlfMSJ.pdf.

33. Copyright Act of 1976 at 17 U.S.C. § 107, http://www.copyright.gov/title17/92chap1.html#107.

34. Henry Mitchell, *The Intellectual Commons,* 16.

35. Lawrence Lessig, "Copyright's First Amendment," 1070.

36. Kembrew McLeod, 163.

37. Lawrence Lessig, "Copyright's First Amendment," 1065.

38. James Boyle, *The Public Domain,* 62.

39. Ibid., 61.

40. James Boyle, "Text is Free, We Make Our Money on Volume(s)," *The Financial Times.* FT.com, January 22, 2007, http://www.ft.com/cms/s/2/b46f5a58-aa2e-11db-83b0-0000779e2340.html#axzz17XNhkiik.

41. James Boyle, *The Public Domain,* 60–61.

42. Neil Postman, "Informing Ourselves to Death," a talk given before the German Informatics Society, October 11, 1990, in Stuttgart, Germany, http://w2.eff.org/Net_culture/Criticisms/informing_ourselves_to_death.paper.

43. Ibid.

44. James Boyle, *The Public Domain,* 60.

45. Walter Ong, *Orality and Literacy,* 2–3.

46. Marshall McLuhan, "Sight, Sound and Fury," in Rosenberg, 489–490.

47. Ibid., 494.

48. Henry Mitchell, *The Intellectual Commons,* 5.

49. The entire act can be read at http://www.copyrighthistory.org/.

50. Lionel Bently, and Jane C. Ginsburg, ""The Sole Right . . . Shall Return to the Authors": Anglo-American Authors' Reversion Rights From the Statute of Anne to Contemporary U.S. Copyright," 12.

51. Ibid., 14.

52. Ibid., 2–3.

53. Daniel Defoe, *Review,* Feb. 2, 1710.

54. Anne Bradstreet, "An Author to her Book." The complete poem can be found at http://www.annebradstreet.com/the_author_to_her_book.htm.

55. Mark Rose, "Copyright and Its Metaphors," 7.

56. Ibid., 15.

57. Ibid.

58. Henry Mitchell, *The Intellectual Commons,* 35.

59. Mark Rose, "Copyright and Its Metaphors," 12–13.

60. Ibid., 15.

61. Sandra Day O'Connor, "Feist Publications, Inc. v. Rural Telephone Service Co.," decided March 27, 1991, http://caselaw.lp.findlaw.com/scripts/getcase.pl?court=us&vol=499&invol=340.

62. Marcus Boon, *In Praise of Copying,* 17–18.

63. Ibid., 3.

64. Ibid., 21.

65. Ibid.

66. Ibid., 49.

67. Lawrence Lessig, "Copyright's First Amendment," 1063.

68. Ibid., 1064.

69. The full text of this letter from Noah Webster to Daniel Webster, dated September 30, 1826, can be found at http://www.copyrighthistory.org/cgi-bin/kleioc/0010/exec/showThumb/%22us_1826_im_001_0001.jpg%22.

70. The October 14, 1826, letter from Daniel Webster to Noah Webster is reproduced at http://www.copyrighthistory.org/cgi-bin/kleioc/0010/exec/showThumb/%22us_1826a%22/start/%22yes%22.

71. Kembrew McLeod, 167.

72. William Wordsworth, "Preface," *Lyrical Ballads,* William Wordsworth and Samuel Taylor Coleridge, http://www.bartleby.com/39/36.html.

73. Henry Mitchell, *The Intellectual Commons,* 15.

74. Kembrew McLeod, 198.

75. Joyce Cary, *The Horse's Mouth,* 15.

76. Roland Barthes, "The Death of the Author," 146.

77. Marcus Boon, *In Praise of Copying,* 48.

78. Ibid., 101.

79. Adam Himmelsbach, "Colleges Tell High Schools Logos Are Off Limits," *New York Times,* November 26, 2010, http://www.nytimes.com/2010/11/27/sports/football/27logos.html?hp.

80. Walter Benjamin, "Doctrine of the Similar," 65.

81. Marcus Boon, *In Praise of Copying,* 30.

82. Federal Trade Commission Staff Discussion Draft: Potential Policy Recommendations to Support the Reinvention of Journalism," http://www.ftc.gov/opp/workshops/news/jun15/docs/new-staff-discussion.pdf.

83. Jeff Jarvis, "FTC Protects Journalism's Past," *Buzz Machine,* May 29, 2010, http://www.buzzmachine.com/2010/05/29/ftc-protects-journalisms-past/.

84. Quoted in Susan Decker and Thom Weidlich, "Myriad Loses Ruling Over Breast-Cancer Gene Patent," *Bloomberg Businessweek,* March 29, 2010, http://www.businessweek.com/news/2010–03–29/myriad-loses-ruling-over-breast-cancer-gene-patents-update1-.html.

85. Kembrew McLeod,137.

86. Ibid.

87. James Boyle, *The Public Domain,* 63.

88. Eugene Robinson, "In WikiLeaks Aftermath, An Assault on Free Speech," *Washington Post,* December 14, 2010, http://www.washingtonpost.com/wp-dyn/content/article/2010/12/13/AR2010121304085.html.

89. Ibid.

90. Caille Millner, "Lines Are Drawn in Online Culture War," *SFGate: San Francisco Chronicle,* December 13, 2010, A-13, http://www.sfgate.com/cgi-bin/article.cgi?f=/c/a/2010/12/12/ED3E1GOG68.DTL#ixzz18TbqJsb6.

91. Tom Hals, "WikiLeaks Shows Reach and Limits of Internet Speech," *Reuters,* December 9, 2010, http://www.reuters.com/article/idUSTRE6B85I42010 1209.

92. Jennifer Elsea, *Criminal Prohibitions on the Publication of Classified Defense Information: A Report for Congress,* Congressional Research Service, December 6, 2010, 21, http://www.fas.org/sgp/crs/secrecy/R41404.pdf.

93. Tony Hey and Anne Trefethen, "The Data Deluge: An e-Science Perspective," 12.

FOUR

1. Kevin Kelly, *What Technology Wants,* 11.

2. Kevin Kelly, "The Evidence of a Global SuperOrganism," *Technium,* http://www.kk.org/thetechnium/archives/2008/10/evidence_of_a_g.php.

3. Edward O. Wilson, *Sociobiology: The New Synthesis,* 399.

4. Bert Holldobler, Edward O. Wilson, and Margaret Cecile Nelson. 2009. *The Superorganism: The Beauty, Elegance, and Strangeness of Insect Societies,* xx.

5. Mark Millonas, 418.

6. Mark Taylor, 152.

7. Ibid., 153.

8. James Surowiecki, *The Wisdom of Crowds,* xx.

9. Chris Higgens, 68–71; James Surowiecki, xx-xxi.

10. John P. Craven, *The Silent War,* 168.

11. Ibid., 167.

12. Ibid., 167–168.

13. James Surowiecki, *The Wisdom of Crowds,* 71.

14. Christine Quinn, "State of the City Address," February 15, 2011, 5. http://council.nyc.gov/html/soc/2011_speech.pdf.

15. Howard Rheingold, *Smart Mobs,* 182.

FIVE

1. Christine Borgman, *Scholarship in the Digital Age,* 38.

2. Walter Lippmann, *Drift and Mastery,* 67.

3. Jave David Bolter and Richard Grusin, *Remediation,* 203.

4. Clifford Stoll, *Silicon Snake Oil,* 178.

5. Ibid., 185.

6. Douglas Greenberg, "Camel Drivers and Gatecrashers," 106.

7. Evgeny Morozov, *The Net Delusion,* 247.

8. Ibid., 253.

9. Luke Allnut in Evgeny Morozov, *The Net Delusion,* 254.

10. Thomas More, *Utopia,* 119.

11. Federich Nietzsche, *Thus Spake Zarathustra,* LVI. Old and New Tables, 12, trans.http://nietzsche.thefreelibrary.com/Thus-Spake-Zarathustra/58–1.

12. Walter Lippman, *The Public Philosophy,* 43.

13. Christine Borgman, *Scholarship in the Digital Age,* 31.

14. Evgeny Morozov, *The Net Delusion,* 273.

15. Stuart Chase, *The Tyranny of Words,* 352.

16. Neil Postman, "Informing Ourselves to Death," a talk given before the German Informatics Society, October 11, 1990, in Stuttgart, Germany, http://w2.eff. org/Net_culture/Criticisms/informing_ourselves_to_death.paper.

17. Andrew Keen, *The Cult of the Amateur,* 196.

18. John Dewey, *The Public and Its Problems,* 202–203.

19. William Gibson, *Neuromancer,* 69.

20. John Perry Barlow, "Crime and Puzzlement," http://w2.eff.org/Misc/ Publications/John_Perry_Barlow/HTML/crime_and_puzzlement_1.html.

21. James Martineau, *Types of Ethical Theory,* 242.

22. Sheldon Wolin, *Democracy, Incorporated,* 262.

23. Edward Wilson, *Consilience,* 278.

24. Malcolm Gladwell, "Small Change," http://www.newyorker.com/reporting/ 2010/10/04/101004fa_fact_gladwell?currentPage=all.

25. Kembrew McLeod, *Freedom of Expression,* 160.

26. Eric Abrahamson and David Freedman, *A Perfect Mess,* 245–246.

27. Eli Pariser, *The Filter Bubble,* 5.

28. Jorge Luis Borges, "Pierre Menard, Author of the Quixote," *Labyrinths,* 39.

29. Ibid., 43.

30. Arthur Danto, *The Transfiguration of the Commonplace,* 35–36.

31. Stuart Chase, *The Tyranny of Words,* 356.

32. William Scheuerman, "Citizenship and Speed," 299.

33. Philip K. Dick, "The Exit Door Leads In," 315.

34. Jeffrey Goldfarb, *Civility & Subversion,* 76–77.

35. Jim Rutenberg, "The Gossip Machine, Churning Out Cash," *New York Times,* 5/22/2011, A1, http://www.nytimes.com/2011/05/22/us/22gossip.html?hp.

36. William James, *The Will to Believe,* 220–221.

37. Malcolm Gladwell, *Blink,* 43–44.

38. Tony Hey and Anne Trefethen, "The Data Deluge: An e-Science Perspective," 9.

39. Franco Moretti, *Graphs, Maps, Trees,* x.

40. Marshall McLuhan, "Sight, Sound and Fury," in *Mass Culture: The Popular Arts in America,* ed., Bernard Rosenberg, and David Manning White. Glencoe, IL: The Free Press of Glencoe, 1957, 491.

41. Theodor Adorno, "Television and the Patterns of Mass Culture," in *Mass Culture: The Popular Arts in America,* ed., Bernard Rosenberg, and David Manning White. Glencoe, IL: The Free Press of Glencoe, 1957, 479.

42. N. Katherine Hayles, *How We Became Posthuman,* 132.

43. Edward Wilson, *On Human Nature,* 89.

44. Lettvin et al., "What the Frog's Eye Tells the Frog's Brain," 234.

45. Ibid., 254–255.

46. N. Katherine Hayles, *How We Became Posthuman,* 136.

47. Ibid., 137.

48. Humberto Maturana and Francisco Varela, *Autopoiesis and Cognition: The Realization of the Living,* xxii.

49. N. Katherine Hayles, *How We Became Posthuman,* 138.

50. Ibid., following Maturana and Varela, x–xi.

51. N. Katherine Hayles, *How We Became Posthuman,* 139.

52. Humberto Maturana and Francisco Varela, *Autopoiesis and Cognition,* 50.

53. N. Katherine Hayles, *How We Became Posthuman,* 141.

54. Walter Lippmann, *Drift and Mastery,* 268–269.

55. Richard Hofstadter, *Anti-Intellectualism in American Life,* 428–429.

56. Henry Jenkins, *Convergence Culture,* 217.

57. George Orwell, "In Front of Your Nose," *Tribune,* March 22, 1946, http://orwell.ru/library/articles/nose/english/e_nose.

58. Norbert Wiener, "The Brain and the Machine (Summary)," 111–112.

SIX

1. Richard Dooling, "The Rise of the Machines," *New York Times,* October 11, 2008, http://www.nytimes.com/2008/10/12/opinion/12dooling.html.

2. George Dyson, "Economic Disequilibrium: Can You Have Your House and Spend It Too?," *Consumerist,* October 27, 2008, http://consumerist.com/2008/10/make-magazine-economic-disequilibrium.html.

3. Richard Dooling, "The Rise of the Machines."

4. Ibid.

5. George Dyson, "Economic Disequilibrium."

6. Richard Dooling, "The Rise of the Machines."

7. Ray Kurzweil, *The Singularity Is Near: When Humans Transcend Biology* (New York: Viking, 2005), 8.

8. Brian Solis, "The State of Social Media 2008," *Brian Solis Defining the Convergence of Media and Influence* (blog), September 29, 2008, http://www.briansolis.com/2008/09/state-of-social-media-2008/.

9. Michael Arrington, "Facebook No Longer The Second Largest Social Network," *TechCrunch,* June 12, 2008, http://techcrunch.com/2008/06/12/facebook-no-longer-the-second-largest-social-network/.

10. Adam Ostrow, "Twitter's Massive 2008: 752 Percent Growth," *Mashable: The Social Media Guide,* January 9, 2009, http://mashable.com/2009/01/09/twitter-growth-2008/.

11. Aaron Barlow, *The Rise of the Blogosphere* (Westport, CT: Praeger, 2007), 182.

12. Malcolm Gladwell, "Small Change: Why the Revolution Will Not Be Tweeted," *New Yorker,* October 4, 2010, http://www.newyorker.com/reporting/2010/10/04/101004fa_fact_gladwell.

13. John Hudson, "The 'Twitter Revolution' Debate: The Egyptian Test Case—Global," *Atlantic Wire,* January 31, 2011, http://www.theatlanticwire.com/global/2011/01/the-twitter-revolution-debate-the-egyptian-test-case/21296/.

14. Matt Welch, "The Arab Spring," *Reason Magazine,* May 2011, http://reason.com/archives/2011/04/05/the-arab-spring.

15. Malcolm Gladwell, "Small Change."

16. Email to Amanda Booher, June 13, 2011.

17. E.M. Forster, *The Machine Stops and Other Stories* (London: André Deutsch, 1997), *Kindle Edition.* Loc: 12323–25.

18. Mark Slouka, *War of the Worlds: Cyberspace and the High-tech Assault on Reality* (New York: BasicBooks, 1995), 84–85.

19. Hubert L. Dreyfus, *On the Internet* (Milton Park, Abingdon, Oxon: Routledge, 2009), 50.

20. Malcolm Gladwell, "Small Change."

21. Clay Shirky, *Here Comes Everybody: The Power of Organizing without Organizations* (New York: Penguin Press, 2008), 53–54.

22. Jean M. Twenge, and W. Keith Campbell, *The Narcissism Epidemic: Living in the Age of Entitlement* (New York: Frec Press, 2009), 107–109.

23. Clay Shirky, *Here Comes Everybody,* 56.

24. Clay Shirky, "Are Lolcats a Sign of Human Progress??" YouTube, June 18, 2010, http://www.youtube.com/watch?v=Z0msKMRxFNw.

25. Jason Helms, "Composing Multimodally about Multimodal Composition" (lecture, Conference of College Composition and Communication, Atlanta, April 6, 2011).

26. Martin Heidegger, *Parmenides* (Bloomington: Indiana University Press, 1992), 28.

27. Langdon Winner, "Do Artifacts Have Politics?," *Daedalus* 109, no. 1 (1980): 25.

SEVEN

1. Neil Postman, "Informing Ourselves to Death," a talk given before the German Informatics Society, October 11, 1990, in Stuttgart, Germany, http://w2.eff.org/Net_culture/Criticisms/informing_ourselves_to_death.paper.

2. Bertrand Russell, *Our Knowledge of the External World,* 164.

3. Ken Robinson, "Changing Paradigms," 2008 Benjamin Franklin Awards lecture, http://www.thersa.org/events/vision/archive/sir-ken-robinson, or (excerpted, with animation) http://www.youtube.com/watch?v=zDZFcDGpL4U.

4. Jacques Barzun, *The House of Intellect,* 139.

5. Tara Brabazon, *The University of Google,* 15.

6. Ibid., 17.

7. Ibid., 16.

8. Ibid., 18.

9. Jenny McCarthy, interview with Allison Kugel, "Jenny McCarthy on Healing Her Son's Autism and Discovering Her Life's Mission," *PR.com,* October 9, 2007, http://www.pr.com/article/1076.

10. Michael Willrich, "Why Parents Fear the Needle," *New York Times,* January 21, 2011, A25. http://www.nytimes.com/2011/01/21/opinion/21willrich.html?ref=opinion.

11. Richard Rorty, *Philosophy and the Mirror of Nature,* 157.

12. Neil Postman, "Informing Ourselves to Death."

13. Laura Herrera, "In Florida, Virtual Classrooms With No Teachers," *New York Times,* January 18, 2011, A15. http://www.nytimes.com/2011/01/18/education/18classrooms.html?pagewanted=2.

14. Jacques Barzun, *The House of Intellect,* 108.

15. Ibid.

16. Dan Vergano, "Experts Claim 2006 Climate Report Plagiarized," *USA Today,* November 22, 2010, http://www.usatoday.com/weather/climate/globalwarming/2010-11-21-climate-report-questioned_N.htm.

17. Tom Wagner, *The Global Achievement Gap,* particularly Chapter 1: "The New World of Work and the Seven Survival Skills," 1–42.

18. Adam Bessie, "Let's Not 'Reform' Public Education," *Truthout,* January 22, 2011, http://www.truth-out.org/lets-not-reform-public-education67006.

19. Diane Ravitch, "The Myth of Charter Schools," *New York Review of Books,* November 11, 2010, http://www.nybooks.com/articles/archives/2010/nov/11/myth-charter-schools/.

20. Kevin Sieff, "Virginia 4th-Grade Textbook Criticized over Claims on Black Confederate Soldiers," *Washington Post,* October 20, 2010, http://www.washingtonpost.com/wp-dyn/content/article/2010/10/19/AR2010101907974.html.

21. Ibid.

22. Jerome Handler and Michael Tuite, "Retouching History: The Modern Falsification of a Civil War Photograph," presented to the Virginia Foundation for the

Humanities on February 15, 2005, and at the Conference on African Americans and the Civil War, Virginia State University, Petersburg, VA, May 28, 2005, http://people.virginia.edu/~jh3v/retouchinghistory/essay.html.

23. Gary Scharrer, "Board Takes Up Books' Take on Religion," *Houston Chronicle,* September 15, 2010, http://www.chron.com/disp/story.mpl/metropoli tan/7203033.html.

24. Jacques Barzun, *The House of Intellect,* 122.

25. John Palfrey and Urs Gasser, *Born Digital,* 241.

26. Ibid., 242.

27. Ibid.

28. Walter Ong, *Orality and Literacy,* 78.

29. Eric Hoffer, *The True Believer,* 78.

30. Stuart Chase, *The Tyranny of Words,* 359.

31. George Orwell, "Politics and the English Language," *Horizon* 13/76, April 1946, 265.

32. Charles Morris, *Signs, Language and Behavior,* 121–122.

33. Wallbuilders.com,   http://www.wallbuilders.com/LIBissuesArticles.asp? id=22345.

34. http://www.facebook.com/group.php?gid=6650593277.

35. Robert Park, *Voodoo Science,* 5.

36. Ibid., 8.

37. Ibid., 138.

38. WallBuilders, David Barton bio, http://wallbuilders.com/SCHbioDB.asp.

39. Ibid.

40. Ken Robinson, "Changing Paradigms," 2008 Benjamin Franklin Awards lecture, http://www.thersa.org/events/vision/archive/sir-ken-robinson, or (excerpted, with animation) http://www.youtube.com/watch?v=zDZFcDGpL4U.

41. Bertrand Russell, *Our Knowledge of the External World,* 163.

42. *21st Century Skills, Education and Competitiveness: A Resource and Policy Guide.* Tucson, AZ: Partnership for 21st Century Skills, 6, http://p21.org/documents/21st_century_skills_education_and_competitiveness_guide.pdf.

43. Ibid.

44. Jacques Barzun, *The House of Intellect,* 109.

45. George Orwell, "In Front of Your Nose," *Tribune,* March 22, 1946, http://orwell.ru/library/articles/nose/english/e_nose.

46. Brendan Nyhan and Jason Reifler, "When Corrections Fail: The Persistence of Political Misperceptions," 323, http://www.springerlink.com/content/064786861r21m257/fulltext.pdf.

47. Ibid.

48. Eliot Eisner, "Benjamin Bloom, 1913–1999," *Prospects: The Quarterly Review of Comparative Education* vol. 30, no. 3, (September 2000): 4, http://www.ibe.unesco.org/publications/ThinkersPdf/bloome.pdf.

49. Fred Keller, " 'Good-Bye, Teacher,' " *Journal of Applied Behavioral Analysis,* 1:78–89.

50. J.A. Kulik, K. Carmichael, and C.L. Kulik, "The Keller Plan in Science Teaching: An Individually Paced, Student-Tutored, and Mastery-Oriented Instructional Method is Evaluated," 379.

51. Trebor Scolz, "Learning to Learn Through Digital Media," *Learning Through Digital Media: Essays on Technology and Pedagogy,* http://mediacommons.fu tureofthebook.org/mcpress/artoflearning/learning-through-digital-media/.

52. Roland Barthes, *Image-Music-Text,* 194.

53. Paulo Freire, *Pedagogy of the Oppressed,* 77.

54. Ibid., 80–81.

55. Laura Herrera, "In Florida, Virtual Classrooms With No Teachers," *New York Times,* January 18, 2011, A15, http://www.nytimes.com/2011/01/18/education/18classrooms.html?pagewanted=2.

56. Fred Keller, " 'Good-Bye, Teacher,' " *Journal of Applied Behavioral Analysis,* 1:78–89, 79.

57. Ibid., 81.

58. Richard Arum and Josipa Roksa, *Academically Adrift,* 54.

59. Ralph Tyler, *Basic Principles of Curriculum and Instruction,* 8.

60. Ibid., 63.

EIGHT

1. Henry Jenkins, *Convergence Culture: Where Old and New Media Collide* (New York: New York University Press, 2008), Kindle Loc: 545.

2. Ibid., Kindle Loc: 717.

3. "Visual Networking Index—Cisco Systems," Cisco Systems, Inc., http://www.cisco.com/en/US/netsol/ns827/networking_solutions_sub_solution.html.

4. Jennifer Valentino-DeVries, "Twitter Servers Can't Keep up with World Cup Traffic," *WSJ Blogs*—WSJ, June 16, 2010, http://blogs.wsj.com/digits/2010/06/16/twitter-servers-cant-keep-up-with-world-cup-traffic/.

5. Jesus Diaz, "Justin Bieber Has Dedicated Servers at Twitter," *Gizmodo,* September 7, 2010, http://gizmodo.com/5632095/justin-bieber-has-dedicated-servers-at-twitter.

6. Eli Pariser, "Beware Online 'Filter Bubbles'" TED: Ideas worth Spreading, March 2011, http://www.ted.com/talks/eli_pariser_beware_online_filter_bubbles.html.

7. Eli Pariser, "Mind Reading: The New Profiling Technique That Learns Exactly What Makes You Tick—and Buy," *Wired,* May 2011, 31–32.

8. Ibid., 32.

9. Jeff Howe, "The Rise of Crowdsourcing," *Wired,* June 2006, http://www.wired.com/wired/archive/14.06/crowds.html.

Bibliography

Aaker, Jennifer L., and Andy Smith. 2010. *The dragonfly effect: Quick, effective, and powerful ways to use social media to drive social change*. San Francisco: Jossey-Bass.

Abrahamson, Eric, and David H. Freedman. 2006. *A perfect mess: The hidden benefits of disorder: How crammed closets, cluttered offices, and on-the-fly planning make the world a better place*. New York: Little, Brown.

Adorno, Theodor. 1954. "Television and the Patterns of Mass Culture." *Quarterly of Film, Radio and Television* vol. 8, 213–235. Rpt. in Rosenberg, 474–488.

Alexander, Gregory S. 1997. *Commodity & propriety: Competing visions of property in American legal thought, 1776–1970*. Chicago: University of Chicago Press.

Arum, Richard, and Josipa Roksa. 2011. *Academically adrift: Limited learning on college campuses*. Chicago: University of Chicago Press.

Ayer, A.J. 1940. *The foundations of empirical knowledge*. London: Macmillan and Co., Limited.

Barlow, Aaron. 2007. *The rise of the blogosphere*. Westport, CT: Praeger.

Barzun, Jacques. 1961. *The house of intellect / Jacques Barzun*. New York: Harper & Brothers.

Bell, Clive. 1928. "How to Make a Civilization." *Civilization*. London: Chatto & Windus. Rpt. In Larrabee and Meyersohn, 31–38.

Benjamin, Walter, Howard Eiland, Kevin McLaughlin, and Rolf Tiedemann. 1999. *The arcades project*. Cambridge, MA: The Belknap Press of Harvard University Press.

Bergson, Henri, and Arthur Mitchell (trans.). 1931. *Creative evolution*. New York: Henry Holt.

Berman, Fran, Geoffrey Fox, and Anthony J. G. Hey. 2003. *Grid computing making the global infrastructure a reality*. Wiley series on parallel and distributed computing. Chichester, England: Wiley.

Bérubé, Michael. 2006. *What's liberal about the liberal arts?* New York: W. W. Norton.

Bester, Alfred. 2003 (1954). "Fondly Fahrenheit." Rpt. in Silverberg, 472–489.

Birkerts, Sven. 1994. *The Gutenberg elegies: The fate of reading in an electronic age*. Boston: Faber and Faber.

Bloom, Benjamin. 1976. *Human characteristics and school learning*. New York: McGraw-Hill.

Bok, Sissela. 1978. *Lying: Moral choice in public and private life*. New York: Pantheon Books.

Bolle, Leen De. 2010. *Deleuze and psychoanalysis: Philosophical essays on Deleuze's debate with psychoanalysis*. Leuven, Belgium: Leuven University Press.

Bolter, Jay David, and Richard Grusin. 2003. *Remediation: Understanding new media*. Cambridge, MA: MIT Press.

Borges, Jorge Luis. 1964. *Labyrinths; selected stories & other writings*. New York: New Directions Pub. Corp.

Borges, Jorge Luis. 1978. *The book of sand*. New York: Dutton.

Borgman, Christine L. 2007. *Scholarship in the digital age: Information, infrastructure, and the Internet*. Cambridge, MA: MIT Press.

Bowker, Geoffrey C., and Susan Leigh Star. 2000. *Sorting things out: Classification and its consequences*. Inside technology. Cambridge, MA: MIT Press.

Boyle, James. 2008. *The public domain: Enclosing the commons of the mind*. New Haven, CT: Yale University Press.

Bradley, Peter. 2007. "Performance and Property: Archive.org, Authorship, and Authenticity." In *The Grateful Dead and philosophy: Getting high minded about love and Haight,* ed. Steven Gimbel, 37–48. Chicago: Open Court.

Braidotti, Rosi. 2006. *Transpositions: On nomadic ethics*. Cambridge, UK: Polity Press.

Brand, Stewart. 1994. *How buildings learn: What happens after they're built*. New York: Viking.

Brown, John Seely, and Paul Duguid. 2000. *The social life of information*. Boston: Harvard Business School Press.

Carr, Nicholas G. 2010. *The shallows: What the Internet is doing to our brains*. New York: W. W. Norton.

Chase, Stuart. 1938. *The tyranny of words*. New York: Harcourt, Brace.

Cheney, Margaret. 1981. *Tesla, man out of time*. Englewood Cliffs, NJ: Prentice-Hall.

Cixous, Helene. 1976. "The Laugh of the Medusa." Translated by Keith Cohen and Paula Cohen. *Signs: Journal of Women in Culture and Society* 1, no. 4: 875–893.

Cixous, Helene. 1993. "We Who Are Free, Are We Free?" Translated by Chris Miller. *Critical Inquiry* 19, no. 2: 201–219.

Corning, William C., and Martin Balaban, ed. 1968. *The mind; biological approaches to its functions.* New York: Interscience Publishers.

Craven, John P. 2001. *The Silent War: The Cold War Battle beneath the sea.* New York: Simon & Schuster, 2001.

Danto, Arthur Coleman. 1981. *The transfiguration of the commonplace: A philosophy of art.* Cambridge, MA: Harvard University Press.

De Landa, Manuel. 1991. *War in the age of intelligent machines.* New York: Zone Books.

Dewey, John. 1927. *The public and its problems.* New York: H. Holt and Company.

Dick, Philip K. 1975. *Confessions of a crap artist: Jack Isidore (of Seville, Calif.): A chronicle of verified scientific fact, 1945–1959: A novel.* New York: Entwhistle Books.

Dreyfus, Hubert L. 2009. *On the Internet.* Milton Park, Abingdon, Oxon: Routledge.

Due, Reidar Andreas. 2007. *Deleuze.* Cambridge, MA: Blackwell Pub.

Eiland, Howard, and Kevin McLaughlin. "Translators' Foreword." In Benjamin. ix–xiv.

Eisenstein, Sergei. 1998. "The Dramaturgy of Film Form." In *The Eisenstein reader,* trans. Richard Taylor, 93–110. London: British Film Institute.

Feuer, Lewis S. 1958. *Spinoza and the rise of liberalism.* Boston: Beacon Press.

Forster, E. M. 1997. *The Machine stops and other stories.* London: André Deutsch.

Freire, Paulo. 1990. *Pedagogy of the oppressed.* New York: Continuum.

Gane, Nicholas, and Hannes Hansen-Magnusson. 2006. "Materiality Is the Message?" *Theory Culture and Society* 23, No. 7–8: 315–328.

Gibson, William. 1984. *Neuromancer.* New York: Ace Books.

Gillespie, Tarleton. 2007. *Wired shut: Copyright and the shape of digital culture.* Cambridge, MA: MIT Press.

Gimbel, Steven, ed. 2007. *The Grateful Dead and philosophy: Getting high minded about love and Haight.* Chicago: Open Court.

Gladwell, Malcolm. 2005. *Blink: The power of thinking without thinking.* New York: Little, Brown and Co.

Gladwell, Malcolm. 2010. "Small Change: Why the Revolution Will Not Be Tweeted." *The New Yorker,* October 4.

Gleick, James. 2011. *The information: A history, a theory, a flood.* New York: Pantheon Books.

Goldfarb, Jeffrey C. 1998. *Civility and subversion: The intellectual in democratic society.* Cambridge: Cambridge University Press.

Gopnik, Adam. 2011. "The Information: How the Internet Gets Inside Us." *New Yorker,* February 14.

Gorman, Lyn, and David McLean. 2009. *Media and society into the 21st century: A historical introduction.* Chichester, UK: Wiley-Blackwell.

Grant, Claire. 2007. *Crime and punishment in contemporary culture*. London: Routledge.

Habermas, Jürgen. 1989. *The structural transformation of the public sphere: An inquiry into a category of bourgeois society*. Studies in contemporary German social thought. Cambridge, MA: MIT Press.

Hardt, Michael. 2002. *Gilles Deleuze*. Minneapolis: University of Minnesota Press.

Harnad, S., and J.M.N. Hey. 1970. *Esoteric knowledge: The scholar and scholarly publishing on the net.*

Harnad, S. and J.M.N. Hey. 1995. "Esoteric knowledge: The scholar and scholarly publishing on the net." In *Networking and the future of libraries 2: Managing the intellectual record*. Proceedings of an International Conference, Bath, April 19–21, 1995, 110–116. Chicago: Library Association Publishing.

Harris, Jan L., and Paul A. Taylor. 2005. *Digital matters: Theory and culture of the matrix*. London: Routledge.

Hayles, N. Katherine. 1999. *How we became posthuman: Virtual bodies in cybernetics, literature, and informatics*. Chicago: University of Chicago Press.

Heidegger, Martin. 1992. *Parmenides*. Bloomington: Indiana University Press.

Hey, Tony, and Anne Trefethen. 2003. "The Data Deluge: An e-Science Perspective." http://eprints.ecs.soton.ac.uk/7648/1/The_Data_Deluge.pdf.

Higgins, Chris. 2002. *Nuclear submarine disasters*. Philadelphia: Chelsea House Publishers.

Hoffer, Eric. 1951. *The true believer: Thoughts on the nature of mass movements*. New York: Harper & Row.

Hofstadter, Douglas R. 1979. *Gödel, Escher, Bach*. New York: Basic Books.

Hofstadter, Richard. 1963. *Anti-intellectualism in American life*. New York: Knopf.

Hölldobler, Bert, Edward O. Wilson, and Margaret Cecile Nelson. 2009. *The superorganism: The beauty, elegance, and strangeness of insect societies*. New York: W. W. Norton.

Hook, Sidney, ed. 1969. *Dimensions of the mind: A symposium (proceedings)*. London: Collier Books.

Howe, Jeff. 2006. "The Rise of Crowdsourcing." *Wired*, 14, June 6.

Hudson, John. 2011. "The 'Twitter Revolution' Debate: The Egyptian Test Case—Global." *The Atlantic Wire*, January 31.

Hyde, Lewis. 2010. *Common as air: Revolution, art, and ownership*. New York: Farrar, Straus and Giroux.

James, William. 1956. *The will to believe and other essays in popular philosophy; human immortality: Two supposed objections to the doctrine*. New York: Dover.

Jenkins, Henry. 2006. *Convergence culture: Where old and new media collide*. New York: New York University Press.

Johns, Adrian. 2009. *Piracy: The intellectual property wars from Gutenberg to Gates*. Chicago: The University of Chicago Press.

Johnson, Paul. 1988. *Intellectuals*. New York: Harper & Row.

Johnson, Steven. 2010. *Where good ideas come from: The natural history of innovation*. New York: Riverhead Books.

Kauffman, Stuart A. 1995. *At home in the universe: The search for laws of self-organization and complexity*. New York: Oxford University Press.

Keen, Andrew. 2007. *The cult of the amateur: How today's Internet is killing our culture*. New York: Doubleday/Currency.

Kelly, Kevin. 1994. *Out of control: The rise of neo-biological civilization*. Reading, MA: Addison-Wesley.

Kelly, Kevin. 2010. *What technology wants*. New York: Viking.

Kerslake, Christian. 2010. "Desire and the Dialectics of Love: Deleuze, Canguilhem, and the Philosophy of Desire." In *Deleuze and psychoanalysis: Philosophical essays on Deleuze's debate with psychoanalysis,* 51–82. Leuven, Belgium: Leuven University Press.,

Kittler, Friedrich A. 2006. *Gramophone, Film, Typewriter*. Stanford, CA: Stanford University Press.

Kuhn, Thomas S. 1962. *Structure of scientific revolutions*. Chicago: University of Chicago Press.

Kulik, J.A., K. Carmichael, and C.L. Kulik. 1974. "The Keller Plan in science teaching: An individually paced, student-tutored, and mastery-oriented instructional method is evaluated." *Science* (New York). 183 (4123): 379–383.

Kurzweil, Ray. 2005. *The singularity is near: When humans transcend biology*. New York: Viking.

Langton, Christopher G., ed. 1994. *Artificial life III: Proceedings of the workshop on artificial life.* Held June 1992 in Santa Fe, New Mexico. Reading, MA: Addison-Wesley, Advanced Book Program.

Larrabee, Eric, and Rolf Meyersohn, ed. 1958. *Mass leisure*. Glencoe, IL: Free Press.

Lessig, Lawrence. 2001. *The future of ideas: The fate of the commons in a connected world*. New York: Random House.

Lessig, Lawrence. 2004. *Free culture: How big media uses technology and the law to lock down culture and control creativity*. New York: Penguin Press.

Lessig, Lawrence. 2008. *Remix: Making art and commerce thrive in the hybrid economy*. New York: Penguin Press.

Lettvin, J.Y., H.R. Maturana, W.S. MacCulloch, and W.H. Pitts. 1968. "What the Frog's Eye Tells the Frog's Brain." In *The mind; biological approaches to its functions,* ed., William C. Corning, and Martin Balaban, 233–258. New York: Interscience Publishers.

Lippmann, Walter. 1914. *Drift and mastery: An attempt to diagnose the current unrest*. New York: Kennerley.

Lippmann, Walter. 1955. *Essays in the public philosophy*. Boston: Little, Brown.

Madrigal, Alexis. 2011. "The Inside Story of How Facebook Responded to Tunisian Hacks." *The Atlantic,* January 24.

Markoff, John. 2006. *What the dormouse said: How the sixties counterculture shaped the personal computer industry.* New York: Penguin Books.

Martineau, James. 1901. *Types of ethical theory,* vol. 2. Oxford: Clarendon Press.

Maturana, Humberto R., and Francisco J. Varela. 1980. *Autopoiesis and cognition: The realization of the living.* Boston studies in the philosophy of science, vol. 42. Dordrecht, Holland: D. Reidel Pub. Co.

McLeod, Kembrew. 2007. *Freedom of expression®: Resistance and repression in the age of intellectual property.* Minneapolis: University of Minnesota Press.

McLuhan, Marshall. 1954 "Sight, Sound, and Fury." *Commonweal,* vol. 60, 168–197. Rpt. in Rosenberg, 489–495.

McLuhan, Marshall. 1964. *Understanding media; the extensions of man.* New York: McGraw-Hill.

McLuhan, Marshall, and Quentin Fiore. 1967. *The medium is the massage.* New York: Bantam Books.

Menand, Louis, ed. 1996. *The future of academic freedom.* Chicago: University of Chicago Press.

Millones, Mark M. 1994. "Swarms, Phase Transitions, and Collective Intelligence." In *Artificial life III: Proceedings of the workshop on artificial life,* ed., Christopher G. Langton. Reading, MA: Addison-Wesley, 417–446.

Mitchell, Henry C. 2005. *The intellectual commons: Toward an ecology of intellectual property.* Lexington studies in social, political, and legal philosophy. Lanham, MD: Lexington Books.

More, Thomas. 2008. *Utopia.* Rockville, MD: Arc Manor.

Moretti, Franco. 2005. *Graphs, maps, trees: Abstract models for a literary history.* London: Verso.

Morris, Charles. 1946. *Signs, language and behavior.* New York: Braziller.

Netanel, Neil. 2008. *Copyright's paradox.* Oxford: Oxford University Press.

Norman, Donald A. 1998. *The invisible computer: Why good products can fail, the personal computer is so complex, and information appliances are the solution.* Cambridge, MA: MIT Press.

Ong, Walter J. 1982. *Orality and literacy: The technologizing of the word.* London: Methuen.

Palfrey, John G., and Urs Gasser. 2008. *Born digital: Understanding the first generation of digital natives.* New York: Basic Books.

Patry, William F. 2009. *Moral panics and the copyright wars.* New York: Oxford University Press.

Pursell, Carroll. 2007. *The machine in America: A social history of technology.* Baltimore, MD: The Johns Hopkins University Press.

Quine, W. V. 1960. *Word and object.* Cambridge: Technology Press of the Massachusetts Institute of Technology.

Rheingold, Howard. 2003. *Smart mobs: The next social revolution*. Cambridge, MA: Perseus Pub.

La Rochefoucauld, François. John Heard, trans. 1982. *Maxims of Le duc de La Rochefoucauld*. Brookline Village, MA: Branden Press.

Rorty, Richard. 1979. *Philosophy and the mirror of nature*. Princeton: Princeton University Press.

Rosenberg, Bernard, and David Manning White. 1957. *Mass culture: The popular arts in America*. Glencoe, IL: The Free Press of Glencoe.

Rushkoff, Douglas. 2010. *Program or Be Programmed: Ten Commands for a Digital Age*. New York: OR Books.

Russell, Bertrand. 1960. *Our knowledge of the external world by Bertrand Russell*. New York: New American Library.

Russell, Bertrand. 2004 (1935). "In Praise of Idleness." *In praise of idleness and other essays*. London: Routledge, 1–15. http://www.netlibrary.com/urlapi.asp?action=summary&v=1&bookid=105266.

Sagan, Carl. 1995. *The demon-haunted world: Science as a candle in the dark*. New York: Random House.

Sawyer, R. Keith. 2006. *Explaining creativity: The science of human innovation*. Oxford: Oxford University Press.

Shirky, Clay. 2008. *Here Comes Everybody: The Power of Organizing without Organizations*. New York: Penguin Press.

Shirky, Clay. 2010. *Cognitive surplus: Creativity and generosity in a connected age*. New York: Penguin Press.

Silverberg, Robert. 2003. *The science fiction hall of fame. The greatest science fiction stories of all time chosen by the members of the Science Fiction Writers of America*, Vol. 1, 1929–1964. New York: Tor.

Slouka, Mark. 1995. *War of the worlds: Cyberspace and the high-tech assault on reality*. New York: BasicBooks.

Stoll, Clifford. 1995. *Silicon snake oil: Second thoughts on the information highway*. New York: Doubleday.

Surowiecki, James. 2004. *The wisdom of the crowds: Why the many are smarter than the few*. London: Abacus.

Taylor, Mark C. 2001. *The moment of complexity: Emerging network culture*. Chicago: University of Chicago Press.

Thorburn, David, and Henry Jenkins. 2003. *Rethinking media change: The aesthetics of transaction*. Cambridge, MA: The MIT Press.

Trouillot, Michel-Rolph. 1995. *Silencing the past: Power and the production of history*. Boston: Beacon Press.

Turkle, Sherry. 2008. *The inner history of devices*. Cambridge, MA: MIT Press.

Twenge, Jean M., and W. Keith Campbell. 2009. *The narcissism epidemic: Living in the age of entitlement*. New York: Free Press.

Ulmer, Gregory L. 1994. *Heuretics: The logic of invention*. Baltimore: Johns Hopkins University Press.

Vaidhyanathan, Siva. 2010. *The Googlization of everything: How one company is transforming culture, commerce, and community—and why we should worry*. London: Profile.

Virilio, Paul. 1997. *Open sky*. London: Verso.

Weiner, Norbert. 1960. "The Brain and the Machine (Summary)." Presented during the Third Annual New York University Institute of Philosophy, New York, May 15–16, 1959. Also in Hook, Sidney, ed. 1969. *Dimensions of the mind: A symposium (proceedings)*. London: Collier Books. 109–112.

Welch, Matt. 2011. "The Arab Spring." *Reason,* May.

Wershler-Henry, Darren. 2007. *The iron whim: A fragmented history of typewriting*. Ithaca, NY: Cornell University Press.

Whorf, Benjamin Lee. 1956. *Language, thought, and reality: Selected writings*. Cambridge: Technology Press of Massachusetts Institute of Technology.

Wilson, Edward O. 1975. *Sociobiology: The new synthesis*. Cambridge, MA: Belknap Press of Harvard University Press.

Wilson, Edward O. 1998. *Consilience: The unity of knowledge*. New York: Knopf.

Wilson, Edward Osborne. 2004. *On human nature*. Cambridge, MA: Harvard University Press.

Winner, Langdon. 1980. "Do Artifacts Have Politics?" *Daedalus* 109, no. 1: 121–136.

Wittkower, D.E. 2008. *IPod and philosophy: ICon of an EPoch*. Chicago: Open Court.

Wolin, Sheldon S. 2010. *Democracy incorporated: Managed democracy and the specter of inverted totalitarianism*. Princeton, NJ: Princeton University Press.

Wu, Tim. 2010. *The master switch: The rise and fall of information empires*. New York: Alfred A. Knopf.

Index

Acker, Jennifer, 177
Adorno, Theodor, 160
Advertising: copyrights and revenues from, 72–73; cultural impact of, 155; digital highway's impact, 139–40; impact of "hypermediacy" on, 137; on the Internet, 165; Lippmann's comments about, 136–37; manipulation themes of, 67; and sociotechnical systems, 136; unauthorized acts and, 82
Amazon, 106–7, 233, 235
American Civil Liberties Union (ACLU), 104
An American Dictionary of the English Language (Noah Webster), 99
American Journal of Distance Education, 223
AMOLED (active-matrix organic light emitting diode) displays, 18
Android operating system: BUMP application, 19
An Essay on Criticism (Pope), 208–9
Ants: African success of eusociality among, 114–15; allelo-mimesis adaptive system, 118; "copy your neighbor" behavior of, 176; emergent behavior of, 112, 133; human vs.

ant colonies, 117, 119, 129; success of eusociality among, 114–15; as superorganism, 115; Taylor's fascination with, 116
Apple, 21, 23, 88, 104–6
The Arcades Project (Benjamin), 41, 55–56, 58, 60
Arroyo, Sarah, 189
Artificial intelligence: and evolutionary computation, 174; growing likelihood of, 60, 167; hive mind concept in, 110; human intelligence and, 167; self-awareness vs., 115; Watson IBM computer example, 111
Arum, Richard, 225
At Home in the Universe (Kauffman), 3
Atlantic Monthly article (2008), 110
"The Author to Her Book" (Bradstreet), 90
Autopoiesis (self-making) concept, 6, 162–63

Barthes, Roland, 101–2, 104, 221–22
Barton, David, 214
Barzun, Jacques: on failure of reliance of testing, 198; on working together minus a teacher, 201, 218; writings of, 205
Bateson, Gregory, 160

Batman Returns, use of flocking simulation program, 3

Baudelaire, Charles: "browser" concept identification, 35; expansive view of the flâneur, 40–41, 45; "The Painter of Modern Life" essay, 36, 37–38

BBC (United Kingdom), 33

Bebe, William, 118

Beck, Glenn, 32

Being and Time (Heidegger), 191

Bell, Clive, 39

Benjamin, Walter, 34, 41, 55–60, 102–3

Bently, Lionel, 88–89

Bergson, Henri, 8, 9

Berkman Center for the Internet and Society, 125

Bernanke, Ben, 171

Berry, David, 45

Bessie, Adam, 203

Biggs, Abraham, 190

Birkerts, Sven, 189

Birther movement, 211

Blackberry cell phones, 37, 171

Blink (Gladwell), 158

"Bloggers vs. journalists" article (Rosen), 34

Blogs/blogging (bloggers, blog posts): Anthony Curtis, 73; blogger profile, 33; Charles Johnson, 31; crap artists disparaging attitudes, 35; denigration by traditional journalists, 33–34; journalist envy issue, 35; *literatura mundana* blog, 44; Pajamas Media, 31; Roger Simon, 31; on Wikipedia, 19

Bloom, Benjamin, 219–20

Boids flocking program (of Reynolds), 2–3

Bolter, Jay, 11

"The Book of Sand" (Borges), 50–52, 54, 57–58, 61

Books: changing forms of, 11–12; desires exhibited by, 6; electronic tools for reading, 12–13; importance in Renaissance culture, 4

Boon, Marcus: advocacy for copying, 65, 94–95, 102; limited impact of, 93;

support of Benjamin, 103; writings on "free access," 67

Borges, Jorge Luis: on context and meaning, 154; on copying original material, 153; on limitations of knowledge acquisition, 53; on problems of the Internet, 50–51

Borgman, Christine: "complex environments" of, 144; on implications of technology for scholarship, 142–43; on sociotechnical systems, 135–36

Bradstreet, Anne, 90

Braidotto, Rosi, 9–10

Browsers: Baudelaire's identification of, 35–36, 37; bloggers as/and use of, 34, 48; comparison with *Star Trek* computers, 198; Russell on promise of, 38–39; Russell's view of, 47; self-centeredness of, 62

Buffett, Warren, 170

BUMP smart phone application, 19

Burdick, Eugene, 12

Burton, Tim: use of flocking simulation program, 3

Business Link program, 130

Campbell, Keith, 187

Carpenter, Loren, 1–2; flight simulator challenge, 2; Pong game challenge, 1

Carr, Nicholas: article on Google, 110; on information and cognition, 27; support of McLuhan, 26

Carter, Geoff, 190

Carter, Jimmy, 170

Cary, Joyce, 101

Cascades: avoidance requirements, 132; influence/nature of, 126; occasional negative effects of, 133

Causal agent (Bergson), 8

Center for Digital Democracy, 107

Center for Digital Research in the Humanities, 43

Chase, Stuart: on complexity of culture, 155; faith in language, 144–45, 208; on map, mapped, user relation, 144

Cheltenham Literature Festival, 33

China: collapse of, 140; cultural calcification in, 145–46; exploitation by international companies, 171; filtering of Internet access, 62
Circular mill, 118–19, 127, 176
Cisco Visual Networking Index, 189
Clark, Andy, 37
Clementi, Tyler, 189, 190
Cognitive Surplus (Shirky), 184, 188–89
Collections of Antipiracy Act, 84
Common Sense (Paine), 85
A Compendious Dictionary of the English Language (Noah Webster), 99
Complex adaptive systems: computational intelligence and, 174; conditions necessary in, 132; displays of emergent behavior, 132; financial bubbles and, 176; financial sector as, 170; human brain as, 26; intelligent group behavior association, 118, 131, 231; Internet as, 117, 133; keys to understanding, 116; mathematical simulations of, 29; social media/participatory culture comparison, 177; Surowiecki's examples, 122; swarm logic rules, 27; as technium component, 6. *See also* Decentralization; Superorganism
Computational power, 157
Computer literacy, 12
Confessions of a Crap Artist (Dick), 32
Constitution (U.S.), 69–70, 81, 95, 107, 109, 147, 208
Content Management Systems (CMS), 45
Cooper, James Fenimore, 40
Copying: Boon's advocacy for, 65, 94–95, 102; Frederick's opinion on, 71; McLeod's opinion on, 77
Copyright Act (1831), 89
Copyrights (copyright law): Congressional compromises, 77; contemporary laws, 71, 78, 80, 87; contraventions of, 72; copier's vs., 73; corporate extension promotion, 81; digital age transition, 48, 78–79; fair use doctrine, 72, 76, 78, 79–80; free distribution vs., 82, 84; growing extent of, 97–98; historical background,

88–89; need for changing conventions, 47; relation of authors to, 69, 98–99; relation of "fair use doctrine," 79; Righthaven company protections of, 66, 72–77; *Sony v. Universal City Studios* (1984), 73; U.S.-related legislation, 69–70, 84; use of, by book purchasers, 49; views of Lessig, 81–82, 95–96; views of Rose, 91, 95; WikiLeaks issue, 105–6, 105–8. *See also* Intellectual property
Crap artists, 31–32; characteristics, 38; disparaging attitudes towards bloggers, 35; loss of Internet control, 33; name derivation, 31–32; parody of, 37; realization of one, 32
Craven, John P., 120–21
Creative Commons organization, 77, 83, 93
Crowd intelligence: application of power of, 112; and cascades, 126, 132–33; cells forming brain (example), 112–13; circular mill and, 118–19, 127, 176; described, 127; growing importance of, 109–10; question of existence of, 112; relation of "emergence" and, 113–14; requirements for functioning, 131. *See also* Ants; Superorganism; Surowiecki, James
Culture: oral vs. literate, 10–11
Cyberspace: described, 42–43

Davis, Diane, 190
"The Death of the Author" (Barthes), 101
Decentralization: as fan community quality, 231–32; and individual/ group decisions, 124, 127, 129, 132; observations of Surowiecki, 119, 123; technology and, 14; and wealth creation, 171
Defoe, Daniel, 89–91
De Landa, Manual, 182
Deleuze, Gilles, 7–9
Democratic Underground: counter lawsuit against Righthaven, 75–76; defense use of fair use doctrine, 79; lawsuit against, 73; Righthaven lawsuit against, 73, 75

Dick, Philip K.: Barlow's doctoral dissertation on, 68; on "crap artists," 31–32; society as envisioned by, 155
Difference and Repetition (Deleuze), 9
Digital highway, 139
Digital humanities, 43–44, 139
Digital literacy, 11–12
Digital Matters: Theory and Culture of the Matrix (Harris & Taylor), 24–25
Digital Millennium Copyright Act, 84
Digital Natives, 206–7
Digital resources, 135, 204. *See also* Internet; Social networking
Digital revolution, 86, 137. *See also* Internet; Social media; Social networking; World Wide Web
Dilettante, observations of, 38
"Directional evolution" description (Kelly), 28
Directors Guild of America, 70
Divergent thinking: as basis for creativity, problem solving, 225–26; benefits for learning/web use, 215–16; benefits for schools, 216–17; scientific method association, 216
"Doctrine of the Similar" essay (Benjamin), 103
Dooling, Richard: evolutionary algorithm concerns, 175; financial industry opinion piece, 169–72
The Dragonfly Effect (Acker & Smith), 177
Drew, Christopher, 119
Drift and Mastery (Lippmann), 136
Dromospheric pollution crisis (Virilio), 17–18
Duchamp, Marcel: alterations of copyrighted work, 71, 74, 93, 153; on limits of knowledge, 53
Due, Reidar, 7
Dyson, George, 169–70

The Earth Is Flat (Friedman), 210
eBooks, 12
Education, preparation for the digital age, 225–27
Elan vital force (Bergson), 8, 9

Electronic Frontier Foundation (EFF), 73
Electronic journals and archives, 47
Electronic tools for reading, 12–13
Emergence: defined, 113–14; Word processing and virtual communities, 132
Emergence: The Connected Lives of Ants, Brains, Cities, and Software (Steven Johnson), 109, 112
Emory, Evan, 190
Everything Bad is Good For You (Steven Johnson), 109, 112
Evolutionary algorithms: association with financial crisis, 170–71; defined, 174; Dooley's outrage about, 175

Facebook: as global civilization infrastructure, 17; gratification gained from, 20; and politics, 106, 125; role in Jasmine Revolution, 126; social transformation caused by, 39; use of, on information appliances, 23
Fair use doctrine, 72, 76, 78, 79–80
The Filter Bubble: What the Internet is Hiding From You (Pariser), 153
Financial crisis (2008), 175–76; Dooling's *NY Times* opinion piece, 169; housing-derivatives market, 126
First Amendment (U.S. Constitution), 107
Fisher v. Dees (1986), 79
Flocking and schooling simulation program (Reynolds), 2–3
FoxNews television, 31
Francis, Sherrin, 190
Frankenstein (Shelley), 50
Franklin, Wayne, 40–41
Frederick, Sherman: on copying as stealing, 71; defense of copyright protection, 66; suing without warning process, 72
Freire, Paolo, 221–22
Freud, Sigmund, 8
Friedman, Thomas, 210
FTP (File Transfer Protocol), 50–51

Gasser, Urs, 205–6
Gates, Bill: false choices presented by, 203; original Windows concepts, 104
Gibson, Steve, 72–73
Gibson, William, 148
Ginsberg, Jane, 88–89
Gladwell, Malcolm: belief in social desires of humans, 186; identification of "thin-slicing," 158; Morozov's support of, 182; *New Yorker* article, 172–73, 177, 182; opinion of social media, 178, 180–81, 184; opinion of the Internet, 42, 151, 179; social media story, 177–78; support of Pariser, 234–35; vs. cyber-utopians, 152
The Global Achievement Gap (Wagner), 202
Google: Brabazon's book about, 199; Carr's article on, 110; comprehending role of, 57; faith in usefulness of, 51; as global civilization infrastructure, 17; news filtering mechanics, 233–34; Pariser on search filtering, 233–34; and politics, 106; and Project Gutenberg, 138; search algorithm, 122, 200; search for "Joseph Wesley Newman," 212–13; Wu's opinion of, 14–15
Graphs, Maps, Trees (Moretti), 159
Grateful Dead, 81–85
Great Britain: copyrights laws, 88–89, 96–98; *Donaldson v. Beckett* (1774), 96; Statute of Anne, 88–89, 93; Statute of Monopolies, 88–89; vaccination issue, 200
Greenberg, Douglas, 139–40
Griffith, D. W., 14
Gropnik, Adam, 34
Groupthink: allelomimesis leading to, 231; of the cascade, 125, 133; described, 110
Grusin, Richard, 11
Guattari, Felix, 7–8
Guggenheim, Davis, 196
Gutenberg, Johannes: development of printing press, 84–85; information revolution started by, 135, 140;

McLuhan's comments on, 86. *See also* Project Gutenberg

Handler, Jerome, 204
Haraway, Donna, 182
Harnad, Steve, 47
Harris, Jan, 24–25
Hayles, Katherine, 160, 162–63, 182
Heidegger, Martin, 191–92
Helms, Jason, 191–92
Here Comes Everybody (Shirky), 109, 178, 184, 188
Hive mind: collective intelligence and, 174; connection with network culture, 3; growing possibility of, 60, 135; use of, in artificial intelligence, 110
Hoffer, Eric, 208
Hofstadter, Richard, 165
Hölldbler, Bert, 115
The House of Intellect (Barzun), 205
Hyper Text Markup Language (HTML), 45–46, 158

Image ownership, 100, 104
Immanence, beliefs in, 7, 9
India, exploitation by international companies, 171
Information appliances, 21
Information technology, 13–14
Intellectual property: argument for absolute, perpetual ownership, 69; argument of O'Connor, 95; contemporary issues, 105; copying, Boon's advocacy for, 65, 94–95, 102; copyrights and, 48; Defoe's property analogy, 89–90; in the digital age, 65–108; Directors Guild vs. CleanFlicks dispute, 70–71, 100–101; growing extent of, 97–98; image ownership issues, 100, 104; Internet enforcement of, 102; McLeod's comments, 68; Mitchell's comments, 88; ownership by authors, 91; Righthaven lawsuits, 102, 105; ruling of Judge Posner, 66–67; view of Jarvis, 103
International Telecommunications Union (ITU), 125

Internet: adoption of, 13–14; analog era vs. era of, 29; authentic ubiquity potential of, 16, 23; convergence of media on, 17; dawn of, 1; dismissiveness of, 32; evolutionary algorithms, 170–71, 174–75; FTP technology, 50–51; Google business model dawn of, 14–15; increasing dominance of time usage, 18; "internet fool" image, 33; Klein/Palin's dismissiveness of, 32; knowledge gathering capability, 35; Lessig's comments on, 56; 19th century Paris arcade comparison, 41; opinions of Gladwell, 42, 151, 179; postal service comparison, 41; security, confidence problems of, 56–57; success of pornography on, 36–37; as a superorganism, 4; use by PR2 robot, 5; use on smart phones, 18–20; "web surfer" description, 36, 39; Wu's opinions on, 14–15. *See also* Google; Social networking
The Invention of Love (Stoppard), 14
The Invisible Computer (Norman), 21
iPad, 12; commercial for, 21, 23; computing power of, 18
iPhone, 17; BUMP application, 19; computing power of, 18; experience of initial awe at, 21; as extension of biological processing, 37; user addiction to, 17
"Is Google Making Us Stupid?" (Carr), 110

James, William, 156–59
Jarvis, Jeff, 103
Jasmine Revolution, 125–26, 182
Jefferson, Thomas, 212
Jenkins, Henry, 166
Jobs, Steve, 104
Johnson, Charles (blogger), 31
Johnson, Samuel, 195
Johnson, Stephen, 159
Johnson, Steven Berlin, 112; on wisdom of groups, crowds, mobs, 102
Jordan, Ervin, 204

Journalists: as bloggers, 177; "Bloggers vs. journalists" article, 34; blogging promotion by, 33; citizen journalists, 176; comparison with videographers, 185; for-sale journalists, 150; jealousy issue with bloggers, 35
Jung, Carl, 8

Kauffman, Stuart, 3
Kay, Alan, 4
Kayles, Katherine, 45
Keen, Andrew, 141, 146–47, 211
Keller, Fred, 220–22. *See also* Personalized System of Instruction
Kelly, Kevin, 1–7, 10; article on the "technium," 113; definition of *want,* 6–7; "directional evolution" description, 28; "glorious network culture" belief, 5; on individual technologies vs. technological ecology, 5–6; on the Internet as "superorganism," 4; 1991 computer conference attendance, 1–2; problems vs. solutions from technology, 29; and the return of *zoe,* 10, 30; on self-organizational patterns of natural systems, 27. *See also* Technium
Kerslake, Christian, 8–9
Kindle reader, 12–13; computing power of, 18
King, Martin Luther, Jr., 100
Kirschenbaum, Matthew, 44–45
Kittler, Friedrich, 24–25, 27
Klein, Jonathan, 31–33
Knight, Hazel, 121
Kornbluth, Cyril, 32
Kubrick, Stanley, 163

Laptop computers: evolution of, 18; as extension of biological processing, 37
Larrabee, Eric, 36
Layars smart phone application, 20
Lederer, William, 12
Leibniz, Gottfried, 7
Leslie, Ester, 60–61
Lessig, Lawrence: on Internet as e2e network, 56; support of Creative

Commons, 83; views on copyrights, 81–82, 95–96
Leston, Robert, 190
Libido: Jung's vs. Freud's definition, 8–9
Lichenstein, Roy, 104
Lippmann, Walter: era of advertising comments, 136; information-gathering, good decision-making beliefs, 142; on mindful reflection, 164
Liquid crystal displays (LCDs), 18
Literacy: computer vs. digital, 11, 12–13, 202; 18th century value of written word, 84, 87; movement from "orality" to, 140; Ong's belief in value of, 85–86; shift away from, 15, 26, 202; technology as end to, 15; as Western culture foundation, 10, 13
Literary Copyright Act (1814), 89
literatura mundana blog, 44
Luke, Robert, 37

Macintosh operating system, 104
Mack, Mary Bono, 69–70
Manovich, Lev, 39
"The Marching Morons" (Kornbluth), 32
Marr, Andrew, 33
Martineau, James: contrast with Wolin, 151; on group mindset, 149–50
Masoff, Joy, 203–7
Mass Leisure (Larrabee & Meyersohn), 36
The Matrix, 3–4
Matsch, Richard, 71
Maturana, Humberto: exploration of autopoiesis, 6, 162; Hayles's use of knowledge of, 162–63; introduction of "allopoietic" term, 163; view of living systems, 162; view on mastery, 164
McBride, Kelly, 72–73
McCarthy, Jenny, 200
McLeod, Kembrew: on copying, 77; on intellectual property, 68; on ownership of images, 100, 104; web comparison to cowboy days, 152
McLuhan, Marshall: on artists as "antenna of the human race," 183; Carr's comments about, 26; comments about Gutenberg, 86; Kittler's agreement

and differences with, 24–25, 27; on literacy of Western civilization, 11–12; "medium is the message" concept, 23–24, 230; on talking being at the core of invention, 159–60; *Understanding Media,* 135
Medium is the Message (McLuhan), 24
Merriam, Charles and George, 99
Metadata: data compared with, 158–59, 164; as a schema, 159
Meyersohn, Rolf, 36
Microsoft: and politics, 106
Mitchell, Arthur, 8
Mitchell, Henry: on authors rights, 91; on copyright law, 69; description of "creation," 98; on intellectual property, 65, 80, 88
Moore, Michael, 223
Moretti, Franco, 159
Morozov, Evgeny: anarchy of the web comments, 148; comparison with Gladwell, 152, 182; comparison with Keen and Stoll, 146–47; views about technology, 141, 143–44
Morris, Charles, 209

Narcissism: cultural narcissism and Web 2.0, 187; Shirky on, 188; and use of social media, 181, 188, 194
The Narcissism Epidemic (Campbell), 187
The Net Delusion: The Dark Side of Internet Freedom (Morozov), 141, 182
Net Neutrality, 48
Network Culture, 4
New Yorker magazine, 172–73
No Child Left Behind legislation, 196
No Electronic Theft Act, 84
Nonorganic life, 9
Nook reader, 12
Norman, Donald: Apple design consultancy position, 23; information processing description, 21; recognition of infancy of computers, 22
Nyhan, Brendan, 219

Obama, Barack, 171, 175, 211
O'Connor, Sandra Day, 95

Ong, Walter: on impact of technology, 86–87; on inability to "refute a text," 207–8; on shift from oral to literate cultures, 10–11, 85–86, 140
"On the Mimetic Faculty" essay (Benjamin), 103
Orality and Literacy (Ong), 85–86
The O'Reilly Factor (FoxNews), 31
The Origin of Order (Kauffman), 3
Orwell, George, 166, 208, 218
Out of Control (Kelly), 1–5, 27, 183; graphics conference description, 1–2; recommended by Wachowski brothers, 3–4; on self-organizational patterns of natural systems, 27

Paine, Thomas, 85
"The Painter of Modern Life" essay (Baudelaire), 36, 37–38
Pajamas Media blog, 31
Palfrey, John, 205–6
Palin, Sarah, 31–32, 177
Palo Alto Research Center (PARC), 104–5
Pariser, Eli: on the chaos of the web, 153; experimental bookstore description, 234–35; on Google's information filtering, 233–34
Park, Robert, 212–13
The Parmenides (Heidegger), 192
Participatory culture technologies. *See* Social media
Partnership for 21st Century Skills, 218
Parviz, Babak, 20
Paulson, Henry, 171
Personalized System of Instruction (PSI) (Keller), 220–22
"Pierre Menard, Author of Quixote" (Borge), 52, 60, 153
Poetics (Aristotle), 85
"Pong" computer game, 1
Pope, Alexander, 208
Pornography, success on the Internet, 36–37
Posner, Richard, 66–67
Postal service, comparison with Internet, 41

Postman, Neil: on coming obsolescence of teachers, 201; on transformation of information, 84–85, 145, 195
Pox: An American History (Willrich), 200
Poynter Institute, 72–73
Presidential election (2008), 31
Program or be Programmed (Rushkoff), 194
Project Gutenberg, 138
PR2 open-source personal robot, 5
Publishing (book publishing): copyright traditions, 84; digital publishing, 83; prediction of end of, 15; scholarly publishing, 43, 46, 108; transformation of form, 47

Quinn, Christine, 128, 130

Race to the Top legislation, 196
Ramsay, Stephen, 43
Rapture for the Geeks: When AI Outsmarts IQ (Dooling), 169
Rather, Dan, 31
Ravitch, Diane, 196, 203
Rebney, Jack, 190
Recording Industry Association of America (RIAA), 73, 96
Reifler, Jason, 219
"Retouching History: The Modern Falsification of a Civil War Photograph" (Tuite), 204
Reynolds, Craig, 2–3
Rhee, Michele, 203
Rheingold, Howard: on complex adaptive systems, 131–32; on wisdom of groups, crowds, mobs, 109
Righthaven: closely held copyright concept development, 76–77; Democratic Underground lawsuit, 75–76, 79; factors allowing narrow interpretations, 80; intellectual property lawsuits, 102, 105; music file sharing cases, 96; protections of copyrights by, 66, 72–77; suing without warning process, 72–73
Robinson, Eugene, 106
Robinson, Kenneth, 196–97, 213, 225

Roksa, Josipa, 225
Rose, Mark: property/limited variability metaphor, 91, 95; questions about property ownership, 90
Rosen, Jay, 34
Royal Society for the Encouragement of Arts, Manufactures, and Commerce, 196–97
Rushkoff, Douglas, 194
Russell, Bertrand, 38, 39

Scholarly publishing, 43, 46, 47, 108
Shelley, Mary, 50
Shirky, Clay: claims about Flickr, 187; Gladwell's comments about, 178–79; limiting view of social media, 173; on narcissism in culture, 188; participatory culture viewpoint, 193–94; social media utopian identity, 172, 182; telematics viewpoint of, 185–86; Web 2.0 viewpoint of, 184–85; on wisdom of groups, crowds, mobs, 109. See also Cognitive Surplus; Here Comes Everybody
The Silent War (Craven), 120
Silicon Snake Oil (Stoll), 137
Simon, Roger, 31
"Small Change: Why the Revolution Will Not be Tweeted" (Gladwell), 173, 177, 182
Smart Mobs (Rheingold), 109, 131
Smart phones: as extension of biological processing, 37
Smith, Andy, 177
Social media: advocacy for, 182, 186; Campbell's investigation of, 187; and collective intelligence research, 131, 177; Gladwell's opinion of, 178, 180–81, 184, 186; Jasmine Revolution role, 126; and narcissism, 181, 188, 194; online variant of traditional activism, 151–52; political role, 175; potential negative consequences, 190; role of, 125; swarm logic domination in, 174; and 2008 financial crisis, 175–76; usefulness vs. non-usefulness, 185; utopian segment, 172; Wu's

viewpoint, 13–14. See also Facebook; Twitter
Social networking: as browsing method, 35; convenience for spreading messages, 180; "feedback loop" aspect, 206; kidnapping use in Mexico, 147; messages absorbed by young people, 187; overhype on role of, 42; self-sabotage by politicians, 177; transformation of the Web, 39; transformation of Web usage, 39
Sociobiology: The New Synthesis (Edward O. Wilson), 114
Sonny Bono Copyright Term Extension Act (1998), 69–70, 84
Sontag, Sherry, 119
Sony Reader, 12
Sony v. Universal City Studios (1984), 73
Space Shuttle Challenger explosion, 122
Spinoza, Baruch, 7, 9
Statute of Anne (English law) (1710), 88–89, 93
Statute of Monopolies (English law) (1624), 88–89
Stephens Media Company, 66
Stiegler, Bernard, 182, 191–92
Stoll, Clifford: arguments against web commerce, 137–39; comparison with Keen and Morozov, 141, 146; on problems posed by the Internet, 211
Stoppard, Tom, 14
Stowe, Harriet Beecher, 49
Strumm, Oliver, 128–31
Suing without warning process, 72. See also Righthaven
Superorganism: defined, 116; Hölldbler's viewpoint, 115; human harnessing of the collective, 122; individual human comparison, 117; Internet as, 4, 117–18; Kelly's viewpoint, 113; technium component of, 6; Wilson's viewpoint, 114–15
The Superorganism: The Beauty, Elegance, and Strangeness of Insect Societies (Wilson), 114–15
Surowiecki, James: on decentralization, 124; on group intelligence, 118–21;

three constants in intelligent organization, 123–24; on wisdom of groups, crowds, mobs, 109, 122

Taylor, Paul, 24–25
Tea Party (political party), 208
Technics and Time: The Myth of Epimetheus (Stiegler), 191
Technium: described, 6, 113, 122; troubling problems for, 29
Technology: AMOLED displays, 18; BUMP application, 19; computational power, 157; digital literacy, 11–12; e-books, 12; electronic tools for reading, 12–13; historical adoption patterns, 13–14, 16; impact on reading, 86–87; Layars smart phone application, 20; responses go growth of, 111–12; smart phones, 17–19, 21, 37; Watson computer, 111; Wu's opinions on, 14–15. *See also* Browsers; Internet
Telematics, 185–86
Tesla, Nikola, 14
Texas Board of Education, 205
Thin-slicing (Gladwell concept), 158
Transcendence, beliefs in, 7
The True Believer (Hoffer), 208
Tuite, Michael, 204
Tumblr, 39
Twain, Mark, 40
Twenge, Jean, 187
21st Century Skills, Education and Competitiveness: A Resource and Policy Guide, 217
Twitter: and politics, 106, 125; role in Jasmine Revolution, 126; social transformation caused by, 39
2001: A Space Odyssey (Kubrick), 163
The Tyranny of Words (Orwell), 208

The Ugly American (Burdick & Lederer), 12
Uncle Tom's Cabin (Stowe), 49
Understanding Media (McLuhan), 135
United Nations Education, Scientific and Cultural Organization (UNESCO), 12
The University of Google (Brabazon), 199

U.S. Copyright Group, 73
U.S. financial crisis, 169

Varela, Francisco: collaboration with Maturana, 162; exploration of autopoiesis, 6, 162
Virilio, Paul: on "dromospheric pollution" crisis, 17–18; opinion on modern telecommunications, 19, 29, 134; *third horizon* concept, 16
Voodoo Science (Park), 212

Wachowski brothers, 3–5
Wagner, Tom, 202; on solution to school problems, 202–3; survival skills advocated by, 202, 206, 215, 216–19, 223
Waiting for Superman documentary (Guggenheim), 196
Wakefield, Andrew, 200
Wallace, Alexandra, 189–90
WallBuilders.com, 214
Wall Street, 169–71
"Wall Street Geeks," 169
Want: definition of, 6–7; early car hand crank example, 13
Warhol, Andy, 104
Watson computer (IBM), 111
Web 2.0: advantages of, 109; control of, by modern users, 38, 41; influence on books, 110; problem with social media claims, 188; Shirky's viewpoint, 184–85; Twenge/Campbell's viewpoint, 187; viewpoint of Shirky, 184–85
Webster, Daniel, 96–97
Webster, Noah, 96–97, 99
"Web surfer" description, 36
Weiner, Norbert, 166–67
What Technology Wants (Kelly), 113
Where Good Ideas Come From: The Natural History of Innovation (Stephen Johnson), 159
Whippet, observations of, 38–39
Who Wants to be a Millionaire TV show, 121
WikiLeaks, 105–8

Wikipedia, 19
Willow Garage (start-up company), 5
Willrich, Michael, 200
Wilson, Charles Erwin, 107
Wilson, Edward O., 114, 115
Windows operating system, 104
Winner, Langdon, 189
Wired magazine, 1, 113, 232, 235. *See also* Kelly, Kevin
The Wisdom of Crowds (Surowiecki), 109
Wolin, Sheldon: contrast with Martineau, 151; on effective democracy, 150
Wong, Jimmy, 190
Wood, Donald, 190
World Wide Web: book knowledge vs., 210; coinciding of digital revolution, 86; HTML mark-up language, 45–46, 158; incompleteness of, 55; navigation by individuals, 39; Pariser on chaos of, 153; post-introduction transformation, 110; pre-Web "Archie" FTP, 50; quill pen compared with, 42; transformative influence on publishing, 47
Wu, Tim: on Google's growing dominance, 14–15; on technology adoption patterns, 13–14, 16

Xerox Corporation, 105

York, Jillian, 125
YouTube, 5, 82, 175, 177–78, 180–81, 185–90

Zoe energy: benefits of, 23; Braidotti's definition, 9; desire of machines, vs. humans, 172; growing awareness of, 17; return being made by, 10; and wants of technology, 27

About the Authors

Aaron Barlow, Associate Professor of English at New York City College of Technology, is the author of *The DVD Revolution: Movies, Culture, and Technology*; *The Rise of the Blogosphere*; *Blogging America: The New Public Sphere*; and *Quentin Tarantino: Life at the Extremes,* all from Praeger.

Robert Leston, Assistant Professor of English at New York City College of Technology, specializes in contemporary American rhetoric and communication.